LLEWELLYN'S

2014

MOON

SIGN

BOOK

Llewellyn's 2014 Moon Sign Book®

ISBN 978-0-7387-2154-5

Cover design by Kevin R. Brown
Cover illustrations: Scrolls: iStockphoto.com/ANGELGILD
    Moon: iStockphoto.com/Magnilion
Editing by Nicole Nugent
Stock photography models used for illustrative purposes only and may not endorse or represent the book's subject.
Copyright 2013 Llewellyn Worldwide Ltd. All rights reserved.
Typography owned by Llewellyn Worldwide Ltd.

Any Internet references contained in this work are current at publication time, but the publisher cannot guarantee that a specific location will continue to be maintained.

Astrological data compiled and programmed by Rique Pottenger. Based on the earlier work of Neil F. Michelsen.

You can order Llewellyn annuals and books from *New Worlds*, Llewellyn's catalog. To request a free copy of the catalog, call toll-free 1-877-NEW-WRLD, or visit our website at www.llewellyn.com.

Llewellyn Publications is a registered trademark of Llewellyn Worldwide Ltd.
2143 Wooddale Drive, Woodbury, MN 55125-2989 USA
Moon Sign Book® is registered in U.S. Patent and Trademark Office.
Moon Sign Book is a trademark of Llewellyn Worldwide Ltd. (Canada).
Printed in the USA

Llewellyn Publications
A Division of Llewellyn Worldwide Ltd.
2143 Wooddale Drive
Woodbury, MN 55125-3989
www.llewellyn.com

Printed in the United States of America

Table of Contents

What's Different About the Moon Sign Book?

Readers have asked why *Llewellyn's Moon Sign Book* says that the Moon is in Taurus when some almanacs indicate that the Moon is in the previous sign of Aries on the same date. It's because there are two different zodiac systems in use today: the tropical and the sidereal. *Llewellyn's Moon Sign Book* is based on the tropical zodiac.

The tropical zodiac takes 0 degrees of Aries to be the Spring Equinox in the Northern Hemisphere. This is the time and date when the Sun is directly overhead at noon along the equator, usually about March 20–21. The rest of the signs are positioned at 30-degree intervals from this point.

The sidereal zodiac, which is based on the location of fixed stars, uses the positions of the fixed stars to determine the starting point of

0 degrees of Aries. In the sidereal system, 0 degrees of Aries always begins at the same point. This does create a problem though, because the positions of the fixed stars, as seen from Earth, have changed since the constellations were named. The term "precession of the equinoxes" is used to describe the change.

Precession of the equinoxes describes an astronomical phenomenon brought about by the Earth's wobble as it rotates and orbits the Sun. The Earth's axis is inclined toward the Sun at an angle of about 23½ degrees, which creates our seasonal weather changes. Although the change is slight, because one complete circle of the Earth's axis takes 25,800 years to complete, we can actually see that the positions of the fixed stars seem to shift. The result is that each year, in the tropical system, the Spring Equinox occurs at a slightly different time.

Does Precession Matter?

There is an accumulative difference of about 23 degrees between the Spring Equinox (0 degrees Aries in the tropical zodiac and 0 degrees Aries in the sidereal zodiac) so that 0 degrees Aries at Spring Equinox in the tropical zodiac actually occurs at about 7 degrees Pisces in the sidereal zodiac system. You can readily see that those who use the other almanacs may be planting seeds (in the garden and in their individual lives) based on the belief that it is occurring in a fruitful sign, such as Taurus, when in fact it would be occurring in Gemini, one of the most barren signs of the zodiac. So, if you wish to plant and plan activities by the Moon, it is helpful to follow *Llewellyn's Moon Sign Book*. Before we go on, there are important things to understand about the Moon, her cycles, and their correlation with everyday living. For more information about gardening by the Moon, see page 61.

Weekly Almanac

Your Guide to Lunar Gardening & Good Timing for Activities

*Gardening for me has been both a delight in good times
and a consolation in times of difficulty.*
~Eileen Campbell

January

December 29–January 4

*Mindful eating begins with making conscious choices about
what you eat, how, and when.*   ~DEBRA MOFFITT

Date	Qtr.	Sign	Activity
Jan 4, 11:58 am– Jan 6, 2:45 pm	1st	Pisces	Plant grains, leafy annuals. Fertilize (chemical). Graft or bud plants. Irrigate. Trim to increase growth.

A New Year's Day New Moon is perfect for laying out this
year's garden plans—and for brightening up a winter afternoon. Make a list of last year's successes and not-quite successes.
Note which ones you want to try again this year, then add one
or two new varieties to keep your garden fresh and your interest
engaged. Next, organize that list by seed starting date. Create a
second column for transplant date and another for harvest dates
for fruits and vegetables. Skip right to the transplant date if you
will only be dealing with seedlings.

_____

_____

_____

_____

January 1
6:14 am EST

JANUARY

S	M	T	W	T	F	S
			1	2	3	4
5	6	7	8	9	10	11
12	13	14	15	16	17	18
19	20	21	22	23	24	25
26	27	28	29	30	31	

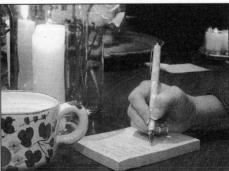

January 5–11 ♑

Manifest plainness, embrace simplicity, reduce selfishness,
have few desires.
        ~LAO-TZU

Date	Qtr.	Sign	Activity
Jan 4, 11:58 am– Jan 6, 2:45 pm	1st	Pisces	Plant grains, leafy annuals. Fertilize (chemical). Graft or bud plants. Irrigate. Trim to increase growth.
Jan 8, 9:24 pm– Jan 11, 7:26 am	2nd	Taurus	Plant annuals for hardiness. Trim to increase growth.

While the Moon is still growing, continue to make your garden plans. Make a rough drawing of your lawn and garden area, trying your best to keep it in scale. If the weather permits, go ahead and measure it out! Note areas that receive more or less sun than average, based on past years' experience. You can do this on paper or on a computer, if you like. (If you use paper, make photocopies of your basic plan to use each year.) Note the approximate square footage available for plants, then estimate how much space you'd like to devote to each kind.

January 7
10:39 pm EST

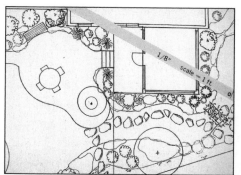

2013 © Bonnie Watton Image from BigStockPhoto.com

JANUARY

S	M	T	W	T	F	S
			1	2	3	4
5	6	7	8	9	10	11
12	13	14	15	16	17	18
19	20	21	22	23	24	25
26	27	28	29	30	31	

January 12–18

The world today doesn't make sense, so why should I paint pictures that do?

~PABLO PICASSO

Date	Qtr.	Sign	Activity
Jan 13, 7:25 pm–Jan 15, 11:52 pm	2nd	Cancer	Plant grains, leafy annuals. Fertilize (chemical). Graft or bud plants. Irrigate. Trim to increase growth.
Jan 15, 11:52 pm–Jan 16, 8:00 am	3rd	Cancer	Plant biennials, perennials, bulbs, and roots. Prune. Irrigate. Fertilize (organic).
Jan 16, 8:00 am–Jan 18, 8:23 pm	3rd	Leo	Cultivate. Destroy weeds and pests. Harvest fruits and root crops for food. Trim to retard growth.
Jan 18, 8:23 pm–Jan 21, 7:43 am	3rd	Virgo	Cultivate, especially medicinal plants. Destroy weeds and pests. Trim to retard growth.

After the Full Moon passes and Luna begins to wane, revisit your garden plans and make revisions as necessary. Figure out how many seeds or seedlings you will need to fill the space you've allocated for each plant. Again, make revisions if, for example, you find you've only planned enough space for two tomato plants but were hoping to can salsa this year. You likely have several weeks to tinker before seed starting dates hit.

_____

_____

_____

_____

○

January 15
11:52 pm EST

JANUARY

S	M	T	W	T	F	S
			1	2	3	4
5	6	7	8	9	10	11
12	13	14	15	16	17	18
19	20	21	22	23	24	25
26	27	28	29	30	31	

2013 © Mehmet Dilsiz Image from BigStockPhoto.com

January 19–25 〜〜

Knowledge is proud that he has learned so much; wisdom is humble that he knows no more.   ⁓WILLIAM COWPER

Date	Qtr.	Sign	Activity
Jan 18, 8:23 pm– Jan 21, 7:43 am	3rd	Virgo	Cultivate, especially medicinal plants. Destroy weeds and pests. Trim to retard growth.
Jan 23, 4:43 pm– Jan 24, 12:19 am	3rd	Scorpio	Plant biennials, perennials, bulbs, and roots. Prune. Irrigate. Fertilize (organic).
Jan 24, 12:19 am– Jan 25, 10:13 pm	4th	Scorpio	Plant biennials, perennials, bulbs, and roots. Prune. Irrigate. Fertilize (organic).
Jan 25, 10:13 pm– Jan 28, 12:04 am	4th	Sagittarius	Cultivate. Destroy weeds and pests. Harvest fruits and root crops for food. Trim to retard growth.

As the time to start seeds approaches, consider what free materials you could use for seed containers: toilet paper tubes, halved citrus rinds, eggshells, newspaper … Buying seed pots can get expensive year after year, but these alternatives can go straight into the ground to decompose naturally. Eggshells will even benefit tomatoes, peppers, and eggplant (all members of the Nightshade family).

◖

January 24
12:19 am EST

JANUARY

S	M	T	W	T	F	S
			1	2	3	4
5	6	7	8	9	10	11
12	13	14	15	16	17	18
19	20	21	22	23	24	25
26	27	28	29	30	31	

2013 © Maria Dryfhout Image from BigStockPhoto.com

~~~ February

January 26–February 1

*It's our choices… that show what we truly are, far more than
our abilities.*

~J. K. ROWLING

Date	Qtr.	Sign	Activity
Jan 25, 10:13 pm– Jan 28, 12:04 am	4th	Sagittarius	Cultivate. Destroy weeds and pests. Harvest fruits and root crops for food. Trim to retard growth.
Jan 28, 12:04 am– Jan 29, 11:33 pm	4th	Capricorn	Plant potatoes and tubers. Trim to retard growth.
Jan 29, 11:33 pm– Jan 30, 4:39 pm	4th	Aquarius	Cultivate. Destroy weeds and pests. Harvest fruits and root crops for food. Trim to retard growth.
Jan 31, 10:45 pm– Feb 2, 11:55 pm	1st	Pisces	Plant grains, leafy annuals. Fertilize (chemical). Graft or bud plants. Irrigate. Trim to increase growth.

During the coldest part of the year, you may see what's called a sun dog. This appears usually right at sunset or sunrise when the air is cold enough to have ice crystals in it. The crystals act as prisms, forming a circular rainbow or halo a distance out from the Sun on the horizon.

January 30
4:39 pm EST

FEBRUARY

S	M	T	W	T	F	S
						1
2	3	4	5	6	7	8
9	10	11	12	13	14	15
16	17	18	19	20	21	22
23	24	25	26	27	28	

2013 © Clive Johnson Image from BigStockPhoto.com

February 2–8 〜〜

Don't go around saying the world owes you a living. The
world owes you nothing. It was here first. ⁓MARK TWAIN

Date	Qtr.	Sign	Activity
Jan 31, 10:45 pm–Feb 2, 11:55 pm	1st	Pisces	Plant grains, leafy annuals. Fertilize (chemical). Graft or bud plants. Irrigate. Trim to increase growth.
Feb 5, 4:47 am–Feb 6, 2:22 pm	1st	Taurus	Plant annuals for hardiness. Trim to increase growth.
Feb 6, 2:22 pm–Feb 7, 1:44 pm	2nd	Taurus	Plant annuals for hardiness. Trim to increase growth.

Groundhog Day supposedly began as a Pennsylvania German custom in the 1700s and 1800s, and it is in Punxsutawney, Pennsylvania, that the largest celebration is held. If Punxsutawney Phil sees his shadow on the morning of February 2, there will be six more weeks of winter; if it is cloudy and he sees no shadow, spring will come early that year. Though Phil emerges from a hole outside of town for the festival, this particular groundhog actually lives in the town's library.

February 6
2:22 pm EST

FEBRUARY

S	M	T	W	T	F	S
						1
2	3	4	5	6	7	8
9	10	11	12	13	14	15
16	17	18	19	20	21	22
23	24	25	26	27	28	

2013 © Pauline Wessel Image from BigStockPhoto.com

～～ **February 9–15**

One heart's enough for me—one heart to love, adore—one heart's enough for me; O, who could wish for more?

~AUGUST MIGNON

Date	Qtr.	Sign	Activity
Feb 10, 1:33 am– Feb 12, 2:15 pm	2nd	Cancer	Plant grains, leafy annuals. Fertilize (chemical). Graft or bud plants. Irrigate. Trim to increase growth.
Feb 14, 6:53 pm– Feb 15, 2:26 am	3rd	Leo	Cultivate. Destroy weeds and pests. Harvest fruits and root crops for food. Trim to retard growth.
Feb 15, 2:26 am– Feb 17, 1:23 pm	3rd	Virgo	Cultivate, especially medicinal plants. Destroy weeds and pests. Trim to retard growth.

Herbs are among the most "profitable" plants to grow, considering the cost of buying herbs in a grocery store. However, you're only saving money if you actually use everything your herb plants produce! Start with familiar types like basil, sage, rosemary, and parsley before venturing into tarragon and marjoram. Aim to use one of your herbs in every meal, even if you only chop a few tablespoons to mix with butter on bread.

○
February 14
6:53 pm EST

FEBRUARY

S	M	T	W	T	F	S
						1
2	3	4	5	6	7	8
9	10	11	12	13	14	15
16	17	18	19	20	21	22
23	24	25	26	27	28	

2013 © jabiru Image from BigStockPhoto.com

February 16–22

People who think only a model type can be a beautiful woman are as lacking in sophistication as those who think only a burger and fries can be a tasty meal. ～VICTORIA MORAN

Date	Qtr.	Sign	Activity
Feb 15, 2:26 am–Feb 17, 1:23 pm	3rd	Virgo	Cultivate, especially medicinal plants. Destroy weeds and pests. Trim to retard growth.
Feb 19, 10:33 pm–Feb 22, 5:12 am	3rd	Scorpio	Plant biennials, perennials, bulbs, and roots. Prune. Irrigate. Fertilize (organic).
Feb 22, 5:12 am–Feb 22, 12:15 pm	3rd	Sagittarius	Cultivate. Destroy weeds and pests. Harvest fruits and root crops for food. Trim to retard growth.
Feb 22, 12:15 pm–Feb 24, 8:50 am	4th	Sagittarius	Cultivate. Destroy weeds and pests. Harvest fruits and root crops for food. Trim to retard growth.

When planting perennials, remember that it will take a few seasons for the plant to mature and fill in. The popular saying is: sleep, creep, leap. The plant will "sleep" the first year, recovering from being transplanted. It will "creep" the second year, growing slowly. With luck, the perennial will "leap" with growth the third season.

_____

_____

_____

_____

February 22
12:15 pm EST

FEBRUARY

S	M	T	W	T	F	S
						1
2	3	4	5	6	7	8
9	10	11	12	13	14	15
16	17	18	19	20	21	22
23	24	25	26	27	28	

March

February 23–March 1

To weakness, strength succeeds, and power from frailty
springs! Press on, press on!   ~PARK BENJAMIN

Date	Qtr.	Sign	Activity
Feb 22, 12:15 pm– Feb 24, 8:50 am	4th	Sagittarius	Cultivate. Destroy weeds and pests. Harvest fruits and root crops for food. Trim to retard growth.
Feb 24, 8:50 am– Feb 26, 9:55 am	4th	Capricorn	Plant potatoes and tubers. Trim to retard growth.
Feb 26, 9:55 am– Feb 28, 9:53 am	4th	Aquarius	Cultivate. Destroy weeds and pests. Harvest fruits and root crops for food. Trim to retard growth.
Feb 28, 9:53 am– Mar 1, 3:00 am	4th	Pisces	Plant biennials, perennials, bulbs, and roots. Prune. Irrigate. Fertilize (organic).
Mar 1, 3:00 am– Mar 2, 10:40 am	1st	Pisces	Plant grains, leafy annuals. Fertilize (chemical). Graft or bud plants. Irrigate. Trim to increase growth.

Precipitation this time of year can be unpredictable—not only in amount but in form. There is snow and rain, of course, but also rain and snow mixed, sleet, mist, freezing rain, drizzle, ice pellets, graupel (soft hail or snow pellets), and hail.

March 1
3:00 am EST

MARCH

S	M	T	W	T	F	S
						1
2	3	4	5	6	7	8
9	10	11	12	13	14	15
16	17	18	19	20	21	22
23	24	25	26	27	28	29
30	31					

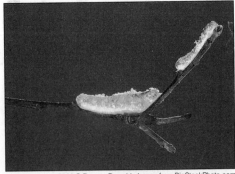

2013 © Evgeny Parushin Image from BigStockPhoto.com

March 2–8

I prefer an accommodating vice to an obstinate virtue.

~Molière

Date	Qtr.	Sign	Activity
Mar 1, 3:00 am– Mar 2, 10:40 am	1st	Pisces	Plant grains, leafy annuals. Fertilize (chemical). Graft or bud plants. Irrigate. Trim to increase growth.
Mar 4, 2:12 pm– Mar 6, 9:37 pm	1st	Taurus	Plant annuals for hardiness. Trim to increase growth.

A well-tended basil plant can easily produce enough for a family of four for a whole summer, plus extra. Pluck off flower heads before they have a chance to sprout to encourage more growth. If your basil stems are thin, go ahead and toss them in with the rest of the leaves, but do trim away thicker stems—they may have a bitter flavor. Use extra basil to make pesto (minus the Parmesan cheese) and freeze it in cubes. To use, simply defrost, add the cheese, and enjoy! Homemade basil may turn brown; if the color bothers you, add parsley to the mix to keep that nice, bright-green hue.

March 8
8:27 am EST

March

S	M	T	W	T	F	S
						1
2	3	4	5	6	7	8
9	10	11	12	13	14	15
16	17	18	19	20	21	22
23	24	25	26	27	28	29
30	31					

2013 © photopips Image from BigStockPhoto.com

March 9–15

This I moreover hold and dare affirm where'er my rhyme
may go: whatever things be sweet or fair, love makes them so.

~Alice Cray

Date	Qtr.	Sign	Activity
Mar 9, 9:33 am– Mar 11, 10:09 pm	2nd	Cancer	Plant grains, leafy annuals. Fertilize (chemical). Graft or bud plants. Irrigate. Trim to increase growth.

Wearing a sunhat can provide a great deal of protection for your eyes and face, as well as neck and ears. You might think a hat would make you feel hotter, but the right fabric will actually keep your head cooler. Choose a closewoven straw or cotton hat with a brim of at least 3 inches. It's a good idea to buy a hat with a chin strap or some other way of fastening the hat to yourself on windy days. Some hats even have flaps on the back to cover your neck when you are bending over the garden beds.

Daylight Saving Time
begins March 9, 2:00 am

MARCH

S	M	T	W	T	F	S
						1
2	3	4	5	6	7	8
9	10	11	12	13	14	15
16	17	18	19	20	21	22
23	24	25	26	27	28	29
30	31					

March 16–22 ✵

Spring is coming, didn't you know? Oh yes, it's up to ten below. ~Anita McLean Washington

(handwritten) 10:00 5:46 pm

(handwritten, vertical) SUNDAY

Date	Qtr.	Sign	Activity
Mar 16, 1:08 pm–Mar 16, 8:46 pm	3rd	Virgo	Cultivate, especially medicinal plants. Destroy weeds and pests. Trim to retard growth.
Mar 19, 5:13 am–Mar 21, 11:39 am	3rd	Scorpio	Plant biennials, perennials, bulbs, and roots. Prune. Irrigate. Fertilize (organic).
Mar 21, 11:39 am–Mar 23, 4:03 pm	3rd	Sagittarius	Cultivate. Destroy weeds and pests. Harvest fruits and root crops for food. Trim to retard growth.

Gluten-free products are making a splash in today's supermarkets. Gluten is a protein found in wheat and other grains that some digestive systems are unable to process. On the gluten-ous list: some oats, rye, barley, and wheats like spelt, farro, durum, bulgur, and semolina. Alternatives include corn, rice, quinoa, wild rice, millet, pure oats, and buckwheat.

(handwritten) 3-16 · Good time for endings
(handwritten) H o'clock   pages 62 - 65

2013 © Marilyn Barbone Image from BigStockPhoto.com

O
March 16
1:08 pm EDT

March

S	M	T	W	T	F	S
						1
2	3	4	5	6	7	8
9	10	11	12	13	14	15
16	17	18	19	20	21	22
23	24	25	26	27	28	29
30	31					

March 23–29

Youth is the time of getting, middle age of improving, and old age of spending.　　　　　～ANNE BRADSTREET

Date	Qtr.	Sign	Activity
Mar 21, 11:39 am– Mar 23, 4:03 pm	3rd	Sagittarius	Cultivate. Destroy weeds and pests. Harvest fruits and root crops for food. Trim to retard growth.
Mar 23, 4:03 pm– Mar 23, 9:46 pm	3rd	Capricorn	Plant potatoes and tubers. Trim to retard growth.
Mar 23, 9:46 pm– Mar 25, 6:39 pm	4th	Capricorn	Plant potatoes and tubers. Trim to retard growth.
Mar 25, 6:39 pm– Mar 27, 8:10 pm	4th	Aquarius	Cultivate. Destroy weeds and pests. Harvest fruits and root crops for food. Trim to retard growth.
Mar 27, 8:10 pm– Mar 29, 9:54 pm	4th	Pisces	Plant biennials, perennials, bulbs, and roots. Prune. Irrigate. Fertilize (organic).
Mar 29, 9:54 pm– Mar 30, 2:45 pm	4th	Aries	Cultivate. Destroy weeds and pests. Harvest fruits and root crops for food. Trim to retard growth.

Potato slips should be planted no sooner than two weeks before the last hard frost. You can check http://tinyurl.com/HardFrostDate to find the date when probability of a 28-degree temperature is 10 percent or less for your specific area.

_____

_____

_____

_____

March 23
9:46 pm EDT

APRIL

S	M	T	W	T	F	S
		1	2	3	4	5
6	7	8	9	10	11	12
13	14	15	16	17	18	19
20	21	22	23	24	25	26
27	28	29	30			

April

March 30–April 5

Never let the fear of striking out get in your way.
~GEORGE HERMAN "BABE" RUTH

Date	Qtr.	Sign	Activity
Mar 29, 9:54 pm– Mar 30, 2:45 pm	4th	Aries	Cultivate. Destroy weeds and pests. Harvest fruits and root crops for food. Trim to retard growth.
Apr 1, 1:20 am– Apr 3, 7:48 am	1st	Taurus	Plant annuals for hardiness. Trim to increase growth.
Apr 5, 5:40 pm– Apr 7, 4:31 am	1st	Cancer	Plant grains, leafy annuals. Fertilize (chemical). Graft or bud plants. Irrigate. Trim to increase growth.

Boulevards along city streets are often piled with snow and road salt thanks to passing plows. Reduce the salt's effect by "washing" these areas down with a garden hose—yes, even during the wet spring thaw. Topdress the area with compost amended with gypsum, which can counteract the sodium found in most road salts. Gypsum can even be applied in the fall to prevent damage over the winter months.

March 30
2:45 pm EDT

APRIL

S	M	T	W	T	F	S
		1	2	3	4	5
6	7	8	9	10	11	12
13	14	15	16	17	18	19
20	21	22	23	24	25	26
27	28	29	30			

2013 © Moshe Barzeski Image from BigStockPhoto.com

April 6–12

Most men, till by losing rendered sager, will back their own opinions by a wager.
~LORD BYRON

Date	Qtr.	Sign	Activity
Apr 7, 4:31 am– Apr 8, 5:50 am	2nd	Cancer	Plant grains, leafy annuals. Fertilize (chemical). Graft or bud plants. Irrigate. Trim to increase growth.

Spring may find you seeing plants in your yard or neighborhood that you don't recognize. Try the USDA's website for identification help on mystery plants: www.plants.usda.gov. The University of Texas at Austin also has a helpful search feature: www.wildflower.org/plants.

Neighborhood garden centers and botanical gardens are good resources to cultivate. Bring a clipping of the plant along with notes on where it's growing and how. You will likely be asked about the plant's height, leaf arrangement, flower color and timing, and how much sun it seems to like. Be sure to make a purchase now and again if you are getting help from a salesperson!

_____

_____

_____

_____

April 7
4:31 am EDT

APRIL

S	M	T	W	T	F	S
		1	2	3	4	5
6	7	8	9	10	11	12
13	14	15	16	17	18	19
20	21	22	23	24	25	26
27	28	29	30			

April 13–19 ♈

Of all our parts, the eyes express the sweetest kind of
bashfulness.
                                    ~ROBERT HERRICK

Date	Qtr.	Sign	Activity
Apr 13, 4:33 am– Apr 15, 3:42 am	2nd	Libra	Plant annuals for fragrance and beauty. Trim to increase growth.
Apr 15, 12:20 pm– Apr 17, 5:44 pm	3rd	Scorpio	Plant biennials, perennials, bulbs, and roots. Prune. Irrigate. Fertilize (organic).
Apr 17, 5:44 pm– Apr 19, 9:28 pm	3rd	Sagittarius	Cultivate. Destroy weeds and pests. Harvest fruits and root crops for food. Trim to retard growth.
Apr 19, 9:28 pm– Apr 22, 12:18 am	3rd	Capricorn	Plant potatoes and tubers. Trim to retard growth.

Now is a great time to start a morning glory from seed. Soak seeds overnight, then plant one seed per pot. Transplant your seedling around Memorial Day, then watch as the plant explodes in July and flowers each morning through the first frost. Morning glories love full sun and will require a structure to climb, or the vines will twist around themselves and protrude into open air. They are excellent for covering an unsightly chain link fence.

2013 © Nicole Nugent

○
April 15
3:42 am EDT

			APRIL			
S	M	T	W	T	F	S
		1	2	3	4	5
6	7	8	9	10	11	12
13	14	15	16	17	18	19
20	21	22	23	24	25	26
27	28	29	30			

April 20–26

Do not allow evil into your heart; it will make a home there.
                          ~AGATHA CHRISTIE, AS HERCULE POIROT

Date	Qtr.	Sign	Activity
Apr 19, 9:28 pm– Apr 22, 12:18 am	3rd	Capricorn	Plant potatoes and tubers. Trim to retard growth.
Apr 22, 12:18 am– Apr 22, 3:52 am	3rd	Aquarius	Cultivate. Destroy weeds and pests. Harvest fruits and root crops for food. Trim to retard growth.
Apr 22, 3:52 am– Apr 24, 2:55 am	4th	Aquarius	Cultivate. Destroy weeds and pests. Harvest fruits and root crops for food. Trim to retard growth.
Apr 24, 2:55 am– Apr 26, 6:01 am	4th	Pisces	Plant biennials, perennials, bulbs, and roots. Prune. Irrigate. Fertilize (organic).
Apr 26, 6:01 am– Apr 28, 10:23 am	4th	Aries	Cultivate. Destroy weeds and pests. Harvest fruits and root crops for food. Trim to retard growth.

Overabundance isn't usually a gardener's problem, but some people are hesitant to grow zucchini for fear of wasting the prolific vegetables. Plan to freeze extra zucchini to use in the winter months. Steam-blanch grated zucchini 1–2 minutes, or water-blanch 1/2-inch slices for 3 minutes. Cool immediately in ice water, then drain and package.

April 22
3:52 am EDT

APRIL

S	M	T	W	T	F	S
		1	2	3	4	5
6	7	8	9	10	11	12
13	14	15	16	17	18	19
20	21	22	23	24	25	26
27	28	29	30			

2013 © alexh Image from BigStockPhoto.com

May
April 27–May 3

O dark, dark, dark, amid the blaze of noon; irrecoverably
dark! Total eclipse, without all hope of day.

~John Milton

Date	Qtr.	Sign	Activity
Apr 26, 6:01 am–Apr 28, 10:23 am	4th	Aries	Cultivate. Destroy weeds and pests. Harvest fruits and root crops for food. Trim to retard growth.
Apr 28, 10:23 am–Apr 29, 2:14 am	4th	Taurus	Plant potatoes and tubers. Trim to retard growth.
Apr 29, 2:14 am–Apr 30, 4:56 pm	1st	Taurus	Plant annuals for hardiness. Trim to increase growth.
May 3, 2:13 am–May 5, 1:55 pm	1st	Cancer	Plant grains, leafy annuals. Fertilize (chemical). Graft or bud plants. Irrigate. Trim to increase growth.

Use frozen zucchini as a side vegetable by partially thawing then sauteeing with seasonings. Add frozen slices to soups and stews near the end of cooking. Use grated frozen zucchini in baking (bread or cake) or as a vegetable layer in lasagna.

2013 © Madlen Image from BigStockPhoto.com

April 29
2:14 am EDT

May

S	M	T	W	T	F	S
				1	2	3
4	5	6	7	8	9	10
11	12	13	14	15	16	17
18	19	20	21	22	23	24
25	26	27	28	29	30	31

May 4–10

*Simply sowing seed, watching life emerge, weeding, pruning,
harvesting and clearing give a satisfying rhythm to life.*

~EILEEN CAMPBELL

Date	Qtr.	Sign	Activity
May 3, 2:13 am– May 5, 1:55 pm	1st	Cancer	Plant grains, leafy annuals. Fertilize (chemical). Graft or bud plants. Irrigate. Trim to increase growth.
May 10, 1:19 pm– May 12, 9:07 pm	2nd	Libra	Plant annuals for fragrance and beauty. Trim to increase growth.

Digging, planting, mulching, and hauling can make for some sore hands and arms. Stretch tired fingers by flexing the digits out and back, then bending only the top knuckles. Return to the flex, then bend all your fingers toward your wrist. Return to the flex once more, then make a tight fist. To stretch wrist and forearm muscles, hold one arm straight out and use the other hand to push the hand up in a "stop" gesture; hold for several seconds. Repeat the stretch with the fingers pointed downward, then switch arms.

*May 6
11:15 pm EDT*

MAY

S	M	T	W	T	F	S
				1	2	3
4	5	6	7	8	9	10
11	12	13	14	15	16	17
18	19	20	21	22	23	24
25	26	27	28	29	30	31

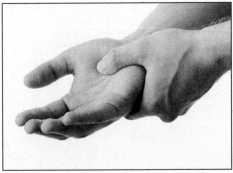

May 11–17

As it fell upon a day in the merry month of May, sitting in a pleasant shade which a grove of myrtles made.

~RICHARD BARNFIELD

Date	Qtr.	Sign	Activity
May 10, 1:19 pm– May 12, 9:07 pm	2nd	Libra	Plant annuals for fragrance and beauty. Trim to increase growth.
May 12, 9:07 pm– May 14, 3:16 pm	2nd	Scorpio	Plant grains, leafy annuals. Fertilize (chemical). Graft or bud plants. Irrigate. Trim to increase growth.
May 14, 3:16 pm– May 15, 1:44 am	3rd	Scorpio	Plant biennials, perennials, bulbs, and roots. Prune. Irrigate. Fertilize (organic).
May 15, 1:44 am– May 17, 4:12 am	3rd	Sagittarius	Cultivate. Destroy weeds and pests. Harvest fruits and root crops for food. Trim to retard growth.
May 17, 4:12 am– May 19, 5:58 am	3rd	Capricorn	Plant potatoes and tubers. Trim to retard growth.

Stand perpendicular to a wall and place one hand on the wall at shoulder height, about a foot behind you. Now take a step forward, straighten your arm, and rotate your body away from the wall. This should produce a gentle stretch in your chest and down your biceps muscle. Hold for several seconds, then switch sides.

2013 © Edyta Pawlowska Image from BigStockPhoto.com

○
May 14
3:16 pm EDT

MAY

S	M	T	W	T	F	S
				1	2	3
4	5	6	7	8	9	10
11	12	13	14	15	16	17
18	19	20	21	22	23	24
25	26	27	28	29	30	31

May 18–24

Dawn is fair, because her mists fade slowly into day, which floods the world with light.   ~ADELAIDE A. PROCTER

Date	Qtr.	Sign	Activity
May 17, 4:12 am– May 19, 5:58 am	3rd	Capricorn	Plant potatoes and tubers. Trim to retard growth.
May 19, 5:58 am– May 21, 8:18 am	3rd	Aquarius	Cultivate. Destroy weeds and pests. Harvest fruits and root crops for food. Trim to retard growth.
May 21, 8:18 am– May 21, 8:59 am	3rd	Pisces	Plant biennials, perennials, bulbs, and roots. Prune. Irrigate. Fertilize (organic).
May 21, 8:59 am– May 23, 12:01 pm	4th	Pisces	Plant biennials, perennials, bulbs, and roots. Prune. Irrigate. Fertilize (organic).
May 23, 12:01 pm– May 25, 5:28 pm	4th	Aries	Cultivate. Destroy weeds and pests. Harvest fruits and root crops for food. Trim to retard growth.

If your garden is far from your garden shed, you might try putting a metal mailbox on a pole in your garden. The mailbox can hold your most commonly used garden tools, keeping them dry and at hand. Have fun decorating the mailbox to match your garden's theme.

May 21
8:59 am EDT

			MAY			
S	M	T	W	T	F	S
				1	2	3
4	5	6	7	8	9	10
11	12	13	14	15	16	17
18	19	20	21	22	23	24
25	26	27	28	29	30	31

May 25–31

Beauty is nature's brag and must be shown.

~John Milton

Date	Qtr.	Sign	Activity
May 23, 12:01 pm– May 25, 5:28 pm	4th	Aries	Cultivate. Destroy weeds and pests. Harvest fruits and root crops for food. Trim to retard growth.
May 25, 5:28 pm– May 28, 12:47 am	4th	Taurus	Plant potatoes and tubers. Trim to retard growth.
May 28, 12:47 am– May 28, 2:40 pm	4th	Gemini	Cultivate. Destroy weeds and pests. Harvest fruits and root crops for food. Trim to retard growth.
May 30, 10:13 am– Jun 1, 9:43 pm	1st	Cancer	Plant grains, leafy annuals. Fertilize (chemical). Graft or bud plants. Irrigate. Trim to increase growth.

To stop critters from munching on your tender new plants, sprinkle some cayenne or red pepper flakes on or around the plants in question. It won't hurt the plant (or affect its flavor) at all, but most animals will dislike the spicy pepper so much that they'll stay away. You may need to apply after each watering at first, but the animals will soon form an aversion for the area. You can cut your applications in half after a few weeks.

May 28
2:40 pm EDT

			MAY			
S	M	T	W	T	F	S
				1	2	3
4	5	6	7	8	9	10
11	12	13	14	15	16	17
18	19	20	21	22	23	24
25	26	27	28	29	30	31

June

June 1–7

The tongue is but three inches long yet it can kill a man six feet tall.

~Japanese Proverb

Date	Qtr.	Sign	Activity
May 30, 10:13 am–Jun 1, 9:43 pm	1st	Cancer	Plant grains, leafy annuals. Fertilize (chemical). Graft or bud plants. Irrigate. Trim to increase growth.
Jun 6, 10:01 pm–Jun 9, 6:38 am	2nd	Libra	Plant annuals for fragrance and beauty. Trim to increase growth.

Green Goddess dressing was once a very popular salad dressing and vegetable dip, before the arrival of ranch. Recipes vary but typically include garlic, mayonnaise, sour cream, parsley, tarragon, chives, lemon juice, and salt and pepper. The dressing was reportedly invented in California in the early 1900s in honor of a play of the same name.

June 5
4:39 pm EDT

June

S	M	T	W	T	F	S
1	2	3	4	5	6	7
8	9	10	11	12	13	14
15	16	17	18	19	20	21
22	23	24	25	26	27	28
29	30					

2013 © ViFi Image from BigStockPhoto.com

June 8–14

The sun has drunk the dew that lay upon the morning grass.

~William Cullen Bryant

Date	Qtr.	Sign	Activity
Jun 6, 10:01 pm–Jun 9, 6:38 am	2nd	Libra	Plant annuals for fragrance and beauty. Trim to increase growth.
Jun 9, 6:38 am–Jun 11, 11:23 am	2nd	Scorpio	Plant grains, leafy annuals. Fertilize (chemical). Graft or bud plants. Irrigate. Trim to increase growth.
Jun 13, 12:11 am–Jun 13, 1:04 pm	3rd	Sagittarius	Cultivate. Destroy weeds and pests. Harvest fruits and root crops for food. Trim to retard growth.
Jun 13, 1:04 pm–Jun 15, 1:27 pm	3rd	Capricorn	Plant potatoes and tubers. Trim to retard growth.

In this, the season of salads, try making your own dressings. Simple vinaigrettes are easy and quick to make, plus you can whip up fresh batches for each meal. Simply whisk 1/4 cup vinegar (any kind you like) with 1/2 cup oil (again, choose your own adventure here). Add salt and pepper to taste, or even a bit of minced onion or shallot. Red wine, balsamic, and cider vinegars make nice tangy dressings for those sweeter baby greens.

○
June 13
12:11 am EDT

JUNE

S	M	T	W	T	F	S
1	2	3	4	5	6	7
8	9	10	11	12	13	14
15	16	17	18	19	20	21
22	23	24	25	26	27	28
29	30					

June 15–21

Ten thousand warblers cheer the day, and one the
live-long night. ~WILLIAM COWPER

Date	Qtr.	Sign	Activity
Jun 13, 1:04 pm– Jun 15, 1:27 pm	3rd	Capricorn	Plant potatoes and tubers. Trim to retard growth.
Jun 15, 1:27 pm– Jun 17, 2:26 pm	3rd	Aquarius	Cultivate. Destroy weeds and pests. Harvest fruits and root crops for food. Trim to retard growth.
Jun 17, 2:26 pm– Jun 19, 2:39 pm	3rd	Pisces	Plant biennials, perennials, bulbs, and roots. Prune. Irrigate. Fertilize (organic).
Jun 19, 2:39 pm– Jun 19, 5:26 pm	4th	Pisces	Plant biennials, perennials, bulbs, and roots. Prune. Irrigate. Fertilize (organic).
Jun 19, 5:26 pm– Jun 21, 11:03 pm	4th	Aries	Cultivate. Destroy weeds and pests. Harvest fruits and root crops for food. Trim to retard growth.
Jun 21, 11:03 pm– Jun 24, 7:05 am	4th	Taurus	Plant potatoes and tubers. Trim to retard growth.

Hang up old CDs (from trees or eaves) to keep birds away! The reflections and shiny surface will keep them from landing where you don't want them, as will the movement of the CDs in the breeze.

—Pam L., Minnesota

June 19
2:39 pm EDT

JUNE

S	M	T	W	T	F	S
1	2	3	4	5	6	7
8	9	10	11	12	13	14
15	16	17	18	19	20	21
22	23	24	25	26	27	28
29	30					

June 22–28

Now the summer came to pass, and flowers through the grass
joyously sprang, while all the tribes of birds sang.

~WALTHER VON DER VOGELWEIDE

Date	Qtr.	Sign	Activity
Jun 21, 11:03 pm– Jun 24, 7:05 am	4th	Taurus	Plant potatoes and tubers. Trim to retard growth.
Jun 24, 7:05 am– Jun 26, 5:05 pm	4th	Gemini	Cultivate. Destroy weeds and pests. Harvest fruits and root crops for food. Trim to retard growth.
Jun 26, 5:05 pm– Jun 27, 4:08 am	4th	Cancer	Plant biennials, perennials, bulbs, and roots. Prune. Irrigate. Fertilize (organic).
Jun 27, 4:08 am– Jun 29, 4:43 am	1st	Cancer	Plant grains, leafy annuals. Fertilize (chemical). Graft or bud plants. Irrigate. Trim to increase growth.

This time of year, garlic scapes make their appearance in fields and farmers' markets. The scape is the flower stalk of the plant, and it is usually removed in June in order to promote larger clove growth. The skinny, curly stalks can be eaten raw or lightly sauteed. They are excellent in salads, in stir fries, or—for those who relish garlic flavor—made into a pesto and served over pasta.

June 27
4:08 am EDT

2013 © Ganna Poltoratska Image from BigStockPhoto.com

JUNE

S	M	T	W	T	F	S
1	2	3	4	5	6	7
8	9	10	11	12	13	14
15	16	17	18	19	20	21
22	23	24	25	26	27	28
29	30					

July

June 29–July 5

Nature is always wise in every part.

~Edmund, Second Baron Thurlow

Date	Qtr.	Sign	Activity
Jun 27, 4:08 am– Jun 29, 4:43 am	1st	Cancer	Plant grains, leafy annuals. Fertilize (chemical). Graft or bud plants. Irrigate. Trim to increase growth.
Jul 4, 5:43 am– Jul 5, 7:59 am	1st	Libra	Plant annuals for fragrance and beauty. Trim to increase growth.
Jul 5, 7:59 am– Jul 6, 3:33 pm	2nd	Libra	Plant annuals for fragrance and beauty. Trim to increase growth.

Use your muffin tin to make large ice cubes for pitchers of beverages before hosting a summer party. The larger cubes will last longer and can hold frozen fruit pieces or herbs more easily; lemon rounds look lovely in a muffin-sized ice cube. You can even use the beverage itself to make large cubes the day beforehand, so the pitcher doesn't get watered down as the cube melts.

July 5
7:59 am EDT

July

S	M	T	W	T	F	S
		1	2	3	4	5
6	7	8	9	10	11	12
13	14	15	16	17	18	19
20	21	22	23	24	25	26
27	28	29	30	31		

2013 © Liang Zhang Image from BigStockPhoto.com

July 6–12 ♋

For love of gardening is a seed that once sown, never dies.

~GERTRUDE JEKYLL

Date	Qtr.	Sign	Activity
Jul 5, 7:59 am– Jul 6, 3:33 pm	2nd	Libra	Plant annuals for fragrance and beauty. Trim to increase growth.
Jul 6, 3:33 pm– Jul 8, 9:24 pm	2nd	Scorpio	Plant grains, leafy annuals. Fertilize (chemical). Graft or bud plants. Irrigate. Trim to increase growth.
Jul 10, 11:24 pm– Jul 12, 7:25 am	2nd	Capricorn	Graft or bud plants. Trim to increase growth.
Jul 12, 7:25 am– Jul 12, 11:07 pm	3rd	Capricorn	Plant potatoes and tubers. Trim to retard growth.
Jul 12, 11:07 pm– Jul 14, 10:40 pm	3rd	Aquarius	Cultivate. Destroy weeds and pests. Harvest fruits and root crops for food. Trim to retard growth.

Craving a super crunchy snack? Try kohlbrabi! The funny-looking roots and tough skin hide a deliciously crisp and slightly sweet interior. Peel the outside and cut into thick fry slices for an easy, healthy side of vegetables. The flavor is similar to a very sweet broccoli stem.

_____

_____

_____

_____

○
July 12
7:25 am EDT

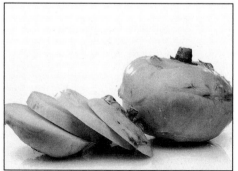

2013 © Peter Zijlstra Image from BigStockPhoto.com

		JULY			
S	M	T	W	T	F	S
		1	2	3	4	5
6	7	8	9	10	11	12
13	14	15	16	17	18	19
20	21	22	23	24	25	26
27	28	29	30	31		

July 13–19

'Twas in the summer time so sweet, when hearts and flowers are both in season.   ~Thomas Moore

Date	Qtr.	Sign	Activity
Jul 12, 11:07 pm– Jul 14, 10:40 pm	3rd	Aquarius	Cultivate. Destroy weeds and pests. Harvest fruits and root crops for food. Trim to retard growth.
Jul 14, 10:40 pm– Jul 17, 12:07 am	3rd	Pisces	Plant biennials, perennials, bulbs, and roots. Prune. Irrigate. Fertilize (organic).
Jul 17, 12:07 am– Jul 18, 10:08 pm	3rd	Aries	Cultivate. Destroy weeds and pests. Harvest fruits and root crops for food. Trim to retard growth.
Jul 18, 10:08 pm– Jul 19, 4:43 am	4th	Aries	Cultivate. Destroy weeds and pests. Harvest fruits and root crops for food. Trim to retard growth.
Jul 19, 4:43 am– Jul 21, 12:36 pm	4th	Taurus	Plant potatoes and tubers. Trim to retard growth.

If weeding is doing a number on your lower back, incorporate a few stretches into your daily routine. Rest on all fours and arch your back up like a cat; then scoop your back down and look up. This is called cat/cow pose in yoga; move slowly and alternate several times to limber up muscles.

_____

_____

_____

_____

◐
July 18
10:08 pm EDT

July

S	M	T	W	T	F	S
		1	2	3	4	5
6	7	8	9	10	11	12
13	14	15	16	17	18	19
20	21	22	23	24	25	26
27	28	29	30	31		

2013 © Vitaliy Markov Image from BigStockPhoto.com

July 20–26

Creativity is ... seeing something that doesn't exist already.

~MICHELE SHEA

Date	Qtr.	Sign	Activity
Jul 19, 4:43 am– Jul 21, 12:36 pm	4th	Taurus	Plant potatoes and tubers. Trim to retard growth.
Jul 21, 12:36 pm– Jul 23, 10:59 pm	4th	Gemini	Cultivate. Destroy weeds and pests. Harvest fruits and root crops for food. Trim to retard growth.
Jul 23, 10:59 pm– Jul 26, 10:55 am	4th	Cancer	Plant biennials, perennials, bulbs, and roots. Prune. Irrigate. Fertilize (organic).
Jul 26, 10:55 am– Jul 26, 6:42 pm	4th	Leo	Cultivate. Destroy weeds and pests. Harvest fruits and root crops for food. Trim to retard growth.

Low-back tension can also be released with child's pose: simply rest on all fours and gently sit your bottom back to your heels. (Use rolled-up towels to pad the space if going all the way back is uncomfortable.) Keep your hands in their orginal position and lower your head, stretching your entire spine. Rest your forehead on the floor if you are able, so you can fully relax.

July 26
6:42 pm EDT

JULY

S	M	T	W	T	F	S
		1	2	3	4	5
6	7	8	9	10	11	12
13	14	15	16	17	18	19
20	21	22	23	24	25	26
27	28	29	30	31		

2013 © iofoto.com Image from BigStockPhoto.com

♋ August

July 27–August 2

Ere I am old, O, let me give my life to learning how to live!

~Caroline A. Briggs

Date	Qtr.	Sign	Activity
Jul 31, 12:09 pm– Aug 2, 10:57 pm	1st	Libra	Plant annuals for fragrance and beauty. Trim to increase growth.
Aug 2, 10:57 pm– Aug 3, 8:50 pm	1st	Scorpio	Plant grains, leafy annuals. Fertilize (chemical). Graft or bud plants. Irrigate. Trim to increase growth.

Most of us struggle to drink as much water as "they" say we should. Find a pair of liter-size bottles and draw lines on them for 8-ounce increments. Label the lines with the following times, top to bottom: 8am, 10am, 12pm, 2pm, 4pm, 6pm, 8pm, 10pm. This is 64 ounces spread equally over 16 hours. You'll be able to tell at a glance if you are "behind" on your water consumption. This 64-ounce amount is a general goal. For a more personal goal, divide your weight in pounds by two; this is how many ounces of total liquids you should aim to consume each day.

AUGUST

S	M	T	W	T	F	S
					1	2
3	4	5	6	7	8	9
10	11	12	13	14	15	16
17	18	19	20	21	22	23
24	25	26	27	28	29	30
31						

2013 © Cheryl Casey Image from BigStockPhoto.com

August 3–9 ♌

He is the greatest artist, then, whether of pencil or or pen,
who follows Nature.

~Henry Wadsworth Longfellow

Date	Qtr.	Sign	Activity
Aug 2, 10:57 pm– Aug 3, 8:50 pm	1st	Scorpio	Plant grains, leafy annuals. Fertilize (chemical). Graft or bud plants. Irrigate. Trim to increase growth.
Aug 3, 8:50 pm– Aug 5, 6:19 am	2nd	Scorpio	Plant grains, leafy annuals. Fertilize (chemical). Graft or bud plants. Irrigate. Trim to increase growth.
Aug 7, 9:38 am– Aug 9, 9:52 am	2nd	Capricorn	Graft or bud plants. Trim to increase growth.

So do soda, coffee, tea, and juice count toward liquid consumption per day? It depends. Unsweetened coffee and tea certainly count in moderation; candy-in-a-cup drinks do not. Juice counts toward a fruit serving, not a liquid serving. Soda is not a good substitute for water, even if it's diet and caffeine-free. Drink a few swallows of water before and after your soda; you won't notice the taste and your body will get the water it needs.

August 3
8:50 pm EDT

AUGUST

S	M	T	W	T	F	S
					1	2
3	4	5	6	7	8	9
10	11	12	13	14	15	16
17	18	19	20	21	22	23
24	25	26	27	28	29	30
31						

August 10–16

Nature never makes excellent things for mean or no uses.

~John Locke

Date	Qtr.	Sign	Activity
Aug 10, 2:09 pm– Aug 11, 8:55 am	3rd	Aquarius	Cultivate. Destroy weeds and pests. Harvest fruits and root crops for food. Trim to retard growth.
Aug 11, 8:55 am– Aug 13, 9:00 am	3rd	Pisces	Plant biennials, perennials, bulbs, and roots. Prune. Irrigate. Fertilize (organic).
Aug 13, 9:00 am– Aug 15, 11:58 am	3rd	Aries	Cultivate. Destroy weeds and pests. Harvest fruits and root crops for food. Trim to retard growth.
Aug 15, 11:58 am– Aug 17, 8:26 am	3rd	Taurus	Plant potatoes and tubers. Trim to retard growth.

Forget paying money to heat up and dry clothes on the hot summer days! String up a clothesline and save about 50 cents per load for an electric dryer, or 30 cents per load for a gas dryer. Lots of clothes can dry in an hour or so on a sunny day. If the fabric seems stiff after line drying, pop the load in the dryer for five minutes to soften it up. You'll also keep your laundry room quite a bit cooler.

_____

_____

_____

August 10
2:09 pm EDT

August

S	M	T	W	T	F	S
					1	2
3	4	5	6	7	8	9
10	11	12	13	14	15	16
17	18	19	20	21	22	23
24	25	26	27	28	29	30
31						

August 17–23

The evil that men do lives after them; the good is oft interred with their bones.
     ~William Shakespeare

Date	Qtr.	Sign	Activity
Aug 15, 11:58 am–Aug 17, 8:26 am	3rd	Taurus	Plant potatoes and tubers. Trim to retard growth.
Aug 17, 8:26 am–Aug 17, 6:41 pm	4th	Taurus	Plant potatoes and tubers. Trim to retard growth.
Aug 17, 6:41 pm–Aug 20, 4:45 am	4th	Gemini	Cultivate. Destroy weeds and pests. Harvest fruits and root crops for food. Trim to retard growth.
Aug 20, 4:45 am–Aug 22, 4:49 pm	4th	Cancer	Plant biennials, perennials, bulbs, and roots. Prune. Irrigate. Fertilize (organic).
Aug 22, 4:49 pm–Aug 25, 5:33 am	4th	Leo	Cultivate. Destroy weeds and pests. Harvest fruits and root crops for food. Trim to retard growth.

Got lots of leftover pill bottles? Those orange-shaded bottles protect their contents from sunlight, making them perfect for small-scale herb storage. You can attach labels or paper to pretty them up, or just write directly on the bottle.

August 17
8:26 am EDT

August

S	M	T	W	T	F	S
					1	2
3	4	5	6	7	8	9
10	11	12	13	14	15	16
17	18	19	20	21	22	23
24	25	26	27	28	29	30
31						

♍ August 24–30

Rejoice! ye fields, rejoice! and wave with gold, when August round her precious gifts is flinging.   ~JOHN RUSKIN

Date	Qtr.	Sign	Activity
Aug 22, 4:49 pm–Aug 25, 5:33 am	4th	Leo	Cultivate. Destroy weeds and pests. Harvest fruits and root crops for food. Trim to retard growth.
Aug 25, 5:33 am–Aug 25, 10:13 am	4th	Virgo	Cultivate, especially medicinal plants. Destroy weeds and pests. Trim to retard growth.
Aug 27, 5:54 pm–Aug 30, 4:53 am	1st	Libra	Plant annuals for fragrance and beauty. Trim to increase growth.
Aug 30, 4:53 am–Sep 1, 1:17 pm	1st	Scorpio	Plant grains, leafy annuals. Fertilize (chemical). Graft or bud plants. Irrigate. Trim to increase growth.

Don't care for cilantro? Don't feel bad; you're not alone. In fact, the chemical makeup of cilantro's aroma is somewhat similar to the chemicals found in soaps and lotions. Your nose smells it and tells your mouth not to eat it because it smells like cleaner, not food. Some people may be genetically predisposed to sense this cilantro-soap similarity. Crushing or chopping the herb and allowing that distinctive aroma to dissipate before garnishing a dish may well change your mind about cilantro's actual taste.

August 25
10:13 am EDT

AUGUST

S	M	T	W	T	F	S
					1	2
3	4	5	6	7	8	9
10	11	12	13	14	15	16
17	18	19	20	21	22	23
24	25	26	27	28	29	30
31						

September ♍
August 31–September 6

Failure is simply the opportunity to begin again, this time
more intelligently.
                                                    ∼Henry Ford

Date	Qtr.	Sign	Activity
Aug 30, 4:53 am–Sep 1, 1:17 pm	1st	Scorpio	Plant grains, leafy annuals. Fertilize (chemical). Graft or bud plants. Irrigate. Trim to increase growth.
Sep 3, 6:15 pm–Sep 5, 7:59 pm	2nd	Capricorn	Graft or bud plants. Trim to increase growth.

The early weeks of September may find you scrambling to harvest and use your herbs before the first frosts arrive. Herbed salts are a good option for shelf-stable storage that will last throughout winter. Rosemary, sage, and thyme are great choices. Simply pulse leaves in a blender until fine. Combine 1 part ground fresh herb with 3 parts salt and store in jars. If using sea salt, process 1/3 of the salt in with the herbs to reduce separation. Sprinkle on meats or vegetables before roasting, or use sparingly in place of table salt.

September 2
7:11 am EDT

Sᴇᴘᴛᴇᴍʙᴇʀ

S	M	T	W	T	F	S
		1	2	3	4	5	6
7	8	9	10	11	12	13
14	15	16	17	18	19	20
21	22	23	24	25	26	27
28	29	30				

2013 © Natika Image from BigStockPhoto.com

♍ September 7–13

There's beauty all around our paths, if but our watchful eyes can trace it midst familiar things, and through their lowly guise.   ~FELICIA HEMANS

Date	Qtr.	Sign	Activity
Sep 7, 7:47 pm– Sep 8, 9:38 pm	2nd	Pisces	Plant grains, leafy annuals. Fertilize (chemical). Graft or bud plants. Irrigate. Trim to increase growth.
Sep 8, 9:38 pm– Sep 9, 7:33 pm	3rd	Pisces	Plant biennials, perennials, bulbs, and roots. Prune. Irrigate. Fertilize (organic).
Sep 9, 7:33 pm– Sep 11, 9:17 pm	3rd	Aries	Cultivate. Destroy weeds and pests. Harvest fruits and root crops for food. Trim to retard growth.
Sep 11, 9:17 pm– Sep 14, 2:26 am	3rd	Taurus	Plant potatoes and tubers. Trim to retard growth.

Even if you have a great lawn already, now is the time to do some overseeding. Grass needs to be revitalized every few years, and overseeding can do this in addition to repairing trouble spots. Ask your garden center expert what type of seed will do best in your lawn (shade, sun, drought-tolerant, etc.). Overseed by hand or with a spreader after mowing to ensure the seed reaches ground level. Water daily until the new grass germinates.

○
September 8
9:38 pm EDT

SEPTEMBER

S	M	T	W	T	F	S
	1	2	3	4	5	6
7	8	9	10	11	12	13
14	15	16	17	18	19	20
21	22	23	24	25	26	27
28	29	30				

2013 © Denise M Montville Image from BigStockPhoto.com

September 14–20 ♍

A breeze came wandering from the sky, light as the whispers of a dream.
                              ~WILLIAM CULLEN BRYANT

Date	Qtr.	Sign	Activity
Sep 11, 9:17 pm– Sep 14, 2:26 am	3rd	Taurus	Plant potatoes and tubers. Trim to retard growth.
Sep 14, 2:26 am– Sep 15, 10:05 pm	3rd	Gemini	Cultivate. Destroy weeds and pests. Harvest fruits and root crops for food. Trim to retard growth.
Sep 15, 10:05 pm– Sep 16, 11:24 am	4th	Gemini	Cultivate. Destroy weeds and pests. Harvest fruits and root crops for food. Trim to retard growth.
Sep 16, 11:24 am– Sep 18, 11:10 pm	4th	Cancer	Plant biennials, perennials, bulbs, and roots. Prune. Irrigate. Fertilize (organic).
Sep 18, 11:10 pm– Sep 21, 11:54 am	4th	Leo	Cultivate. Destroy weeds and pests. Harvest fruits and root crops for food. Trim to retard growth.

Cooler weather and abundant tomatoes make this a great time of year for some fancy grilled cheese sandwiches. Add sliced tomato and basil, arugula and turkey, or shredded buffalo chicken and crumbled bacon to your usual recipe.

September 15
10:05 pm EDT

SEPTEMBER

S	M	T	W	T	F	S
	1	2	3	4	5	6
7	8	9	10	11	12	13
14	15	16	17	18	19	20
21	22	23	24	25	26	27
28	29	30				

2013 © Elena Elisseeva Image from BigStockPhoto.com

♎ September 21–27

*Divinest autumn! who may paint thee best, forever changeful
o'er the changeful globe?*   ~R. H. STODDARD

Date	Qtr.	Sign	Activity
Sep 18, 11:10 pm– Sep 21, 11:54 am	4th	Leo	Cultivate. Destroy weeds and pests. Harvest fruits and root crops for food. Trim to retard growth.
Sep 21, 11:54 am– Sep 23, 11:59 pm	4th	Virgo	Cultivate, especially medicinal plants. Destroy weeds and pests. Trim to retard growth.
Sep 24, 2:14 am– Sep 26, 10:29 am	1st	Libra	Plant annuals for fragrance and beauty. Trim to increase growth.
Sep 26, 10:29 am– Sep 28, 6:50 pm	1st	Scorpio	Plant grains, leafy annuals. Fertilize (chemical). Graft or bud plants. Irrigate. Trim to increase growth.

Almost everyone recognizes the distinctive look and smell of lavender plants. Lavender likes plenty of hot sun and soil that drains well. Most varieties are technically perennial, though they will behave as an annual in areas that see freezing temperatures in winter. Harvest lavender as you would any other flower: a day or so before the blooms really pop.

*September 24
2:14 am EDT*

SEPTEMBER

S	M	T	W	T	F	S
		1	2	3	4	5	6
7	8	9	10	11	12	13
14	15	16	17	18	19	20
21	22	23	24	25	26	27
28	29	30				

2013 © Ivonne Wierink Image from BigStockPhoto.com

October ♎

September 28–October 4

*I remember, I remember the rose—red and white; the
violets and the lily-cups, those flowers made of light!*

~Thomas Hood

Date	Qtr.	Sign	Activity
Sep 26, 10:29 am–Sep 28, 6:50 pm	1st	Scorpio	Plant grains, leafy annuals. Fertilize (chemical). Graft or bud plants. Irrigate. Trim to increase growth.
Oct 1, 12:41 am–Oct 1, 3:33 pm	1st	Capricorn	Graft or bud plants. Trim to increase growth.
Oct 1, 3:33 pm–Oct 3, 4:00 am	2nd	Capricorn	Graft or bud plants. Trim to increase growth.

Dry lavender as you would most other herbs, either by hanging in a well-ventilated area or snipping the buds into a paper bag. After a few weeks, you can use the dried flowers for decoration, cooking, or fragrance. Sachets can be made with small organza bags (found in craft stores).

2013 © Ivonne Wierink Image from BigStockPhoto.com

October 1
3:33 pm EDT

October

S	M	T	W	T	F	S
			1	2	3	4
5	6	7	8	9	10	11
12	13	14	15	16	17	18
19	20	21	22	23	24	25
26	27	28	29	30	31	

♎ October 5–11

I don't know anything about music. In my line, you don't have to.

~Elvis Presley

Date	Qtr.	Sign	Activity
Oct 5, 5:24 am– Oct 7, 6:07 am	2nd	Pisces	Plant grains, leafy annuals. Fertilize (chemical). Graft or bud plants. Irrigate. Trim to increase growth.
Oct 8, 6:51 am– Oct 9, 7:44 am	3rd	Aries	Cultivate. Destroy weeds and pests. Harvest fruits and root crops for food. Trim to retard growth.
Oct 9, 7:44 am– Oct 11, 11:51 am	3rd	Taurus	Plant potatoes and tubers. Trim to retard growth.
Oct 11, 11:51 am– Oct 13, 7:30 pm	3rd	Gemini	Cultivate. Destroy weeds and pests. Harvest fruits and root crops for food. Trim to retard growth.

If your lavender plants have been especially abundant, make lavender water. Put about a cup of dried lavender buds in a spice bag or square of cheesecloth, then place in a glass container. Pour 1 pint of boiling water (distilled is best) over the flowers, cover, and let cool completely. Squeeze the flowers before discarding to get out all the scent. Store the lavender water in tight-sealing glass bottles or a spray bottle.

○
October 8
6:51 am EDT

October

S	M	T	W	T	F	S
			1	2	3	4
5	6	7	8	9	10	11
12	13	14	15	16	17	18
19	20	21	22	23	24	25
26	27	28	29	30	31	

October 12–18 ♎

A single word even may be a spark of inextinguishable thought.

~PERCY BYSSHE SHELLEY

Date	Qtr.	Sign	Activity
Oct 11, 11:51 am– Oct 13, 7:30 pm	3rd	Gemini	Cultivate. Destroy weeds and pests. Harvest fruits and root crops for food. Trim to retard growth.
Oct 13, 7:30 pm– Oct 15, 3:12 pm	3rd	Cancer	Plant biennials, perennials, bulbs, and roots. Prune. Irrigate. Fertilize (organic).
Oct 15, 3:12 pm– Oct 16, 6:29 am	4th	Cancer	Plant biennials, perennials, bulbs, and roots. Prune. Irrigate. Fertilize (organic).
Oct 16, 6:29 am– Oct 18, 7:08 pm	4th	Leo	Cultivate. Destroy weeds and pests. Harvest fruits and root crops for food. Trim to retard growth.
Oct 18, 7:08 pm– Oct 21, 7:12 am	4th	Virgo	Cultivate, especially medicinal plants. Destroy weeds and pests. Trim to retard growth.

You might not think twice of using dirt to help douse a campfire, but never use potting soil from your container plants to do so. Potting soil contains peat and vermiculite, which can smolder, melt containers, and cause nearby objects to catch fire. There have been many cases of people putting out a cigarette in a potted plant only to start a serious housefire.

October 15
3:12 pm EDT

2013 © Eva Gruendemann Image from BigStockPhoto.com

OCTOBER

S	M	T	W	T	F	S
			1	2	3	4
5	6	7	8	9	10	11
12	13	14	15	16	17	18
19	20	21	22	23	24	25
26	27	28	29	30	31	

♎ October 19–25

How bravely Autumn paints upon the sky the gorgeous fame
of Summer which is fled!   ∼THOMAS HOOD

Date	Qtr.	Sign	Activity
Oct 18, 7:08 pm– Oct 21, 7:12 am	4th	Virgo	Cultivate, especially medicinal plants. Destroy weeds and pests. Trim to retard growth.
Oct 23, 5:10 pm– Oct 23, 5:57 pm	4th	Scorpio	Plant biennials, perennials, bulbs, and roots. Prune. Irrigate. Fertilize (organic).
Oct 23, 5:57 pm– Oct 26, 12:40 am	1st	Scorpio	Plant grains, leafy annuals. Fertilize (chemical). Graft or bud plants. Irrigate. Trim to increase growth.

Your garden is likely dormant, but you can display your love for it with your Halloween costume. A flower costume could be as simple as dressing in green clothes and pinning fake or real flowers to yourself, or wearing a garland of them around your neck. Cheekier options include black-eyed Susan—paint one eye black and wear a "Susan" nametag; tiger lily—tiger-stripe facepaint and a "Lily" nametag; or marigold—a gold outfit with a "Mary" nametag. Halloween doesn't have to be just for kids!

●

October 23
5:57 pm EDT

OCTOBER

S	M	T	W	T	F	S
			1	2	3	4
5	6	7	8	9	10	11
12	13	14	15	16	17	18
19	20	21	22	23	24	25
26	27	28	29	30	31	

November ♏

October 26–November 1

Cats yawn because they realize that there's nothing to do.

~Jack Kerouac

Date	Qtr.	Sign	Activity
Oct 23, 5:57 pm– Oct 26, 12:40 am	1st	Scorpio	Plant grains, leafy annuals. Fertilize (chemical). Graft or bud plants. Irrigate. Trim to increase growth.
Oct 28, 6:03 am– Oct 30, 9:52 am	1st	Capricorn	Graft or bud plants. Trim to increase growth.
Nov 1, 12:37 pm– Nov 3, 1:53 pm	2nd	Pisces	Plant grains, leafy annuals. Fertilize (chemical). Graft or bud plants. Irrigate. Trim to increase growth.

Group costumes can be lots of fun. Four people could dress as the seasons (seasonal colors and small objects like flowers, leaves, snowflakes, raindrops). Music fans could whip up costumes to go as crimson and clover, or as parsley, sage, rosemary, and thyme—green shirts with fresh herbs attached could do the trick easily. A couple could be the Sun and Moon: one wears bright yellow and sunglasses while the other wears silver and black.

October 30
10:48 pm EDT

November

S	M	T	W	T	F	S
						1
2	3	4	5	6	7	8
9	10	11	12	13	14	15
16	17	18	19	20	21	22
23	24	25	26	27	28	29
30						

2013 © Karamysheva Alexandra Image from BigStockPhoto.com

♏ November 2–8

Nothing in the whole world felt as good as being able to make something from a sudden idea.   ∼Beverly Cleary

Date	Qtr.	Sign	Activity
Nov 1, 12:37 pm– Nov 3, 1:53 pm	2nd	Pisces	Plant grains, leafy annuals. Fertilize (chemical). Graft or bud plants. Irrigate. Trim to increase growth.
Nov 5, 4:33 pm– Nov 6, 5:23 pm	2nd	Taurus	Plant annuals for hardiness. Trim to increase growth.
Nov 6, 5:23 pm– Nov 7, 8:45 pm	3rd	Taurus	Plant potatoes and tubers. Trim to retard growth.
Nov 7, 8:45 pm– Nov 10, 3:38 am	3rd	Gemini	Cultivate. Destroy weeds and pests. Harvest fruits and root crops for food. Trim to retard growth.

It's time to store away the summer gardening tools. Be sure to prepare your metal tools, such as shovels and hoes, for winter: Rub off all dirt clumps and give them a bath in warm water. Dry with a rag, then buff away any rust (and only the rust) with sand paper or steel wool. Bring any dull tools to your local hardware store for a sharpening, so they're ready to go in spring. Finally, protect the metal pieces with a coat of WD-40 or mineral oil.

○
November 6, 5:23 pm EST
Daylight Saving Time ends
November 2, 2:00 am

NOVEMBER

S	M	T	W	T	F	S
						1
2	3	4	5	6	7	8
9	10	11	12	13	14	15
16	17	18	19	20	21	22
23	24	25	26	27	28	29
30						

November 9–15 ♏

Though we travel the world over to find the beautiful, we must carry it with us or we find it not.

~RALPH WALDO EMERSON

Date	Qtr.	Sign	Activity
Nov 7, 8:45 pm– Nov 10, 3:38 am	3rd	Gemini	Cultivate. Destroy weeds and pests. Harvest fruits and root crops for food. Trim to retard growth.
Nov 10, 3:38 am– Nov 12, 1:44 pm	3rd	Cancer	Plant biennials, perennials, bulbs, and roots. Prune. Irrigate. Fertilize (organic).
Nov 12, 1:44 pm– Nov 14, 10:16 am	3rd	Leo	Cultivate. Destroy weeds and pests. Harvest fruits and root crops for food. Trim to retard growth.
Nov 14, 10:16 am– Nov 15, 2:08 am	4th	Leo	Cultivate. Destroy weeds and pests. Harvest fruits and root crops for food. Trim to retard growth.
Nov 15, 2:08 am– Nov 17, 2:30 pm	4th	Virgo	Cultivate, especially medicinal plants. Destroy weeds and pests. Trim to retard growth.

To easily recall the herbs in Italian seasoning blends, think **STROMB**oli. **S**age (or savory, if you prefer), **T**hyme, **R**osemary, **O**regano, **M**arjoram, and **B**asil. Any or all of these can be combined in roughly equal parts for an "Italian" flavor.

◑

November 14
10:16 am EST

NOVEMBER

S	M	T	W	T	F	S
						1
2	3	4	5	6	7	8
9	10	11	12	13	14	15
16	17	18	19	20	21	22
23	24	25	26	27	28	29
30						

2013 © Jennifer Davis Image from BigStockPhoto.com

♏ November 16–22

If you believe everything, you are not a believer in anything at all.

*～*Idries Shah

Date	Qtr.	Sign	Activity
Nov 15, 2:08 am– Nov 17, 2:30 pm	4th	Virgo	Cultivate, especially medicinal plants. Destroy weeds and pests. Trim to retard growth.
Nov 20, 12:31 am– Nov 22, 7:19 am	4th	Scorpio	Plant biennials, perennials, bulbs, and roots. Prune. Irrigate. Fertilize (organic).
Nov 22, 7:19 am– Nov 22, 7:32 am	4th	Sagittarius	Cultivate. Destroy weeds and pests. Harvest fruits and root crops for food. Trim to retard growth.

If you live near the equator or in the hotter areas of the United States, now is your planting season! Plant seeds for most vegetables and flowers, as well as flower bulbs, in November. Keep an eye on the weather and protect plants if a rare frost is forecast—use cloches, foam covers, or old bedsheets to cover outdoor plants. Shrubs and trees need less water now that the temperatures are not extremely hot, so cut back on watering. Trim away dead branches after the leaves fall.

November 22
7:32 am EST

November

S	M	T	W	T	F	S
						1
2	3	4	5	6	7	8
9	10	11	12	13	14	15
16	17	18	19	20	21	22
23	24	25	26	27	28	29
30						

November 23–29

Books should to one of these four ends conduce—for wisdom,
piety, delight, or use.　　　　　　　　　~SIR JOHN DENHAM

Date	Qtr.	Sign	Activity
Nov 24, 11:31 am–Nov 26, 2:23 pm	1st	Capricorn	Graft or bud plants. Trim to increase growth.
Nov 28, 5:03 pm–Nov 29, 5:06 am	1st	Pisces	Plant grains, leafy annuals. Fertilize (chemical). Graft or bud plants. Irrigate. Trim to increase growth.
Nov 29, 5:06 am–Nov 30, 8:14 pm	2nd	Pisces	Plant grains, leafy annuals. Fertilize (chemical). Graft or bud plants. Irrigate. Trim to increase growth.

This Thanksgiving, create a "Thankful List" either with your family and friends or as a personal activity. Give each person a piece of paper, then have everyone write until the paper is absolutely full. These can be small things like a new pair of shoes or a sale on something you needed, or large things like the health of a loved one or the creation of a new friendship. Big or small, this list will remind you that there is much to be grateful for in your life, no matter where or who you are.

2013 © Cathy Yeulet Image from BigStockPhoto.com

November 29
5:06 am EST

NOVEMBER

S	M	T	W	T	F	S
						1
2	3	4	5	6	7	8
9	10	11	12	13	14	15
16	17	18	19	20	21	22
23	24	25	26	27	28	29
30						

December
November 30–December 6

How beautiful is night! A dewy freshness fills the air.

~ROBERT SOUTHEY

Date	Qtr.	Sign	Activity
Nov 29, 5:06 am– Nov 30, 8:14 pm	2nd	Pisces	Plant grains, leafy annuals. Fertilize (chemical). Graft or bud plants. Irrigate. Trim to increase growth.
Dec 3, 12:15 am– Dec 5, 5:28 am	2nd	Taurus	Plant annuals for hardiness. Trim to increase growth.
Dec 6, 7:27 am– Dec 7, 12:34 pm	3rd	Gemini	Cultivate. Destroy weeds and pests. Harvest fruits and root crops for food. Trim to retard growth.

According to the National Christmas Tree Association, 33 million live Christmas trees are sold each year in a billion-dollar industry. The average tree takes about seven years to grow, and its main carbon impact comes from the fuel used to transport the tree from farm to store to home. About 9.5 million fake trees are sold each year. Studies show that a fake tree is more environmentally friendly—but only if it is used for ten or more years.

_____

_____

_____

_____

○
December 6
7:27 am EST

DECEMBER

S	M	T	W	T	F	S
	1	2	3	4	5	6
7	8	9	10	11	12	13
14	15	16	17	18	19	20
21	22	23	24	25	26	27
28	29	30	31			

2013 © Lori Sparkia Image from BigStockPhoto.com

December 7–13

When friends rejoice both far and near, how can I keep from singing?

~ROBERT LOWRY, ATTRIBUTED

Date	Qtr.	Sign	Activity
Dec 6, 7:27 am– Dec 7, 12:34 pm	3rd	Gemini	Cultivate. Destroy weeds and pests. Harvest fruits and root crops for food. Trim to retard growth.
Dec 7, 12:34 pm– Dec 9, 10:14 pm	3rd	Cancer	Plant biennials, perennials, bulbs, and roots. Prune. Irrigate. Fertilize (organic).
Dec 9, 10:14 pm– Dec 12, 10:19 am	3rd	Leo	Cultivate. Destroy weeds and pests. Harvest fruits and root crops for food. Trim to retard growth.
Dec 12, 10:19 am– Dec 14, 7:51 am	3rd	Virgo	Cultivate, especially medicinal plants. Destroy weeds and pests. Trim to retard growth.

Anchor your cutting board to prevent slips, nicks, and messes while cutting tough winter squashes. Place a jar grip pad under your cutting board, or create a semi-permanent solution by affixing small rubber dots to the underside corners of a board. You can usually find these near the picture-hanging hooks and stickers in stores. Many kinds are self-adhesive, but you can use superglue to ensure they'll stay on through many washings.

2013 © Bragin Alexey Image from BigStockPhoto.com

DECEMBER

S	M	T	W	T	F	S
	1	2	3	4	5	6
7	8	9	10	11	12	13
14	15	16	17	18	19	20
21	22	23	24	25	26	27
28	29	30	31			

December 14–20

Soft as snowflakes falling, still as moonlight roadways, winter midnights calling, sleep!   ~ANITA McLEAN WASHINGTON

Date	Qtr.	Sign	Activity
Dec 12, 10:19 am–Dec 14, 7:51 am	3rd	Virgo	Cultivate, especially medicinal plants. Destroy weeds and pests. Trim to retard growth.
Dec 14, 7:51 am–Dec 14, 11:05 pm	4th	Virgo	Cultivate, especially medicinal plants. Destroy weeds and pests. Trim to retard growth.
Dec 17, 9:52 am–Dec 19, 4:55 pm	4th	Scorpio	Plant biennials, perennials, bulbs, and roots. Prune. Irrigate. Fertilize (organic).
Dec 19, 4:55 pm–Dec 21, 8:25 pm	4th	Sagittarius	Cultivate. Destroy weeds and pests. Harvest fruits and root crops for food. Trim to retard growth.

Butternut squash can be made easier to peel and slice by microwaving it for a short time. Pierce the flesh in a few spots, then zap for about 90 seconds per pound. Handle carefully in case of hot juices, then cut a flat slice off the top and bottom to create a more stable surface. Now peel using a sturdy metal peeler and proceed with halving and deseeding the squash. Each pound of squash yields about 2 cups cubed.

December 14
7:51 am EST

DECEMBER

S	M	T	W	T	F	S
	1	2	3	4	5	6
7	8	9	10	11	12	13
14	15	16	17	18	19	20
21	22	23	24	25	26	27
28	29	30	31			

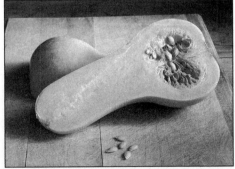

December 21–27 ♑

Yet still the simple gift I prize, for I am sure the giver loved me.

~LORD BYRON

Date	Qtr.	Sign	Activity
Dec 19, 4:55 pm– Dec 21, 8:25 pm	4th	Sagittarius	Cultivate. Destroy weeds and pests. Harvest fruits and root crops for food. Trim to retard growth.
Dec 21, 8:25 pm– Dec 21, 8:36 pm	4th	Capricorn	Plant potatoes and tubers. Trim to retard growth.
Dec 21, 8:36 pm– Dec 23, 9:52 pm	1st	Capricorn	Graft or bud plants. Trim to increase growth.
Dec 25, 11:07 pm– Dec 28, 1:35 am	1st	Pisces	Plant grains, leafy annuals. Fertilize (chemical). Graft or bud plants. Irrigate. Trim to increase growth.

Butternut squash has a sweet flavor that combines very well with a kick of heat from red pepper or red curry. This vegetable can be baked or boiled and made into soup using broth. Top a slightly spicy butternut squash soup with cooked cheese ravioli (frozen works just fine) and a dash of dried sage for a quick and impressive winter meal. Leftover soup freezes well, so don't be afraid to make a large pot using several squashes.

*December 21
8:36 pm EST*

DECEMBER

S	M	T	W	T	F	S
	1	2	3	4	5	6
7	8	9	10	11	12	13
14	15	16	17	18	19	20
21	22	23	24	25	26	27
28	29	30	31			

♑ December 28–January 3, 2015

*Ring out the old, ring in the new—ring, happy bells, across
the snow.*

~Alfred, Lord Tennyson

Date	Qtr.	Sign	Activity
Dec 25, 11:07 pm– Dec 28, 1:35 am	1st	Pisces	Plant grains, leafy annuals. Fertilize (chemical). Graft or bud plants. Irrigate. Trim to increase growth.
Dec 30, 5:56 am– Jan 1, 12:09 pm	2nd	Taurus	Plant annuals for hardiness. Trim to increase growth.
Jan 3, 8:08 pm– Jan 4, 11:53 pm	2nd	Cancer	Plant grains, leafy annuals. Fertilize (chemical). Graft or bud plants. Irrigate. Trim to increase growth.

Remember those hot, muggy days of summer when you hung out clothes to dry in order to save money and energy? You can still line dry your laundry in the winter—indoors. If your area sees dry air in the winter, hanging clothes on drying racks or indoor clotheslines can add a welcome touch of moisture to the air without needing to purchase or plug in a humidifier.

December 28
1:31 pm EST

DECEMBER

S	M	T	W	T	F	S
		1	2	3	4	5	6
7	8	9	10	11	12	13
14	15	16	17	18	19	20
21	22	23	24	25	26	27
28	29	30	31			

Gardening by the Moon

Today, people often reject the notion of gardening according to the Moon's phase and sign. The usual nonbeliever is not a scientist but the city dweller who has never had any real contact with nature and little experience of natural rhythms.

Camille Flammarion, the French astronomer, testifies to the success of Moon planting, though:

"Cucumbers increase at Full Moon, as well as radishes, turnips, leeks, lilies, horseradish, and saffron; onions, on the contrary, are much larger and better nourished during the decline and old age of the Moon than at its increase, during its youth and fullness, which is the reason the Egyptians abstained from onions, on account of their antipathy to the Moon. Herbs gathered while the Moon increases are of great efficiency. If the vines are trimmed at night when the Moon is in the sign of the Lion, Sagittarius, the Scorpion, or the Bull, it will save them from field rats, moles, snails, flies, and other animals."

Dr. Clark Timmins is one of the few modern scientists to have conducted tests in Moon planting. Following is a summary of his experiments:

Beets: When sown with the Moon in Scorpio, the germination rate was 71 percent; when sown in Sagittarius, the germination rate was 58 percent.

Scotch marigold: When sown with the Moon in Cancer, the germination rate was 90 percent; when sown in Leo, the rate was 32 percent.

Carrots: When sown with the Moon in Scorpio, the germination rate was 64 percent; when sown in Sagittarius, the germination rate was 47 percent.

Tomatoes: When sown with the Moon in Cancer, the germination rate was 90 percent; but when sown with the Moon in Leo, the germination rate was 58 percent.

Two things should be emphasized. First, remember that this is only a summary of the results of the experiments; the experiments themselves were conducted in a scientific manner to eliminate any variation in soil, temperature, moisture, and so on, so that only the Moon sign is varied. Second, note that these astonishing results were obtained without regard to the phase of the Moon—the other factor we use in Moon planting, and which presumably would have increased the differential in germination rates.

Dr. Timmins also tried transplanting Cancer- and Leo-planted tomato seedlings while the Cancer Moon was waxing. The result was 100 percent survival. When transplanting was done with the waning Sagittarius Moon, there was 0 percent survival. Dr. Timmins' tests show that the Cancer-planted tomatoes had blossoms twelve days earlier than those planted under Leo; the Cancer-planted tomatoes had an average height of twenty inches at that time compared to fifteen inches for the Leo-planted; the first ripe tomatoes were gathered from the Cancer plantings eleven days ahead of the Leo plantings; and a count of the hanging fruit and its size and weight shows an advantage to the Cancer plants over the Leo plants of 45 percent.

Dr. Timmins also observed that there have been similar tests that did not indicate results favorable to the Moon planting theory. As a scientist, he asked why one set of experiments indicated a positive verification of Moon planting, and others did not. He checked these other tests and found that the experimenters had not followed the geocentric system for determining the Moon sign positions, but the heliocentric. When the times used in these other tests were converted to the geocentric system, the dates chosen often were found to be in barren, rather than fertile, signs. Without going into a technical explanation, it is sufficient to point out that geocentric and heliocentric positions often vary by as much as four days. This is a large enough differential to place the Moon in Cancer, for example, in the heliocentric system, and at the same time in Leo by the geocentric system.

Most almanacs and calendars show the Moon's signs heliocentrically—and thus incorrectly for Moon planting—while the *Moon Sign Book* is calculated correctly for planting purposes, using the geocentric system. Some readers are confused because the *Moon Sign Book* talks about first, second, third, and fourth quarters, while other almanacs refer to these same divisions as New Moon, first quarter, Full Moon, and fourth quarter. Thus the almanacs say first quarter when the *Moon Sign Book* says second quarter.

There is nothing complicated about using astrology in agriculture and horticulture in order to increase both pleasure and profit, but there is one very important rule that is often neglected—use common sense! Of course this is one rule that should be remembered in every activity we undertake, but in the case of gardening and farming by the Moon, if it is not possible to use the best dates for planting or harvesting, we must select the next best and just try to do the best we can.

This brings up the matter of the other factors to consider in your gardening work. The dates we give as best for a certain activity apply to the entire country (with slight time correction), but in your section of the country you may be buried under three feet of snow on a date we say is good to plant your flowers. So we have factors of weather, season, temperature, and moisture variations, soil conditions, your own available time and opportunity, and so forth. Some astrologers like to think it is all a matter of science, but gardening is also an art. In art, you develop an instinctive identification with your work and influence it with your feelings and wishes.

The *Moon Sign Book* gives you the place of the Moon for every day of the year so that you can select the best times once you have become familiar with the rules and practices of lunar agriculture. We give you specific, easy-to-follow directions so that you can get right down to work.

We give you the best dates for planting, and also for various related activities, including cultivation, fertilizing, harvesting, irrigation, and getting rid of weeds and pests. But we cannot tell you exactly when it's good to plant. Many of these rules were learned by observation and experience; as the body of experience grew, we could see various patterns emerging that allowed us to make judgments about new things. That's what you should do, too. After you have worked with lunar agriculture for a while and have gained a working knowledge, you will probably begin to try new things—and we hope you will share your experiments and findings with us. That's how the science grows.

Here's an example of what we mean. Years ago Llewellyn George suggested that we try to combine our bits of knowledge about what to expect in planting under each of the Moon signs in order to benefit from several lunar factors in one plant. From this came our rule for developing "thoroughbred seed." To develop thoroughbred seed, save the seed for three successive years from plants grown by the correct Moon sign and phase. You can plant in the first quarter phase and in the sign of Cancer for fruitfulness; the second year, plant seeds from the first year plants in Libra for beauty; and in the third year, plant the seeds from the second year plants in Taurus to produce hardiness. In a similar manner you can combine the fruitfulness of Cancer, the good root growth of Pisces, and the sturdiness and good vine growth of Scorpio. And don't forget the characteristics of Capricorn: hardy like Taurus, but drier and perhaps more resistant to drought and disease.

Unlike common almanacs, we consider both the Moon's phase and the Moon's sign in making our calculations for the proper timing of our work. It is perhaps a little easier to understand this if we remind you that we are all living in the center of a vast electromagnetic field that is the Earth and its environment in space. Everything that occurs within this electromagnetic field has an effect on everything else within the field. The Moon and the Sun are the most important of the factors affecting the life of the Earth, and it is their relative positions to the Earth that we project for each day of the year.

Many people claim that not only do they achieve larger crops gardening by the Moon, but that their fruits and vegetables are much tastier. A number of organic gardeners have also become lunar gardeners using the natural rhythm of life forces that we experience through the relative movements of the Sun and Moon. We provide a few basic rules and then give you day-by-day guidance for your gardening work. You will be able to choose the best dates to meet your own needs and opportunities.

Planting by the Moon's Phases

During the increasing or waxing light—from New Moon to Full Moon—plant annuals that produce their yield above the ground. An annual is a plant that completes its entire life cycle within one growing season and has to be seeded each year. During the decreasing or waning light—from Full Moon to New Moon—plant biennials, perennials, and bulb and root plants. Biennials include crops that are planted one season to winter over and produce crops the next, such as winter wheat. Perennials and bulb and root plants include all plants that grow from the same root each year.

A simpler, less-accurate rule is to plant crops that produce above the ground during the waxing Moon, and to plant crops that produce below the ground during the waning Moon. Thus the old adage, "Plant potatoes during the dark of the Moon." Llewellyn George's system divided the lunar month into quarters. The first two from New Moon to Full Moon are the first and second quarters, and the last two from Full Moon to New Moon the third and fourth quarters. Using these divisions, we can increase our accuracy in timing our efforts to coincide with natural forces.

First Quarter

Plant annuals producing their yield above the ground, which are generally of the leafy kind that produce their seed outside the fruit. Some examples are asparagus, broccoli, brussels sprouts, cabbage, cauliflower, celery, cress, endive, kohlrabi, lettuce, parsley, and spinach. Cucumbers are an exception, as they do best in the first quarter rather than the second, even though the seeds are inside the fruit. Also plant cereals and grains.

Second Quarter

Plant annuals producing their yield above the ground, which are generally of the viney kind that produce their seed inside the fruit. Some examples include beans, eggplant, melons, peas, peppers, pumpkins, squash, tomatoes, etc. These are not hard-and-fast divisions. If you can't plant during the first quarter, plant during the second, and vice versa. There are many plants that

seem to do equally well planted in either quarter, suc'
melon, hay, and cereals and grains.

Third Quarter

Plant biennials, perennials, bulbs, root plants, trees, shrubs, berries, grapes, strawberries, beets, carrots, onions, parsnips, rutabagas, potatoes, radishes, peanuts, rhubarb, turnips, winter wheat, etc.

Fourth Quarter

This is the best time to cultivate, turn sod, pull weeds, and destroy pests of all kinds, especially when the Moon is in Aries, Leo, Virgo, Gemini, Aquarius, and Sagittarius.

The Moon in the Signs

Moon in Aries

Barren, dry, fiery, and masculine. Use for destroying noxious weeds.

Moon in Taurus

Productive, moist, earthy, and feminine. Use for planting many crops when hardiness is important, particularly root crops. Also used for lettuce, cabbage, and similar leafy vegetables.

Moon in Gemini

Barren and dry, airy and masculine. Use for destroying noxious growths, weeds, and pests, and for cultivation.

Moon in Cancer

Fruitful, moist, feminine. Use for planting and irrigation.

Moon in Leo

Barren, dry, fiery, masculine. Use for killing weeds or cultivation.

Moon in Virgo

Barren, dry, earthy, and feminine. Use for cultivation and destroying weeds and pests.

Moon in Libra

Semi-fruitful, moist, and airy. Use for planting crops that need good pulp growth. A very good sign for flowers and vines. Also used for seeding hay, corn fodder, and the like.

Moon in Scorpio

Very fruitful and moist, watery and feminine. Nearly as productive as Cancer; use for the same purposes. Especially good for vine growth and sturdiness.

Moon in Sagittarius

Barren and dry, fiery and masculine. Use for planting onions, seeding hay, and for cultivation.

Moon in Capricorn

Productive and dry, earthy and feminine. Use for planting potatoes and other tubers.

Moon in Aquarius

Barren, dry, airy, and masculine. Use for cultivation and destroying noxious growths and pests.

Moon in Pisces

Very fruitful, moist, watery, and feminine. Especially good for root growth.

A Guide to Planting

Plant	Quarter	Sign
Annuals	1st or 2nd	
Apple tree	2nd or 3rd	Cancer, Pisces, Virgo
Artichoke	1st	Cancer, Pisces
Asparagus	1st	Cancer, Scorpio, Pisces
Aster	1st or 2nd	Virgo, Libra
Barley	1st or 2nd	Cancer, Pisces, Libra, Capricorn, Virgo
Beans (bush & pole)	2nd	Cancer, Taurus, Pisces, Libra
Beans (kidney, white, & navy)	1st or 2nd	Cancer, Pisces
Beech tree	2nd or 3rd	Virgo, Taurus
Beets	3rd	Cancer, Capricorn, Pisces, Libra
Biennials	3rd or 4th	
Broccoli	1st	Cancer, Scorpio, Pisces, Libra
Brussels sprouts	1st	Cancer, Scorpio, Pisces, Libra
Buckwheat	1st or 2nd	Capricorn
Bulbs	3rd	Cancer, Scorpio, Pisces
Bulbs for seed	2nd or 3rd	
Cabbage	1st	Cancer, Scorpio, Pisces, Taurus, Libra
Canes (raspberry, blackberry, & gooseberry)	2nd	Cancer, Scorpio, Pisces
Cantaloupe	1st or 2nd	Cancer, Scorpio, Pisces, Taurus, Libra
Carrots	3rd	Cancer, Scorpio, Pisces, Taurus, Libra
Cauliflower	1st	Cancer, Scorpio, Pisces, Libra
Celeriac	3rd	Cancer, Scorpio, Pisces
Celery	1st	Cancer, Scorpio, Pisces
Cereals	1st or 2nd	Cancer, Scorpio, Pisces, Libra
Chard	1st or 2nd	Cancer, Scorpio, Pisces
Chicory	2nd or 3rd	Cancer, Scorpio, Pisces
Chrysanthemum	1st or 2nd	Virgo
Clover	1st or 2nd	Cancer, Scorpio, Pisces

Plant	Quarter	Sign
Coreopsis	2nd or 3rd	Libra
Corn	1st	Cancer, Scorpio, Pisces
Corn for fodder	1st or 2nd	Libra
Cosmo	2nd or 3rd	Libra
Cress	1st	Cancer, Scorpio, Pisces
Crocus	1st or 2nd	Virgo
Cucumber	1st	Cancer, Scorpio, Pisces
Daffodil	1st or 2nd	Libra, Virgo
Dahlia	1st or 2nd	Libra, Virgo
Deciduous trees	2nd or 3rd	Cancer, Scorpio, Pisces, Virgo, Libra
Eggplant	2nd	Cancer, Scorpio, Pisces, Libra
Endive	1st	Cancer, Scorpio, Pisces, Libra
Flowers	1st	Cancer, Scorpio, Pisces, Libra, Taurus, Virgo
Garlic	3rd	Libra, Taurus, Pisces
Gladiola	1st or 2nd	Libra, Virgo
Gourds	1st or 2nd	Cancer, Scorpio, Pisces, Libra
Grapes	2nd or 3rd	Cancer, Scorpio, Pisces, Virgo
Hay	1st or 2nd	Cancer, Scorpio, Pisces, Libra, Taurus
Herbs	1st or 2nd	Cancer, Scorpio, Pisces
Honeysuckle	1st or 2nd	Scorpio, Virgo
Hops	1st or 2nd	Scorpio, Libra
Horseradish	1st or 2nd	Cancer, Scorpio, Pisces
Houseplants	1st	Cancer, Scorpio, Pisces, Libra
Hyacinth	3rd	Cancer, Scorpio, Pisces
Iris	1st or 2nd	Cancer, Virgo
Kohlrabi	1st or 2nd	Cancer, Scorpio, Pisces, Libra
Leek	2nd or 3rd	Sagittarius
Lettuce	1st	Cancer, Scorpio, Pisces, Libra, Taurus
Lily	1st or 2nd	Cancer, Scorpio, Pisces
Maple tree	2nd or 3rd	Taurus, Virgo, Cancer, Pisces
Melon	2nd	Cancer, Scorpio, Pisces
Moon vine	1st or 2nd	Virgo

Plant	Quarter	Sign
Morning glory	1st or 2nd	Cancer, Scorpio, Pisces, Virgo
Oak tree	2nd or 3rd	Taurus, Virgo, Cancer, Pisces
Oats	1st or 2nd	Cancer, Scorpio, Pisces, Libra
Okra	1st or 2nd	Cancer, Scorpio, Pisces, Libra
Onion seed	2nd	Cancer, Scorpio, Sagittarius
Onion set	3rd or 4th	Cancer, Pisces, Taurus, Libra
Pansies	1st or 2nd	Cancer, Scorpio, Pisces
Parsley	1st	Cancer, Scorpio, Pisces, Libra
Parsnip	3rd	Cancer, Scorpio, Taurus, Capricorn
Peach tree	2nd or 3rd	Cancer, Taurus, Virgo, Libra
Peanuts	3rd	Cancer, Scorpio, Pisces
Pear tree	2nd or 3rd	Cancer, Scorpio, Pisces, Libra
Peas	2nd	Cancer, Scorpio, Pisces, Libra
Peony	1st or 2nd	Virgo
Peppers	2nd	Cancer, Scorpio, Pisces
Perennials	3rd	
Petunia	1st or 2nd	Libra, Virgo
Plum tree	2nd or 3rd	Cancer, Pisces, Taurus, Virgo
Poppies	1st or 2nd	Virgo
Portulaca	1st or 2nd	Virgo
Potatoes	3rd	Cancer, Scorpio, Libra, Taurus, Capricorn
Privet	1st or 2nd	Taurus, Libra
Pumpkin	2nd	Cancer, Scorpio, Pisces, Libra
Quince	1st or 2nd	Capricorn
Radishes	3rd	Cancer, Scorpio, Pisces, Libra, Capricorn
Rhubarb	3rd	Cancer, Pisces
Rice	1st or 2nd	Scorpio
Roses	1st or 2nd	Cancer, Virgo
Rutabaga	3rd	Cancer, Scorpio, Pisces, Taurus
Saffron	1st or 2nd	Cancer, Scorpio, Pisces
Sage	3rd	Cancer, Scorpio, Pisces

Plant	Quarter	Sign
Salsify	1st	Cancer, Scorpio, Pisces
Shallot	2nd	Scorpio
Spinach	1st	Cancer, Scorpio, Pisces
Squash	2nd	Cancer, Scorpio, Pisces, Libra
Strawberries	3rd	Cancer, Scorpio, Pisces
String beans	1st or 2nd	Taurus
Sunflowers	1st or 2nd	Libra, Cancer
Sweet peas	1st or 2nd	Any
Tomatoes	2nd	Cancer, Scorpio, Pisces, Capricorn
Trees, shade	3rd	Taurus, Capricorn
Trees, ornamental	2nd	Libra, Taurus
Trumpet vine	1st or 2nd	Cancer, Scorpio, Pisces
Tubers for seed	3rd	Cancer, Scorpio, Pisces, Libra
Tulips	1st or 2nd	Libra, Virgo
Turnips	3rd	Cancer, Scorpio, Pisces, Taurus, Capricorn, Libra
Valerian	1st or 2nd	Virgo, Gemini
Watermelon	1st or 2nd	Cancer, Scorpio, Pisces, Libra
Wheat	1st or 2nd	Cancer, Scorpio, Pisces, Libra

Companion Planting Guide

Plant	Companions	Hindered by
Asparagus	Tomatoes, parsley, basil	None known
Beans	Tomatoes, carrots, cucumbers, garlic, cabbage, beets, corn	Onions, gladiolas
Beets	Onions, cabbage, lettuce, mint, catnip	Pole beans
Broccoli	Beans, celery, potatoes, onions	Tomatoes
Cabbage	Peppermint, sage, thyme, tomatoes	Strawberries, grapes
Carrots	Peas, lettuce, chives, radishes, leeks, onions, sage	Dill, anise
Citrus trees	Guava, live oak, rubber trees, peppers	None known
Corn	Potatoes, beans, peas, melon, squash, pumpkin, sunflowers, soybeans	Quack grass, wheat, straw, mulch
Cucumbers	Beans, cabbage, radishes, sunflowers, lettuce, broccoli, squash	Aromatic herbs
Eggplant	Green beans, lettuce, kale	None known
Grapes	Peas, beans, blackberries	Cabbage, radishes
Melons	Corn, peas	Potatoes, gourds
Onions, leeks	Beets, chamomile, carrots, lettuce	Peas, beans, sage
Parsnip	Peas	None known
Peas	Radishes, carrots, corn, cucumbers, beans, tomatoes, spinach, turnips	Onion, garlic
Potatoes	Beans, corn, peas, cabbage, hemp, cucumbers, eggplant, catnip	Raspberries, pumpkins, tomatoes, sunflowers
Radishes	Peas, lettuce, nasturtiums, cucumbers	Hyssop
Spinach	Strawberries	None known
Squash/Pumpkin	Nasturtiums, corn, mint, catnip	Potatoes
Tomatoes	Asparagus, parsley, chives, onions, carrots, marigolds, nasturtiums, dill	Black walnut roots, fennel, potatoes
Turnips	Peas, beans, brussels sprouts	Potatoes

Plant	Companions	Uses
Anise	Coriander	Flavor candy, pastry, cheeses, cookies
Basil	Tomatoes	Dislikes rue; repels flies and mosquitoes
Borage	Tomatoes, squash	Use in teas
Buttercup	Clover	Hinders delphinium, peonies, monkshood, columbine
Catnip		Repels flea beetles
Chamomile	Peppermint, wheat, onions, cabbage	Roman chamomile may control damping-off disease; use in herbal sprays
Chervil	Radishes	Good in soups and other dishes
Chives	Carrots	Use in spray to deter black spot on roses
Coriander	Plant anywhere	Hinders seed formation in fennel
Cosmos		Repels corn earworms
Dill	Cabbage	Hinders carrots and tomatoes
Fennel	Plant in borders	Disliked by all garden plants
Horseradish		Repels potato bugs
Horsetail		Makes fungicide spray
Hyssop		Attracts cabbage flies; harmful to radishes
Lavender	Plant anywhere	Use in spray to control insects on cotton, repels clothes moths
Lovage		Lures horn worms away from tomatoes
Marigolds		Pest repellent; use against Mexican bean beetles and nematodes
Mint	Cabbage, tomatoes	Repels ants, flea beetles, cabbage worm butterflies
Morning glory	Corn	Helps melon germination
Nasturtium	Cabbage, cucumbers	Deters aphids, squash bugs, pumpkin beetles
Okra	Eggplant	Attracts leafhopper (lure insects from other plants)
Parsley	Tomatoes, asparagus	Freeze chopped up leaves to flavor foods
Purslane		Good ground cover
Rosemary		Repels cabbage moths, bean beetles, carrot flies
Savory		Plant with onions for added sweetness
Tansy		Deters Japanese beetles, striped cucumber beetles, squash bugs
Thyme		Repels cabbage worms
Yarrow		Increases essential oils of neighbors

Moon Void-of-Course

By Kim Rogers-Gallagher

The Moon circles the Earth in about twenty-eight days, moving through each zodiac sign in two-and-a-half days. As she passes through the thirty degrees of each sign, she "visits" with the planets in numerical order, forming aspects with them. Because she moves one degree in just two to two-and-a-half hours, her influence on each planet lasts only a few hours. She eventually reaches the planet that's in the highest degree of any sign and forms what will be her final aspect before leaving the sign. From this point until she enters the next sign, she is referred to as void-of-course.

Think of it this way: the Moon is the emotional "tone" of the day, carrying feelings with her particular to the sign she's "wearing" at the moment. After she has contacted each of the planets, she symbolically "rests" before changing her costume, so her instinct is temporarily on hold. It's during this time that many people feel "fuzzy" or "vague." Plans or decisions made now often do not pan out. Without the instinctual "knowing" the Moon provides as she touches each planet, we tend to be unrealistic or exercise poor judgment. The traditional definition of the void Moon is that "nothing will come of this." Actions initiated under a void Moon are often wasted, irrelevant, or incorrect—usually because information is hidden, missing, or has been overlooked.

Although it's not a good time to initiate plans, routine tasks seem to go along just fine. This period is ideal for reflection. On the lighter side, remember there are good uses for the void Moon. It is the period when the universe seems to be most open to loopholes. It's a great time to make plans you don't want to fulfill or schedule things you don't want to do. See the table on pages 76–81 for a schedule of the Moon's void-of-course times.

Last Aspect   Moon Enters New Sign

		January		
2	6:12 am	2	Aquarius	12:03 pm
3	8:47 pm	4	Pisces	11:58 am
6	4:44 am	6	Aries	2:45 pm
8	11:22 am	8	Taurus	9:24 pm
11	5:58 am	11	Gemini	7:26 am
12	4:33 pm	13	Cancer	7:25 pm
15	11:52 pm	16	Leo	8:00 am
18	3:51 am	18	Virgo	8:23 pm
20	3:55 pm	21	Libra	7:43 am
22	10:50 pm	23	Scorpio	4:43 pm
25	8:55 am	25	Sagittarius	10:13 pm
27	5:02 pm	28	Capricorn	12:04 am
29	11:47 am	29	Aquarius	11:33 pm
31	11:45 am	31	Pisces	10:45 pm
		February		
2	11:35 am	2	Aries	11:55 pm
4	6:14 pm	5	Taurus	4:47 am
6	11:49 pm	7	Gemini	1:44 pm
9	4:08 pm	10	Cancer	1:33 am
12	5:51 am	12	Leo	2:15 pm
14	10:13 pm	15	Virgo	2:26 am
17	12:04 am	17	Libra	1:23 pm
19	4:52 pm	19	Scorpio	10:33 pm
21	5:10 pm	22	Sagittarius	5:12 am
24	4:25 am	24	Capricorn	8:50 am
26	5:51 am	26	Aquarius	9:55 am
28	5:55 am	28	Pisces	9:53 am

Last Aspect   Moon Enters New Sign

		March		
2	6:04 am	2	Aries	10:40 am
4	12:31 pm	4	Taurus	2:12 pm
6	8:55 am	6	Gemini	9:37 pm
9	3:53 am	9	Cancer	9:33 am
11	3:50 pm	11	Leo	10:09 pm
14	3:24 am	14	Virgo	10:17 am
16	1:08 pm	16	Libra	8:46 pm
18	9:07 pm	19	Scorpio	5:13 am
20	11:12 pm	21	Sagittarius	11:39 am
23	6:40 am	23	Capricorn	4:03 pm
25	8:35 am	25	Aquarius	6:39 pm
27	9:13 am	27	Pisces	8:10 pm
29	9:44 am	29	Aries	9:54 pm
31	4:07 pm	4/1	Taurus	1:20 am
		April		
3	2:43 am	3	Gemini	7:48 am
5	10:55 am	5	Cancer	5:40 pm
7	2:14 pm	8	Leo	5:50 am
10	2:26 am	10	Virgo	6:08 pm
12	1:12 pm	13	Libra	4:33 am
15	3:42 am	15	Scorpio	12:20 pm
17	3:09 am	17	Sagittarius	5:44 pm
19	9:17 pm	19	Capricorn	9:28 pm
21	7:21 pm	22	Aquarius	12:18 am
23	12:10 pm	24	Pisces	2:55 am
25	4:03 pm	26	Aries	6:01 am
27	7:02 am	28	Taurus	10:23 am
30	11:53 am	30	Gemini	4:56 pm

Last Aspect   **Moon Enters New Sign**

		May		
1	7:32 pm	3	Cancer	2:13 am
5	4:46 am	5	Leo	1:55 pm
7	6:50 am	8	Virgo	2:24 am
9	6:08 pm	10	Libra	1:19 pm
11	8:51 pm	12	Scorpio	9:07 pm
14	3:16 pm	15	Sagittarius	1:44 am
16	3:43 am	17	Capricorn	4:12 am
19	3:02 am	19	Aquarius	5:58 am
20	6:21 pm	21	Pisces	8:18 am
23	2:25 am	23	Aries	12:01 pm
25	11:58 am	25	Taurus	5:28 pm
27	5:10 am	28	Gemini	12:47 am
29	5:59 am	30	Cancer	10:13 am
		June		
1	2:32 am	1	Leo	9:43 pm
3	10:42 am	4	Virgo	10:20 am
6	5:13 am	6	Libra	10:01 pm
8	3:47 pm	9	Scorpio	6:38 am
10	10:21 pm	11	Sagittarius	11:23 am
13	12:11 am	13	Capricorn	1:04 pm
15	2:35 am	15	Aquarius	1:27 pm
17	2:07 pm	17	Pisces	2:26 pm
19	3:05 pm	19	Aries	5:26 pm
21	6:24 pm	21	Taurus	11:03 pm
23	9:49 pm	24	Gemini	7:05 am
26	7:56 am	26	Cancer	5:05 pm
28	9:02 pm	29	Leo	4:43 am

Last Aspect   Moon Enters New Sign

		July		
1	6:00 am	1	Virgo	5:24 pm
4	12:21 am	4	Libra	5:43 am
6	11:31 am	6	Scorpio	3:33 pm
8	6:32 pm	8	Sagittarius	9:24 pm
10	8:19 pm	10	Capricorn	11:24 pm
12	9:56 pm	12	Aquarius	11:07 pm
14	3:23 pm	14	Pisces	10:40 pm
16	8:57 pm	17	Aries	12:07 am
18	10:18 pm	19	Taurus	4:43 am
21	10:12 am	21	Gemini	12:36 pm
23	8:53 pm	23	Cancer	10:59 pm
25	9:53 am	26	Leo	10:55 am
27	8:37 pm	28	Virgo	11:37 pm
31	10:47 am	31	Libra	12:09 pm
		August		
1	10:58 pm	2	Scorpio	10:57 pm
4	1:43 pm	5	Sagittarius	6:19 am
6	10:52 am	7	Capricorn	9:38 am
9	4:09 am	9	Aquarius	9:52 am
10	6:12 pm	11	Pisces	8:55 am
12	12:01 pm	13	Aries	9:00 am
15	11:50 am	15	Taurus	11:58 am
17	8:26 am	17	Gemini	6:41 pm
19	10:54 pm	20	Cancer	4:45 am
21	3:34 pm	22	Leo	4:49 pm
24	4:26 am	25	Virgo	5:33 am
26	10:29 pm	27	Libra	5:54 pm
29	12:00 pm	30	Scorpio	4:53 am

Last Aspect   Moon Enters New Sign

		September		
1	11:40 am	1	Sagittarius	1:17 pm
3	2:06 pm	3	Capricorn	6:15 pm
5	11:08 am	5	Aquarius	7:59 pm
7	1:19 pm	7	Pisces	7:47 pm
9	3:10 pm	9	Aries	7:33 pm
10	8:58 pm	11	Taurus	9:17 pm
13	9:31 am	14	Gemini	2:26 am
15	10:05 pm	16	Cancer	11:24 am
18	2:38 pm	18	Leo	11:10 pm
21	12:33 am	21	Virgo	11:54 am
23	8:15 am	23	Libra	11:59 pm
26	8:39 am	26	Scorpio	10:29 am
28	4:31 pm	28	Sagittarius	6:50 pm
9/29	11:29 pm	10/1	Capricorn	12:41 am
		October		
2	12:18 pm	3	Aquarius	4:00 am
4	2:32 pm	5	Pisces	5:24 am
6	3:38 pm	7	Aries	6:07 am
8	10:20 am	9	Taurus	7:44 am
10	8:49 pm	11	Gemini	11:51 am
13	1:58 pm	13	Cancer	7:30 pm
15	7:27 pm	16	Leo	6:29 am
18	9:10 am	18	Virgo	7:08 pm
20	11:30 pm	21	Libra	7:12 am
23	1:22 pm	23	Scorpio	5:10 pm
25	12:11 pm	26	Sagittarius	12:40 am
27	12:18 pm	28	Capricorn	6:03 am
29	11:01 pm	30	Aquarius	9:52 am

Last Aspect   Moon Enters New Sign

		November		
1	2:22 am	1	Pisces	12:37 pm
3	4:05 am	3	Aries	1:53 pm
5	8:25 am	5	Taurus	4:33 pm
7	11:17 am	7	Gemini	8:45 pm
9	11:22 am	10	Cancer	3:38 am
12	4:16 am	12	Leo	1:44 pm
14	9:53 pm	15	Virgo	2:08 am
17	6:11 am	17	Libra	2:30 pm
19	9:25 am	20	Scorpio	12:31 am
22	12:53 am	22	Sagittarius	7:19 am
23	10:16 pm	24	Capricorn	11:31 am
26	10:30 am	26	Aquarius	2:23 pm
28	12:14 pm	28	Pisces	5:03 pm
30	3:47 pm	30	Aries	8:14 pm
		December		
2	9:42 pm	3	Taurus	12:15 am
5	1:45 am	5	Gemini	5:28 am
7	4:52 am	7	Cancer	12:34 pm
9	7:14 pm	9	Leo	10:14 pm
12	7:48 am	12	Virgo	10:19 am
14	9:11 pm	14	Libra	11:05 pm
17	12:40 am	17	Scorpio	9:52 am
19	4:11 pm	19	Sagittarius	4:55 pm
21	7:34 am	21	Capricorn	8:25 pm
22	10:17 pm	23	Aquarius	9:52 pm
25	10:11 am	25	Pisces	11:07 pm
27	10:44 am	28	Aries	1:35 am
29	7:46 pm	30	Taurus	5:56 am

The Moon's Rhythm

The Moon journeys around Earth in an elliptical orbit that takes about 27.33 days, which is known as a sidereal month (period of revolution of one body about another). She can move up to 15 degrees or as few as 11 degrees in a day, with the fastest motion occurring when the Moon is at perigee (closest approach to Earth). The Moon is never retrograde, but when her motion is slow, the effect is similar to a retrograde period.

Astrologers have observed that people born on a day when the Moon is fast will process information differently from those who are born when the Moon is slow in motion. People born when the Moon is fast process information quickly and tend to react quickly, while those born during a slow Moon will be more deliberate.

The time from New Moon to New Moon is called the synodic month (involving a conjunction), and the average time span between this Sun-Moon alignment is 29.53 days. Since 29.53

won't divide into 365 evenly, we can have a month with two Full Moons or two New Moons.

Moon Aspects

The aspects the Moon will make during the times you are considering are also important. A trine or sextile, and sometimes a conjunction, are considered favorable aspects. A trine or sextile between the Sun and Moon is an excellent foundation for success. Whether or not a conjunction is considered favorable depends upon the planet the Moon is making a conjunction to. If it's joining the Sun, Venus, Mercury, Jupiter, or even Saturn, the aspect is favorable. If the Moon joins Pluto or Mars, however, that would not be considered favorable. There may be exceptions, but it would depend on what you are electing to do. For example, a trine to Pluto might hasten the end of a relationship you want to be free of.

It is important to avoid times when the Moon makes an aspect to or is conjoining any retrograde planet, unless, of course, you want the thing started to end in failure.

After the Moon has completed an aspect to a planet, that planetary energy has passed. For example, if the Moon squares Saturn at 10:00 am, you can disregard Saturn's influence on your activity if it will occur after that time. You should always look ahead at aspects the Moon will make on the day in question, though, because if the Moon opposes Mars at 11:30 pm on that day, you can expect events that stretch into the evening to be affected by the Moon-Mars aspect. A testy conversation might lead to an argument, or more.

Moon Signs

Much agricultural work is ruled by earth signs—Virgo, Capricorn, and Taurus; and the air signs—Gemini, Aquarius, and Libra—rule flying and intellectual pursuits.

Each planet has one or two signs in which its characteristics are enhanced or "dignified," and the planet is said to "rule" that sign. The Sun rules Leo and the Moon rules Cancer, for example. The ruling planet for each sign is listed below. These should not be considered complete lists. We recommend that you purchase a book of planetary rulerships for more complete information.

Aries Moon

The energy of an Aries Moon is masculine, dry, barren, and fiery. Aries provides great start-up energy, but things started at this time may be the result of impulsive action that lacks research or necessary support. Aries lacks staying power.

Use this assertive, outgoing Moon sign to initiate change, but have a plan in place for someone to pick up the reins when you're impatient to move on to the next thing. Work that requires skillful, but not necessarily patient, use of tools—hammering, cutting down trees, etc.—is appropriate in Aries. Expect things to occur rapidly but to also quickly pass. If you are prone to injury or accidents, exercise caution and good judgment in Aries-related activities.

RULER: Mars

IMPULSE: Action

RULES: Head and face

Taurus Moon

A Taurus Moon's energy is feminine, semi-fruitful, and earthy. The Moon is exalted—very strong—in Taurus. Taurus is known as the farmer's sign because of its associations with farmland and precipitation that is the typical day-long "soaker" variety. Taurus energy is good to incorporate into your plans when patience, practicality, and perseverance are needed. Be aware, though, that you may also experience stubbornness in this sign.

Things started in Taurus tend to be long lasting and to increase in value. This can be very supportive energy in a marriage election. On the downside, the fixed energy of this sign resists change or the letting go of even the most difficult situations. A divorce following a marriage that occurred during a Taurus Moon may be difficult and costly to end. Things begun now tend to become habitual and hard to alter. If you want to make changes in something you started, it would be better to wait for Gemini. This is a good time to get a loan, but expect the people in charge of money to be cautious and slow to make decisions.

RULER: Venus

IMPULSE: Stability

RULES: Neck, throat, and voice

Gemini Moon

A Gemini Moon's energy is masculine, dry, barren, and airy. People are more changeable than usual and may prefer to follow intellectual pursuits and play mental games rather than apply themselves to practical concerns.

This sign is not favored for agricultural matters, but it is an excellent time to prepare for activities, to run errands, and write letters. Plan to use a Gemini Moon to exchange ideas, meet people, go on vacations that include walking or biking, or be in situations that require versatility and quick thinking on your feet.

RULER: Mercury

IMPULSE: Versatility

RULES: Shoulders, hands, arms, lungs, and nervous system

Cancer Moon

A Cancer Moon's energy is feminine, fruitful, moist, and very strong. Use this sign when you want to grow things—flowers, fruits, vegetables, commodities, stocks, or collections—for example. This sensitive sign stimulates rapport between people. Considered the most fertile of the signs, it is often associated with mothering. You can use this moontime to build personal friendships that support mutual growth.

Cancer is associated with emotions and feelings. Prominent Cancer energy promotes growth, but it can also turn people pouty and prone to withdrawing into their shells.

RULER: The Moon

IMPULSE: Tenacity

RULES: Chest area, breasts, and stomach

Leo Moon

A Leo Moon's energy is masculine, hot, dry, fiery, and barren. Use it whenever you need to put on a show, make a presentation, or entertain colleagues or guests. This is a proud yet playful energy that exudes self-confidence and is often associated with romance.

This is an excellent time for fund-raisers and ceremonies or to be straightforward, frank, and honest about something. It is advisable not to put yourself in a position of needing public approval or where you might have to cope with underhandedness, as trouble in these areas can bring out the worst Leo traits. There is a tendency in this sign to become arrogant or self-centered.

RULER: The Sun

IMPULSE: I am

RULES: Heart and upper back

Virgo Moon

A Virgo Moon is feminine, dry, barren, earthy energy. It is favorable for anything that needs painstaking attention—especially those things where exactness rather than innovation is preferred.

Use this sign for activities when you must analyze information or when you must determine the value of something. Virgo is the sign of bargain hunting. It's friendly toward agricultural matters with an emphasis on animals and harvesting vegetables. It is an excellent time to care for animals, especially training them and veterinary work.

This sign is most beneficial when decisions have already been made and now need to be carried out. The inclination here is to see details rather than the bigger picture.

There is a tendency in this sign to overdo. Precautions should be taken to avoid becoming too dull from all work and no play. Build a little relaxation and pleasure into your routine from the beginning.

RULER: Mercury

IMPULSE: Discriminating

RULES: Abdomen and intestines

Libra Moon

A Libra Moon's energy is masculine, semi-fruitful, and airy. This energy will benefit any attempt to bring beauty to a place or thing. Libra is considered good energy for starting things of an intellectual nature. Libra is the sign of partnership and unions, which makes it an excellent time to form partnerships of any kind, to make agreements, and to negotiate. Even though this sign is good for initiating things, it is crucial to work with a partner who will provide incentive and encouragement, however. A Libra Moon accentuates teamwork (particularly teams of two) and artistic work (especially work that involves color). Make use of this sign when you are decorating your home or shopping for better-quality clothing.

RULER: Venus

IMPULSE: Balance

RULES: Lower back, kidneys, and buttocks

Scorpio Moon

The Scorpio Moon is feminine, fruitful, cold, and moist. It is useful when intensity (that sometimes borders on obsession) is needed. Scorpio is considered a very psychic sign. Use this Moon sign when you must back up something you strongly believe in, such as union or employer relations. There is strong group loyalty here, but a Scorpio Moon is also a good time to end connections thoroughly. This is also a good time to conduct research.

The desire nature is so strong here that there is a tendency to manipulate situations to get what one wants or to not see one's responsibility in an act.

RULER: Pluto, Mars (traditional)

IMPULSE: Transformation

RULES: Reproductive organs, genitals, groin, and pelvis

Sagittarius Moon

The Moon's energy is masculine, dry, barren, and fiery in Sagittarius, encouraging flights of imagination and confidence in the flow of life. Sagittarius is the most philosophical sign. Candor and honesty are enhanced when the Moon is here. This is an excellent time to "get things off your chest" and to deal with institutions of higher learning, publishing companies, and the law. It's also a good time for sport and adventure.

Sagittarians are the crusaders of this world. This is a good time to tackle things that need improvement, but don't try to be the diplomat while influenced by this energy. Opinions can run strong, and the tendency to proselytize is increased.

RULER: Jupiter

IMPULSE: Expansion

RULES: Thighs and hips

Capricorn Moon

In Capricorn the Moon's energy is feminine, semi-fruitful, and earthy. Because Cancer and Capricorn are polar opposites, the Moon's energy is thought to be weakened here. This energy encourages the need for structure, discipline, and organization. This is a good time to set goals and plan for the future, tend to family business, and to take care of details requiring patience or a businesslike manner. Institutional activities are favored. This sign should be avoided if you're seeking favors, as those in authority can be insensitive under this influence.

RULER: Saturn

IMPULSE: Ambitious

RULES: Bones, skin, and knees

Aquarius Moon

An Aquarius Moon's energy is masculine, barren, dry, and airy. Activities that are unique, individualistic, concerned with humanitarian issues, society as a whole, and making improvements are favored under this Moon. It is this quality of making improvements that has caused this sign to be associated with inventors and new inventions.

An Aquarius Moon promotes the gathering of social groups for friendly exchanges. People tend to react and speak from an intellectual rather than emotional viewpoint when the Moon is in this sign.

RULER: Uranus and Saturn

IMPULSE: Reformer

RULES: Calves and ankles

Pisces Moon

A Pisces Moon is feminine, fruitful, cool, and moist. This is an excellent time to retreat, meditate, sleep, pray, or make that dreamed-of escape into a fantasy vacation. However, things are not always what they seem to be with the Moon in Pisces. Personal boundaries tend to be fuzzy, and you may not be seeing things clearly. People tend to be idealistic under this sign, which can prevent them from seeing reality.

There is a live-and-let-live philosophy attached to this sign, which in the idealistic world may work well enough, but chaos is frequently the result. That's why this sign is also associated with alcohol and drug abuse, drug trafficking, and counterfeiting. On the lighter side, many musicians and artists are ruled by Pisces. It's only when they move too far away from reality that the dark side of substance abuse, suicide, or crime takes away life.

Ruler: Jupiter and Neptune

Impulse: Empathetic

Rules: Feet

More About Zodiac Signs

Element (Triplicity)

Each of the zodiac signs is classified as belonging to an element; these are the four basic elements:

Fire Signs

Aries, Sagittarius, and Leo are action-oriented, outgoing, energetic, and spontaneous.

Earth Signs

Taurus, Capricorn, and Virgo are stable, conservative, practical, and oriented to the physical and material realm.

Air Signs

Gemini, Aquarius, and Libra are sociable and critical, and they tend to represent intellectual responses rather than feelings.

Water Signs

Cancer, Scorpio, and Pisces are emotional, receptive, intuitive, and can be very sensitive.

Quality (Quadruplicity)

Each zodiac sign is further classified as being cardinal, mutable, or fixed. There are four signs in each quadruplicity, one sign from each element.

Cardinal Signs

Aries, Cancer, Libra, and Capricorn represent beginnings and newly initiated action. They initiate each new season in the cycle of the year.

Fixed Signs

Taurus, Leo, Scorpio, and Aquarius want to maintain the status quo through stubbornness and persistence; they represent that "between" time. For example, Leo is the month when summer really feels like summer.

Mutable Signs

Pisces, Gemini, Virgo, and Sagittarius adapt to change and tolerate situations. They represent the last month of each season, when things are changing in preparation for the coming season.

Nature and Fertility

In addition to a sign's element and quality, each sign is further classified as either fruitful, semi-fruitful, or barren. This classification is the most important for readers who use the gardening information in the *Moon Sign Book* because the timing of most events depends on the fertility of the sign occupied by the Moon. The water signs of Cancer, Scorpio, and Pisces are the most fruitful. The semi-fruitful signs are the earth signs Taurus and Capricorn, and the air sign Libra. The barren signs correspond to fire-signs Aries, Leo, and Sagittarius; air-signs Gemini and Aquarius; and earth-sign Virgo.

2013 © Liang Zhang Image from BigStockPhoto.com

Good Timing

By Sharon Leah

Electional astrology is the art of electing times to begin any undertaking. Say, for example, you want to start a business. That business will experience ups and downs, as well as reach its potential, according to the promise held in the universe at the time the business was started—its birth time. The horoscope (birth chart) set for the date, time, and place that a business starts would indicate the outcome—its potential to succeed.

So, you might ask yourself the question: If the horoscope for a business start can show success or failure, why not begin at a time that is more favorable to the venture? Well, you can.

While no time is perfect, there are better times and better days to undertake specific activities. There are thousands of examples that prove electional astrology is not only practical, but that it can make a difference in our lives. There are rules for electing times to begin various activities—even shopping. You'll find detailed instructions about how to make elections beginning on page 107.

Personalizing Elections

The election rules in this almanac are based upon the planetary positions at the time for which the election is made. They do not depend on any type of birth chart. However, a birth chart based upon the time, date, and birthplace of an event has advantages. No election is effective for every person. For example, you may leave home to begin a trip at the same time as a friend, but each of you will have a different experience according to whether or not your birth chart favors the trip.

Not all elections require a birth chart, but the timing of very important events—business starts, marriages, etc.—would benefit from the additional accuracy a birth chart provides. To order a birth chart for yourself or a planned event, visit our Web site at www. llewellyn.com.

Some Things to Consider

You've probably experienced good timing in your life. Maybe you were at the right place at the right time to meet a friend whom you hadn't seen in years. Frequently, when something like that happens, it is the result of following an intuitive impulse—that "gut instinct." Consider for a moment that you were actually responding to planetary energies. Electional astrology is a tool that can help you to align with energies, present and future, that are available to us through planetary placements.

Significators

Decide upon the important significators (planet, sign, and house ruling the matter) for which the election is being made. The Moon is the most important significator in any election, so the Moon should always be fortified (strong by sign and making favorable aspects to other planets). The Moon's aspects to other planets are more important than the sign the Moon is in.

Other important considerations are the significators of the Ascendant and Midheaven—the house ruling the election matter and the ruler of the sign on that house cusp. Finally, any planet or sign that has a general rulership over the matter in question should be taken into consideration.

Nature and Fertility

Determine the general nature of the sign that is appropriate for your election. For example, much agricultural work is ruled by the earth signs of Virgo, Capricorn, and Taurus; while the air signs—Gemini, Aquarius, and Libra—rule intellectual pursuits.

One Final Comment

Use common sense. If you must do something, like plant your garden or take an airplane trip on a day that doesn't have the best aspects, proceed anyway, but try to minimize problems. For example, leave early for the airport to avoid being left behind due to delays in the security lanes. When you have no other choice, do the best that you can under the circumstances at the time.

If you want to personalize your elections, please turn to page 107 for more information. If you want a quick and easy answer, you can refer to Llewellyn's Astro Almanac on the following pages.

Llewellyn's Astro Almanac

The Astro Almanac tables, beginning on the next page, can help you find the dates best suited to particular activities. The dates provided are determined from the Moon's sign, phase, and aspects to other planets. Please note that the Astro Almanac does not take personal factors, such as your Sun and Moon sign, into account. The dates are general, and they will apply for everyone. Some activities will not have ideal dates during a particular month.

Activity	January
Animals (Neuter or spay)	26, 27, 28
Animals (Sell or buy)	6, 10
Automobile (Buy)	1, 12, 20, 29
Brewing	24, 25
Build (Start foundation)	3, 31
Business (Conducting for self and others)	5, 10, 21, 26
Business (Start new)	1, 10
Can Fruits and Vegetables	24, 25
Can Preserves	24, 25
Concrete (Pour)	17, 18
Construction (Begin new)	10, 19, 21, 26
Consultants (Begin work with)	1, 5, 10, 11, 15, 19, 22, 24, 27, 31
Contracts (Bid on)	5, 10, 11, 15, 31
Cultivate	30
Decorating	3, 4, 11, 12, 13, 30, 31
Demolition	16, 17, 26, 27
Electronics (Buy)	3, 12, 22, 30
Entertain Guests	6, 10
Floor Covering (Laying new)	16–23, 30
Habits (Break)	no ideal dates
Hair (Cut to increase growth)	1, 5, 8–12, 28
Hair (Cut to decrease growth)	16, 26, 27
Harvest (Grain for storage)	16, 17, 18
Harvest (Root crops)	16, 17, 18, 26, 27
Investments (New)	10, 21
Loan (Ask for)	8, 9, 10, 11
Massage (Relaxing)	10
Mow Lawn (Decrease growth)	16–29
Mow Lawn (Increase growth)	2–14, 31
Mushrooms (Pick)	14, 15, 16
Negotiate (Business for the elderly)	1, 5, 15, 20, 29
Prune for Better Fruit	23–27
Prune to Promote Healing	1, 28, 29
Wean Children	1, 2, 3, 4, 26–31
Wood Floors (Installing)	1, 28, 29
Write Letters or Contracts	3, 12, 17, 26, 30, 31

Activity	February
Animals (Neuter or spay)	22, 23, 24, 25, 28
Animals (Sell or buy)	1
Automobile (Buy)	8, 17, 25
Brewing	20, 21
Build (Start foundation)	5, 6
Business (Conducting for self and others)	4, 9, 20, 24
Business (Start new)	6
Can Fruits and Vegetables	20, 21
Can Preserves	20, 21
Concrete (Pour)	27
Construction (Begin new)	4, 6, 9, 16, 24
Consultants (Begin work with)	1, 5, 6, 10, 11, 16, 19, 20, 23, 27
Contracts (Bid on)	1, 5, 6, 10, 11
Cultivate	27, 28
Decorating	7, 8, 9
Demolition	14, 22, 23
Electronics (Buy)	8, 19, 27
Entertain Guests	6, 16, 19
Floor Covering (Laying new)	15–19, 26, 27
Habits (Break)	24, 27, 28
Hair (Cut to increase growth)	1, 5–9, 12
Hair (Cut to decrease growth)	22, 23, 24, 25
Harvest (Grain for storage)	22
Harvest (Root crops)	22, 23, 26, 27
Investments (New)	9, 20
Loan (Ask for)	5, 6, 7, 12, 13, 14
Massage (Relaxing)	6
Mow Lawn (Decrease growth)	15–28
Mow Lawn (Increase growth)	1–13
Mushrooms (Pick)	13, 14, 15
Negotiate (Business for the elderly)	2, 25
Prune for Better Fruit	20, 21, 22, 23
Prune to Promote Healing	24, 25, 26
Wean Children	22–28
Wood Floors (Installing)	24, 25, 26
Write Letters or Contracts	8, 13, 22, 27

Activity	March
Animals (Neuter or spay)	21, 22, 23, 24, 28, 29, 30
Animals (Sell or buy)	2, 5, 6, 15
Automobile (Buy)	7, 8, 16, 24, 25
Brewing	20, 28, 29
Build (Start foundation)	5, 6
Business (Conducting for self and others)	5, 11, 21, 26
Business (Start new)	5, 15, 16
Can Fruits and Vegetables	1, 20, 28, 29
Can Preserves	20
Concrete (Pour)	26, 27
Construction (Begin new)	5, 11, 15, 21, 26
Consultants (Begin work with)	1, 3, 5, 8, 10, 15, 19, 20, 24, 28
Contracts (Bid on)	3, 5, 8, 10, 15
Cultivate	22, 23, 26, 27, 30
Decorating	6, 7, 8, 9
Demolition	21, 22, 30
Electronics (Buy)	7, 8, 26
Entertain Guests	6, 17
Floor Covering (Laying new)	17, 18, 19, 26, 27
Habits (Break)	26, 27
Hair (Cut to increase growth)	1, 4–8, 11
Hair (Cut to decrease growth)	21, 22, 23, 24, 28
Harvest (Grain for storage)	21, 22, 23
Harvest (Root crops)	21, 22, 23, 26, 27
Investments (New)	11, 21
Loan (Ask for)	4, 5, 6, 11, 12, 13, 14
Massage (Relaxing)	17, 27
Mow Lawn (Decrease growth)	17–29
Mow Lawn (Increase growth)	2–15, 31
Mushrooms (Pick)	15, 16, 17
Negotiate (Business for the elderly)	1, 11, 29
Prune for Better Fruit	19–23
Prune to Promote Healing	24, 25
Wean Children	22–27
Wood Floors (Installing)	23, 24, 25
Write Letters or Contracts	7, 12, 22, 26, 28

Activity	April
Animals (Neuter or spay)	18, 19, 21, 24, 25
Animals (Sell or buy)	1, 5, 11, 30
Automobile (Buy)	4, 12, 21
Brewing	16, 17, 24, 25
Build (Start foundation)	1, 2, 29, 30
Business (Conducting for self and others)	4, 9, 19, 24
Business (Start new)	1, 11, 12, 29
Can Fruits and Vegetables	16, 17, 24, 25
Can Preserves	16, 17
Concrete (Pour)	22
Construction (Begin new)	1, 4, 9, 11, 19, 29
Consultants (Begin work with)	1, 2, 6, 8, 11, 16, 19, 24, 25, 29
Contracts (Bid on)	1, 2, 6, 8, 11, 30
Cultivate	18, 19, 22, 23, 24, 26, 27
Decorating	3, 4, 5, 13, 14, 15
Demolition	18, 26, 27
Electronics (Buy)	4, 22
Entertain Guests	5, 30
Floor Covering (Laying new)	22, 23, 28
Habits (Break)	23, 24, 26
Hair (Cut to increase growth)	1, 2, 3, 4, 8, 29, 30
Hair (Cut to decrease growth)	18, 19, 20, 21, 25, 28
Harvest (Grain for storage)	17, 18, 19
Harvest (Root crops)	18, 19, 22, 23, 26, 27
Investments (New)	9, 19
Loan (Ask for)	1, 2, 3, 8, 9, 10, 29, 30
Massage (Relaxing)	5, 30
Mow Lawn (Decrease growth)	16–27
Mow Lawn (Increase growth)	1–14, 30
Mushrooms (Pick)	14, 15, 16
Negotiate (Business for the elderly)	7, 12, 21, 25
Prune for Better Fruit	15–19
Prune to Promote Healing	20, 21
Wean Children	18–24
Wood Floors (Installing)	20, 21
Write Letters or Contracts	4, 9, 18, 22, 29

Activity	May
Animals (Neuter or spay)	15, 16, 18, 21, 22, 23
Animals (Sell or buy)	5, 9, 30
Automobile (Buy)	1, 9, 18, 29
Brewing	22, 23
Build (Start foundation)	6
Business (Conducting for self and others)	4, 9, 19, 23
Business (Start new)	9
Can Fruits and Vegetables	22
Can Preserves	26
Concrete (Pour)	20, 26
Construction (Begin new)	4, 9, 19, 23, 27
Consultants (Begin work with)	4, 5, 9, 11, 14, 20, 22, 25, 27, 30
Contracts (Bid on)	4, 5, 9, 11, 14, 30
Cultivate	15, 16, 24, 25, 28
Decorating	1, 2, 10, 11, 12, 28, 29
Demolition	15, 16, 23, 24
Electronics (Buy)	1, 11, 20, 29
Entertain Guests	5, 25, 30
Floor Covering (Laying new)	19, 20, 26, 27, 28
Habits (Break)	23, 25
Hair (Cut to increase growth)	1, 2, 5, 29
Hair (Cut to decrease growth)	15, 16, 17, 18, 22, 25, 26, 27, 28
Harvest (Grain for storage)	15, 16, 19, 20
Harvest (Root crops)	15, 16, 19, 20, 23, 24, 25
Investments (New)	9, 19
Loan (Ask for)	5, 6, 7, 8
Massage (Relaxing)	5, 20, 30
Mow Lawn (Decrease growth)	15–27
Mow Lawn (Increase growth)	1–13, 29, 30, 31
Mushrooms (Pick)	13, 14, 15
Negotiate (Business for the elderly)	4, 9, 18, 22, 31
Prune for Better Fruit	14, 15, 16
Prune to Promote Healing	17, 18, 19
Wean Children	15–20
Wood Floors (Installing)	17, 18, 19
Write Letters or Contracts	1, 6, 16, 20, 29, 30

Activity	June
Animals (Neuter or spay)	13, 15, 18, 19
Animals (Sell or buy)	6, 10, 29
Automobile (Buy)	4, 5, 14, 25, 26
Brewing	18, 19
Build (Start foundation)	2, 3, 29, 30
Business (Conducting for self and others)	2, 8, 17, 22
Business (Start new)	5, 6
Can Fruits and Vegetables	18, 19
Can Preserves	22, 23
Concrete (Pour)	16, 22, 23
Construction (Begin new)	2, 6, 8, 17, 22, 23
Consultants (Begin work with)	1, 4, 6, 9, 10, 17, 19, 21, 23, 26, 28
Contracts (Bid on)	1, 4, 6, 9, 10, 28
Cultivate	20, 21, 24, 25, 26
Decorating	7, 8
Demolition	19, 20
Electronics (Buy)	16, 17, 25, 26
Entertain Guests	24, 29
Floor Covering (Laying new)	15, 16, 22, 23, 24, 25
Habits (Break)	24, 25, 26
Hair (Cut to increase growth)	1, 11, 29
Hair (Cut to decrease growth)	14, 18, 21–25
Harvest (Grain for storage)	15, 16, 19
Harvest (Root crops)	13, 15, 16, 17, 19, 20, 21, 24, 25, 26
Investments (New)	8, 17
Loan (Ask for)	1, 2, 3, 4, 29, 30
Massage (Relaxing)	29
Mow Lawn (Decrease growth)	14–26
Mow Lawn (Increase growth)	1–11, 28, 29, 30
Mushrooms (Pick)	12, 13, 14
Negotiate (Business for the elderly)	5, 14, 18
Prune for Better Fruit	no ideal dates
Prune to Promote Healing	14, 15
Wean Children	12–17
Wood Floors (Installing)	13, 14, 15
Write Letters or Contracts	3, 12, 16, 25, 26, 30

Activity	July
Animals (Neuter or spay)	15, 16
Animals (Sell or buy)	4, 8, 30, 31
Automobile (Buy)	3, 12, 22, 30, 31
Brewing	15, 24, 25
Build (Start foundation)	1, 27, 28
Business (Conducting for self and others)	2, 7, 16, 21
Business (Start new)	3, 4, 12, 30
Can Fruits and Vegetables	15, 24, 25
Can Preserves	20, 24, 25
Concrete (Pour)	13, 14, 20
Construction (Begin new)	2, 4, 17, 21, 31
Consultants (Begin work with)	1, 4, 6, 8, 15, 17, 19, 21, 25, 26, 31
Contracts (Bid on)	1, 4, 6, 8, 31
Cultivate	22, 23
Decorating	4, 5, 6, 31
Demolition	17, 18, 26
Electronics (Buy)	6, 14, 22
Entertain Guests	5, 19, 24
Floor Covering (Laying new)	13, 14, 19, 20, 21, 22, 23, 26
Habits (Break)	21, 22, 23
Hair (Cut to increase growth)	8, 9
Hair (Cut to decrease growth)	10, 11, 15, 16, 19, 20, 21, 22, 26
Harvest (Grain for storage)	13, 14, 17, 18
Harvest (Root crops)	13, 14, 17, 18, 21, 22, 23
Investments (New)	7, 16
Loan (Ask for)	1, 27, 28
Massage (Relaxing)	5, 14, 19, 24
Mow Lawn (Decrease growth)	13–25
Mow Lawn (Increase growth)	1–11, 27–31
Mushrooms (Pick)	11, 12, 13
Negotiate (Business for the elderly)	25, 30
Prune for Better Fruit	no ideal dates
Prune to Promote Healing	12
Wean Children	9–14
Wood Floors (Installing)	12
Write Letters or Contracts	10, 14, 22, 27

Activity	August
Animals (Neuter or spay)	11, 12
Animals (Sell or buy)	4, 5, 28, 29
Automobile (Buy)	8, 19, 26
Brewing	12, 21
Build (Start foundation)	3, 30, 31
Business (Conducting for self and others)	1, 6, 14, 19, 30
Business (Start new)	8, 26
Can Fruits and Vegetables	12, 21
Can Preserves	16, 17, 21
Concrete (Pour)	16, 17, 23, 24
Construction (Begin new)	1, 5, 6, 13, 14, 18, 19, 28
Consultants (Begin work with)	5, 6, 13, 15, 18, 21, 23, 26, 28
Contracts (Bid on)	2, 5, 6, 26, 28
Cultivate	18, 19, 20, 23, 24
Decorating	1, 2, 9, 10, 28, 29
Demolition	13, 14, 22, 23, 24
Electronics (Buy)	10, 19
Entertain Guests	18, 23, 29
Floor Covering (Laying new)	15–19, 22, 23, 24, 25
Habits (Break)	18, 19, 20, 22, 23
Hair (Cut to increase growth)	5, 6, 7, 8
Hair (Cut to decrease growth)	12, 15–19, 22
Harvest (Grain for storage)	13, 14
Harvest (Root crops)	10, 13, 14, 18, 19, 22, 23, 24
Investments (New)	6, 14
Loan (Ask for)	no ideal dates
Massage (Relaxing)	23, 29
Mow Lawn (Decrease growth)	11–24
Mow Lawn (Increase growth)	1–9, 26, 28, 29, 30, 31
Mushrooms (Pick)	9, 10, 11
Negotiate (Business for the elderly)	8, 12, 21, 26
Prune for Better Fruit	no ideal dates
Prune to Promote Healing	no ideal dates
Wean Children	5–11
Wood Floors (Installing)	no ideal dates
Write Letters or Contracts	6, 10, 19, 24, 26

Activity	September
Animals (Neuter or spay)	no ideal dates
Animals (Sell or buy)	3, 25, 28
Automobile (Buy)	5, 15, 23
Brewing	9, 17, 18
Build (Start foundation)	1, 26, 27, 28
Business (Conducting for self and others)	4, 13, 18, 29
Business (Start new)	5
Can Fruits and Vegetables	9, 17, 18
Can Preserves	12, 17, 18
Concrete (Pour)	12, 19, 20
Construction (Begin new)	2, 4, 10, 13, 15, 18, 25, 29
Consultants (Begin work with)	1, 2, 6, 10, 15, 20, 21, 25, 26, 29
Contracts (Bid on)	1, 2, 6, 25, 26, 29
Cultivate	16, 19, 20, 21, 22, 23
Decorating	5, 6, 7, 24, 25, 26
Demolition	10, 19, 20
Electronics (Buy)	6, 15, 26
Entertain Guests	12, 17, 23
Floor Covering (Laying new)	12, 13, 14, 15, 19–23
Habits (Break)	16, 19, 20
Hair (Cut to increase growth)	1, 2, 3, 4, 29
Hair (Cut to decrease growth)	11–15, 18
Harvest (Grain for storage)	9, 10, 11, 14, 15
Harvest (Root crops)	10, 11, 14, 15, 19, 20
Investments (New)	4, 13
Loan (Ask for)	11
Massage (Relaxing)	12, 17
Mow Lawn (Decrease growth)	9–22
Mow Lawn (Increase growth)	1–7, 25–30
Mushrooms (Pick)	7, 8, 9
Negotiate (Business for the elderly)	no ideal dates
Prune for Better Fruit	no ideal dates
Prune to Promote Healing	no ideal dates
Wean Children	2–7, 29
Wood Floors (Installing)	no ideal dates
Write Letters or Contracts	2, 6, 15, 20, 26, 29

Activity	October
Animals (Neuter or spay)	no ideal dates
Animals (Sell or buy)	3, 27
Automobile (Buy)	1, 2, 12, 13, 20, 29
Brewing	14, 15
Build (Start foundation)	24, 25, 30
Business (Conducting for self and others)	3, 13, 18, 28
Business (Start new)	2, 29
Can Fruits and Vegetables	14, 15
Can Preserves	10, 14, 15
Concrete (Pour)	10, 17, 18
Construction (Begin new)	3, 8, 12, 13, 18, 22, 27, 28
Consultants (Begin work with)	1, 5, 8, 12, 13, 17, 18, 22, 27, 31
Contracts (Bid on)	1, 5, 27, 31
Cultivate	16–21
Decorating	3, 4, 5, 30, 31
Demolition	8, 16, 17
Electronics (Buy)	4, 12, 13, 22, 31
Entertain Guests	12, 18
Floor Covering (Laying new)	9–13, 16–23
Habits (Break)	16, 17, 18
Hair (Cut to increase growth)	1, 2, 6, 26, 27, 28, 29
Hair (Cut to decrease growth)	9, 10, 11, 12, 16
Harvest (Grain for storage)	11, 12, 13
Harvest (Root crops)	8, 11, 12, 13, 16, 17, 18
Investments (New)	3, 13
Loan (Ask for)	no ideal dates
Massage (Relaxing)	3, 18
Mow Lawn (Decrease growth)	9–22
Mow Lawn (Increase growth)	1–7, 24–31
Mushrooms (Pick)	7, 8, 9
Negotiate (Business for the elderly)	2, 6, 15, 20, 29
Prune for Better Fruit	23
Prune to Promote Healing	no ideal dates
Wean Children	1–5, 26–31
Wood Floors (Installing)	no ideal dates
Write Letters or Contracts	4, 12, 17, 22, 27, 31

Activity	November
Animals (Neuter or spay)	no ideal dates
Animals (Sell or buy)	5, 23, 27
Automobile (Buy)	8, 16, 17, 26
Brewing	10, 11, 12, 20, 21
Build (Start foundation)	27, 28
Business (Conducting for self and others)	2, 11, 17, 26
Business (Start new)	26
Can Fruits and Vegetables	10, 11, 20, 21
Can Preserves	7, 10, 11, 20, 21
Concrete (Pour)	7, 13
Construction (Begin new)	5, 9, 11, 17, 19, 23, 26
Consultants (Begin work with)	5, 9, 10, 14, 16, 19, 21, 23, 26
Contracts (Bid on)	1, 5, 23, 26
Cultivate	14, 15, 16, 17
Decorating	1, 26, 27, 28
Demolition	12, 13, 14, 15
Electronics (Buy)	8, 27
Entertain Guests	12, 17
Floor Covering (Laying new)	7, 8, 9, 12–19
Habits (Break)	15
Hair (Cut to increase growth)	2, 5, 22, 23, 24, 25, 29
Hair (Cut to decrease growth)	7, 8, 9, 12
Harvest (Grain for storage)	7, 8, 9, 12, 13
Harvest (Root crops)	8, 9, 12, 13, 14
Investments (New)	2, 11
Loan (Ask for)	5, 6
Massage (Relaxing)	12, 17, 27
Mow Lawn (Decrease growth)	7–21
Mow Lawn (Increase growth)	1–5, 23–30
Mushrooms (Pick)	5, 6, 7
Negotiate (Business for the elderly)	26, 30
Prune for Better Fruit	20, 21, 22
Prune to Promote Healing	no ideal dates
Wean Children	1, 22–28
Wood Floors (Installing)	no ideal dates
Write Letters or Contracts	8, 21, 23, 27

Activity	December
Animals (Neuter or spay)	20, 21
Animals (Sell or buy)	27, 29
Automobile (Buy)	6, 14, 22
Brewing	8, 9, 18, 19
Build (Start foundation)	24, 25
Business (Conducting for self and others)	1, 11, 17, 26, 30
Business (Start new)	4, 31
Can Fruits and Vegetables	8, 9, 18, 19
Can Preserves	8, 9, 18, 19
Concrete (Pour)	10, 11
Construction (Begin new)	1, 2, 6, 11, 16, 17, 21, 29, 30
Consultants (Begin work with)	1, 2, 6, 11, 16, 17, 21, 22, 27, 29
Contracts (Bid on)	1, 2, 22, 27, 29
Cultivate	14
Decorating	5, 6, 23, 24, 25
Demolition	10, 11, 20
Electronics (Buy)	6, 24
Entertain Guests	no ideal dates
Floor Covering (Laying new)	10–17
Habits (Break)	no ideal dates
Hair (Cut to increase growth)	3, 4, 5, 22, 26, 27, 30, 31
Hair (Cut to decrease growth)	9, 20, 21
Harvest (Grain for storage)	9, 10, 11, 12
Harvest (Root crops)	6, 7, 10, 11, 20
Investments (New)	1, 11, 30
Loan (Ask for)	3, 4, 5
Massage (Relaxing)	no ideal dates
Mow Lawn (Decrease growth)	7–20
Mow Lawn (Increase growth)	1–5, 22–31
Mushrooms (Pick)	5, 6, 7
Negotiate (Business for the elderly)	9, 14, 23
Prune for Better Fruit	17, 18, 19, 20
Prune to Promote Healing	no ideal dates
Wean Children	20–25
Wood Floors (Installing)	no ideal dates
Write Letters or Contracts	6, 10, 20

Choose the Best Time for Your Activities

When rules for elections refer to "favorable" and "unfavorable" aspects to your Sun or other planets, please refer to the Favorable and Unfavorable Days Tables and Lunar Aspectarian for more information. You'll find instructions beginning on page 129 and the tables beginning on page 136.

The material in this section came from several sources including: *The New A to Z Horoscope Maker and Delineator* by Llewellyn George (Llewellyn, 1999), *Moon Sign Book* (Llewellyn, 1945), and *Electional Astrology* by Vivian Robson (Slingshot Publishing, 2000). Robson's book was originally published in 1937.

Advertise (Internet)

The Moon should be conjunct, sextile, or trine Mercury or Uranus and in the sign of Gemini, Capricorn, or Aquarius.

Advertise (Print)

Write ads on a day favorable to your Sun. The Moon should be conjunct, sextile, or trine Mercury or Venus. Avoid hard aspects to Mars and Saturn. Ad campaigns produce the best results when the Moon is well aspected in Gemini (to enhance communication) or Capricorn (to build business).

Animals

Take home new pets when the day is favorable to your Sun, or when the Moon is trine, sextile, or conjunct Mercury, Venus, or Jupiter, or in the sign of Virgo or Pisces. However, avoid days when the Moon is either square or opposing the Sun, Mars, Saturn, Uranus, Neptune, or Pluto. When selecting a pet, have the Moon well aspected by the planet that rules the animal. Cats are ruled by the Sun, dogs by Mercury, birds by Venus, horses by Jupiter, and fish by Neptune. Buy large animals when the Moon is in Sagittarius or Pisces and making favorable aspects to Jupiter or Mercury. Buy animals smaller than sheep when the Moon is in Virgo with favorable aspects to Mercury or Venus.

Animals (Breed)

Animals are easiest to handle when the Moon is in Taurus, Cancer, Libra, or Pisces, but try to avoid the Full Moon. To encourage healthy births, animals should be mated so births occur when the Moon is increasing in Taurus, Cancer, Pisces, or Libra. Those born during a semi-fruitful sign (Taurus and Capricorn) will produce leaner meat. Libra yields beautiful animals for showing and racing.

Animals (Declaw)

Declaw cats for medical purposes in the dark of the Moon. Avoid the week before and after the Full Moon and the sign of Pisces.

Animals (Neuter or spay)

Have livestock and pets neutered or spayed when the Moon is in Sagittarius, Capricorn, or Pisces, after it has passed through Scorpio, the sign that rules reproductive organs. Avoid the week before and after the Full Moon.

Animals (Sell or buy)

In either buying or selling, it is important to keep the Moon and Mercury free from any aspect to Mars. Aspects to Mars will create discord and increase the likelihood of wrangling over price and quality. The Moon should be passing from the first quarter to full and sextile or trine Venus or Jupiter. When buying racehorses, let the Moon be in an air sign. The Moon should be in air signs when you buy birds. If the birds are to be pets, let the Moon be in good aspect to Venus.

Animals (Train)

Train pets when the Moon is in Virgo or trine to Mercury.

Animals (Train dogs to hunt)

Let the Moon be in Aries in conjunction with Mars, which makes them courageous and quick to learn. But let Jupiter also be in aspect to preserve them from danger in hunting.

Automobiles

When buying an automobile, select a time when the Moon is conjunct, sextile, or trine to Mercury, Saturn, or Uranus and in the sign of Gemini or Capricorn. Avoid times when Mercury is in retrograde motion.

Baking Cakes

Your cakes will have a lighter texture if you see that the Moon is in Gemini, Libra, or Aquarius and in good aspect to Venus or Mercury. If you are decorating a cake or confections are being made, have the Moon placed in Libra.

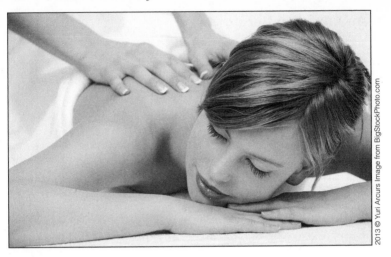

Beauty Treatments (Massage, etc.)

See that the Moon is in Taurus, Cancer, Leo, Libra, or Aquarius and in favorable aspect to Venus. In the case of plastic surgery, aspects to Mars should be avoided, and the Moon should not be in the sign ruling the part to be operated on.

Borrow (Money or goods)

See that the Moon is not placed between 15 degrees Libra and 15 degrees Scorpio. Let the Moon be waning and in Leo, Scorpio (16 to 30 degrees), Sagittarius, or Pisces. Venus should be in good aspect to the Moon, and the Moon should not be square, opposing, or conjunct either Saturn or Mars.

Brewing

Start brewing during the third or fourth quarter, when the Moon is in Cancer, Scorpio, or Pisces.

Build (Start foundation)

Turning the first sod for the foundation marks the beginning of the building. For best results, excavate the site when the Moon is in the first quarter of a fixed sign and making favorable aspects to Saturn.

Business (Start new)

When starting a business, have the Moon be in Taurus, Virgo, or Capricorn and increasing. The Moon should be sextile or trine Jupiter or Saturn, but avoid oppositions or squares. The planet ruling the business should be well aspected, too.

Buy Goods

Buy during the third quarter, when the Moon is in Taurus for quality or in a mutable sign (Gemini, Sagittarius, Virgo, or Pisces) for savings. Good aspects to Venus or the Sun are desirable. If you are buying for yourself, it is good if the day is favorable for your Sun sign. You may also apply rules for buying specific items.

Canning

Can fruits and vegetables when the Moon is in either the third or fourth quarter and in the water sign Cancer or Pisces. Preserves and jellies use the same quarters and the signs Cancer, Pisces, or Taurus.

Clothing

Buy clothing on a day that is favorable for your Sun sign and when Venus or Mercury is well aspected. Avoid aspects to Mars and Saturn. Buy your clothing when the Moon is in Taurus if you want to remain satisfied. Do not buy clothing or jewelry when the Moon is in Scorpio or Aries. See that the Moon is sextile or trine the Sun during the first or second quarters.

Collections

Try to make collections on days when your Sun is well aspected. Avoid days when the Moon is opposing or square Mars or Saturn. If possible, the Moon should be in a cardinal sign (Aries, Cancer, Libra, or Capricorn). It is more difficult to collect when the Moon is in Taurus or Scorpio.

Concrete

Pour concrete when the Moon is in the third quarter of the fixed sign Taurus, Leo, or Aquarius.

Construction (Begin new)

The Moon should be sextile or trine Jupiter. According to Hermes, no building should be begun when the Moon is in Scorpio or Pisces. The best time to begin building is when the Moon is in Aquarius.

Consultants (Work with)

The Moon should be conjunct, sextile, or trine Mercury or Jupiter.

Contracts (Bid on)

The Moon should be in Gemini or Capricorn and either the Moon or Mercury should be conjunct, sextile, or trine Jupiter.

Copyrights/Patents

The Moon should be conjunct, trine, or sextile either Mercury or Jupiter.

Coronations and Installations

Let the Moon be in Leo and in favorable aspect to Venus, Jupiter, or Mercury. The Moon should be applying to these planets.

Cultivate

Cultivate when the Moon is in a barren sign and waning, ideally the fourth quarter in Aries, Gemini, Leo, Virgo, or Aquarius. The third quarter in the sign of Sagittarius will also work.

Cut Timber

Timber cut during the waning Moon does not become worm-eaten; it will season well and not warp, decay, or snap during burning. Cut when the Moon is in Taurus, Gemini, Virgo, or Capricorn—especially in August. Avoid the water signs. Look for favorable aspects to Mars.

Decorating or Home Repairs

Have the Moon waxing and in the sign of Libra, Gemini, or Aquarius. Avoid squares or oppositions to either Mars or Saturn. Venus in good aspect to Mars or Saturn is beneficial.

Demolition

Let the waning Moon be in Leo, Sagittarius, or Aries.

Dental and Dentists

Visit the dentist when the Moon is in Virgo, or pick a day marked favorable for your Sun sign. Mars should be marked sextile, conjunct, or trine; avoid squares or oppositions to Saturn, Uranus, or Jupiter.

Teeth are best removed when the Moon is in Gemini, Virgo, Sagittarius, or Pisces and during the first or second quarter. Avoid the Full Moon! The day should be favorable for your lunar cycle, and Mars and Saturn should be marked conjunct, trine, or sextile. Fillings should be done in the third or fourth quarters in the sign of Taurus, Leo, Scorpio, or Pisces. The same applies for dentures.

Dressmaking

William Lilly wrote in 1676: "Make no new clothes, or first put them on when the Moon is in Scorpio or afflicted by Mars, for they will be apt to be torn and quickly worn out." Design, repair, and sew clothes in the first and second quarters of Taurus, Leo, or Libra on a day marked favorable for your Sun sign. Venus, Jupiter, and Mercury should be favorably aspected, but avoid hard aspects to Mars or Saturn.

Egg-setting (see p. 161)

Eggs should be set so chicks will hatch during fruitful signs. To set eggs, subtract the number of days given for incubation or gestation from the fruitful dates. Chickens incubate in twenty-one days, turkeys and geese in twenty-eight days.

A freshly laid egg loses quality rapidly if it is not handled properly. Use plenty of clean litter in the nests to reduce the number of dirty or cracked eggs. Gather eggs daily in mild weather and at least two times daily in hot or cold weather. The eggs should be placed in a cooler immediately after gathering and stored at 50 to 55° F. Do not store eggs with foods or products that give off pungent odors since eggs may absorb the odors.

Eggs saved for hatching purposes should not be washed. Only clean and slightly soiled eggs should be saved for hatching. Dirty eggs should not be incubated. Eggs should be stored in a cool place with the large ends up. It is not advisable to store the eggs longer than one week before setting them in an incubator.

Electricity and Gas (Install)

The Moon should be in a fire sign, and there should be no squares, oppositions, or conjunctions with Uranus (ruler of electricity), Neptune (ruler of gas), Saturn, or Mars. Hard aspects to Mars can cause fires.

Electronics (Buying)

Choose a day when the Moon is in an air sign (Gemini, Libra, Aquarius) and well aspected by Mercury and/or Uranus when buying electronics.

Electronics (Repair)

The Moon should be sextile or trine Mars or Uranus and in a fixed sign (Taurus, Leo, Scorpio, Aquarius).

Entertain Friends

Let the Moon be in Leo or Libra and making good aspects to Venus. Avoid squares or oppositions to either Mars or Saturn by the Moon or Venus.

Eyes and Eyeglasses

Have your eyes tested and glasses fitted on a day marked favorable for your Sun sign, and on a day that falls during your favorable lunar cycle. Mars should not be in aspect with the Moon. The same applies for any treatment of the eyes, which should also be started during the Moon's first or second quarter.

Fence Posts

Set posts when the Moon is in the third or fourth quarter of the fixed sign Taurus or Leo.

Fertilize and Compost

Fertilize when the Moon is in a fruitful sign (Cancer, Scorpio, Pisces). Organic fertilizers are best when the Moon is waning. Use chemical fertilizers when the Moon is waxing. Start compost when the Moon is in the fourth quarter in a water sign.

Find Hidden Treasure

Let the Moon be in good aspect to Jupiter or Venus. If you erect a horoscope for this election, place the Moon in the Fourth House.

Find Lost Articles

Search for lost articles during the first quarter and when your Sun sign is marked favorable. Also check to see that the planet ruling the lost item is trine, sextile, or conjunct the Moon. The Moon rules household utensils; Mercury rules letters and books; and Venus rules clothing, jewelry, and money.

Fishing

During the summer months, the best time of the day to fish is from sunrise to three hours after and from two hours before sunset until one hour after. Fish do not bite in cooler months until the air is warm, from noon to 3 pm. Warm, cloudy days are good. The most favorable winds are from the south and southwest.

Easterly winds are unfavorable. The best days of the month for fishing are when the Moon changes quarters, especially if the change occurs on a day when the Moon is in a water sign (Cancer, Scorpio, Pisces). The best period in any month is the day after the Full Moon.

Friendship

The need for friendship is greater when the Moon is in Aquarius or when Uranus aspects the Moon. Friendship prospers when Venus or Uranus is trine, sextile, or conjunct the Moon. The Moon in Gemini facilitates the chance meeting of acquaintances and friends.

Grafting or Budding

Grafting is the process of introducing new varieties of fruit on less desirable trees. For this process you should use the increasing phase of the Moon in fruitful signs such as Cancer, Scor-

pio, or Pisces. Capricorn may be used, too. Cut your grafts while trees are dormant, from December to March. Keep them in a cool, dark place, not too dry or too damp. Do the grafting before the sap starts to flow and while the Moon is waxing, preferably while it is in Cancer, Scorpio, or Pisces. The type of plant should determine both cutting and planting times.

Habit (Breaking)

To end an undesirable habit, and this applies to ending everything from a bad relationship to smoking, start on a day when the Moon is in the fourth quarter and in the barren sign of Gemini, Leo, or Aquarius. Aries, Virgo, and Capricorn may be suitable as well, depending on the habit you want to be rid of. Make sure that your lunar cycle is favorable. Avoid lunar aspects to Mars or Jupiter. However, favorable aspects to Pluto are helpful.

Haircuts

Cut hair when the Moon is in Gemini, Sagittarius, Pisces, Taurus, or Capricorn, but not in Virgo. Look for favorable aspects to Venus. For faster growth, cut hair when the Moon is increasing in Cancer or Pisces. To make hair grow thicker, cut when the Moon is full in the signs of Taurus, Cancer, or Leo. If you want your hair to grow more slowly, have the Moon be decreasing in Aries, Gemini, or Virgo, and have the Moon square or opposing Saturn.

Permanents, straightening, and hair coloring will take well if the Moon is in Taurus or Leo and trine or sextile Venus. Avoid hair treatments if Mars is marked as square or in opposition, especially if heat is to be used. For permanents, a trine to Jupiter is helpful. The Moon also should be in the first quarter. Check the lunar cycle for a favorable day in relation to your Sun sign.

Harvest Crops

Harvest root crops when the Moon is in a dry sign (Aries, Leo, Sagittarius, Gemini, Aquarius) and waning. Harvest grain for storage just after the Full Moon, avoiding Cancer, Scorpio, or Pisces. Harvest in the third and fourth quarters in dry signs. Dry crops in the third quarter in fire signs.

Health

A diagnosis is more likely to be successful when the Moon is in Aries, Cancer, Libra, or Capricorn and less so when in Gemini, Sagittarius, Pisces, or Virgo. Begin a recuperation program or enter a hospital when the Moon is in a cardinal or fixed sign and the day is favorable to your Sun sign. For surgery, see "Surgical Procedures." Buy medicines when the Moon is in Virgo or Scorpio.

Home (Buy new)

If you desire a permanent home, buy when the New Moon is in a fixed sign—Taurus or Leo, for example. Each sign will affect your decision in a different way. A house bought when the Moon is in Taurus is likely to be more practical and have a country look—right down to the split-rail fence. A house purchased when the Moon is in Leo will more likely be a real showplace.

If you're buying for speculation and a quick turnover, be certain that the Moon is in a cardinal sign (Aries, Cancer, Libra, Capricorn). Avoid buying when the Moon is in a fixed sign (Leo, Scorpio, Aquarius, Taurus).

Home (Make repairs)

In all repairs, avoid squares, oppositions, or conjunctions to the planet ruling the place or thing to be repaired. For example, bathrooms are ruled by Scorpio and Cancer. You would not want to start a project in those rooms when the Moon or Pluto is receiving hard aspects. The front entrance, hall, dining room, and porch are ruled by the Sun. So you would want to avoid times when Saturn or Mars are square, opposing, or conjunct the Sun. Also, let the Moon be waxing.

Home (Sell)

Make a strong effort to list your property for sale when the Sun is marked favorable in your sign and in good aspect to Jupiter. Avoid adverse aspects to as many planets as possible.

Home Furnishings (Buy new)

Saturn days (Saturday) are good for buying, and Jupiter days (Thursday) are good for selling. Items bought on days when Saturn is well aspected tend to wear longer and purchases tend to be more conservative.

Job (Start new)

Jupiter and Venus should be sextile, trine, or conjunct the Moon. A day when your Sun is receiving favorable aspects is preferred.

Legal Matters

Good Moon-Jupiter aspects improve the outcome in legal decisions. To gain damages through a lawsuit, begin the process during the increasing Moon. To avoid paying damages, a court date during the decreasing Moon is desirable. Good Moon-Sun aspects strengthen your chance of success. A well-aspected Moon in Cancer or Leo, making good aspects to the Sun, brings the best results in custody cases. In divorce cases, a favorable Moon-Venus aspect is best.

Loan (Ask for)

A first and second quarter phase favors the lender, the third and fourth quarters favor the borrower. Good aspects of Jupiter and Venus to the Moon are favorable to both, as is having the Moon in Leo or Taurus.

Machinery, Appliances, or Tools (Buy)

Tools, machinery, and other implements should be bought on days when your lunar cycle is favorable and when Mars and

Uranus are trine, sextile, or conjunct the Moon. Any quarter of the Moon is suitable. When buying gas or electrical appliances, the Moon should be in Aquarius.

Make a Will

Let the Moon be in a fixed sign (Taurus, Leo, Scorpio, or Aquarius) to ensure permanence. If the Moon is in a cardinal sign (Aries, Cancer, Libra, or Capricorn), the will could be altered. Let the Moon be waxing—increasing in light—and in good aspect to Saturn, Venus, or Mercury. In case the will is made in an emergency during illness and the Moon is slow in motion, void-of-course, combust, or under the Sun's beams, the testator will die and the will remain unaltered. There is some danger that it will be lost or stolen, however.

Marriage

The best time for marriage to take place is when the Moon is increasing, but not yet full. Good signs for the Moon to be in are Taurus, Cancer, Leo, or Libra.

The Moon in Taurus produces the most steadfast marriages, but if the partners later want to separate, they may have a difficult time. Make sure that the Moon is well aspected, especially to Venus or Jupiter. Avoid aspects to Mars, Uranus, or Pluto and the signs Aries, Gemini, Virgo, Scorpio, or Aquarius.

The values of the signs are as follows:

- Aries is not favored for marriage
- Taurus from 0 to 19 degrees is good, the remaining degrees are less favorable
- Cancer is unfavorable unless you are marrying a widow
- Leo is favored, but it may cause one party to deceive the other as to his or her money or possessions
- Virgo is not favored except when marrying a widow
- Libra is good for engagements but not for marriage

- Scorpio from 0 to 15 degrees is good, but the last 15 degrees are entirely unfortunate. The woman may be fickle, envious, and quarrelsome
- Sagittarius is neutral
- Capricorn, from 0 to 10 degrees, is difficult for marriage; however, the remaining degrees are favorable, especially when marrying a widow
- Aquarius is not favored
- Pisces is favored, although marriage under this sign can incline a woman to chatter a lot

These effects are strongest when the Moon is in the sign. If the Moon and Venus are in a cardinal sign, happiness between the couple may not continue long.

On no account should the Moon apply to Saturn or Mars, even by good aspect.

Medical Treatment for the Eyes

Let the Moon be increasing in light and motion and making favorable aspects to Venus or Jupiter and be unaspected by Mars. Keep the Moon out of Taurus, Capricorn, or Virgo. If an aspect between the Moon and Mars is unavoidable, let it be separating.

Medical Treatment for the Head

If possible, have Mars and Saturn free of hard aspects. Let the Moon be in Aries or Taurus, decreasing in light, in conjunction or aspect with Venus or Jupiter and free of hard aspects. The Sun should not be in any aspect to the Moon.

Medical Treatment for the Nose

Let the Moon be in Cancer, Leo, or Virgo and not aspecting Mars or Saturn and also not in conjunction with a retrograde or weak planet.

Mining

Saturn rules mining. Begin work when Saturn is marked conjunct, trine, or sextile. Mine for gold when the Sun is marked conjunct, trine, or sextile. Mercury rules quicksilver, Venus rules copper, Jupiter rules tin, Saturn rules lead and coal, Uranus rules radioactive elements, Neptune rules oil, the Moon rules water. Mine for these items when the ruling planet is marked conjunct, trine, or sextile.

Move to New Home

If you have a choice, and sometimes you don't, make sure that Mars is not aspecting the Moon. Move on a day favorable to your Sun sign or when the Moon is conjunct, sextile, or trine the Sun.

Mow Lawn

Mow in the first and second quarters (waxing phase) to increase growth and lushness, and in the third and fourth quarters (waning phase) to decrease growth.

Negotiate

When you are choosing a time to negotiate, consider what the meeting is about and what you want to have happen. If it is agreement or compromise between two parties that you desire, have the Moon be in the sign of Libra. When you are making contracts, it is best to have the Moon in the same element. For example, if your concern is communication, then elect a time when the Moon is in an air sign. If, on the other hand, your concern is about possessions, an earth sign would be more appropriate. Fixed signs are unfavorable, with the exception of Leo; so are cardinal signs, except for Capricorn. If you are negotiating the end of something, use the rules that apply to ending habits.

Occupational Training

When you begin training, see that your lunar cycle is favorable that day and that the planet ruling your occupation is marked conjunct or trine.

Paint

Paint buildings during the waning Libra or Aquarius Moon. If the weather is hot, paint when the Moon is in Taurus. If the weather is cold, paint when the Moon is in Leo. Schedule the painting to start in the fourth quarter as the wood is drier and paint will penetrate wood better. Avoid painting around the New Moon, though, as the wood is likely to be damp, making the paint subject to scalding when hot weather hits it. If the temperature is below 70° F, it is not advisable to paint while the Moon is in Cancer, Scorpio, or Pisces as the paint is apt to creep, check, or run.

Party (Host or attend)

A party timed so the Moon is in Gemini, Leo, Libra, or Sagittarius, with good aspects to Venus and Jupiter, will be fun and well attended. There should be no aspects between the Moon and Mars or Saturn.

Pawn

Do not pawn any article when Jupiter is receiving a square or opposition from Saturn or Mars or when Jupiter is within 17 degrees of the Sun, for you will have little chance to redeem the items.

Pick Mushrooms

Mushrooms, one of the most promising traditional medicines in the world, should be gathered at the Full Moon.

Plant

Root crops, like carrots and potatoes, are best if planted in the sign Taurus or Capricorn. Beans, peas, tomatoes, peppers, and other fruit-bearing plants are best if planted in a sign that supports seed growth. Leaf plants, like lettuce, broccoli, or cauliflower, are best planted when the Moon is in a water sign.

It is recommended that you transplant during a decreasing Moon, when forces are streaming into the lower part of the plant. This helps root growth.

Promotion (Ask for)

Choose a day favorable to your Sun sign. Mercury should be marked conjunct, trine, or sextile. Avoid days when Mars or Saturn is aspected.

Prune

Prune during the third and fourth quarter of a Scorpio Moon to retard growth and to promote better fruit. Prune when the Moon is in cardinal Capricorn to promote healing.

Reconcile with People

If the reconciliation is with a woman, let Venus be strong and well aspected. If elders or superiors are involved, see that Saturn is receiving good aspects; if the reconciliation is between young people or between an older and younger person, see that Mercury is well aspected.

Romance

There is less control of when a romance starts, but romances begun under an increasing Moon are more likely to be permanent or satisfying, while those begun during the decreasing Moon tend to transform the participants. The tone of the relationship can be guessed from the sign the Moon is in. Romances begun with the Moon in Aries may be impulsive. Those begun in Capricorn will take greater effort to bring to a desirable conclusion, but they may be very rewarding. Good aspects between the Moon and Venus will have a positive influence on the relationship. Avoid unfavor-

2013 © Benis Arapovic Image from BigStockPhoto.com

able aspects to Mars, Uranus, and Pluto. A decreasing Moon, particularly the fourth quarter, facilitates ending a relationship and causes the least pain.

Roof a Building

Begin roofing a building during the third or fourth quarter, when the Moon is in Aries or Aquarius. Shingles laid during the New Moon have a tendency to curl at the edges.

Sauerkraut

The best-tasting sauerkraut is made just after the Full Moon in the fruitful signs of Cancer, Scorpio, or Pisces.

Select a Child's Sex

Count from the last day of menstruation to the first day of the next cycle and divide the interval between the two dates in half. Pregnancy in the first half produces females, but copulation should take place with the Moon in a feminine sign. Pregnancy in the latter half, up to three days before the beginning of menstruation, produces males, but copulation should take place with the Moon in a masculine sign. The three-day period before the next period again produces females.

Sell or Canvass

Begin these activities during a day favorable to your Sun sign. Otherwise, sell on days when Jupiter, Mercury, or Mars is trine, sextile, or conjunct the Moon. Avoid days when Saturn is square or opposing the Moon, for that always hinders business and causes discord. If the Moon is passing from the first quarter to full, it is best to have the Moon swift in motion and in good aspect with Venus and/or Jupiter.

Sign Papers

Sign contracts or agreements when the Moon is increasing in a fruitful sign and on a day when the Moon is making favorable aspects to Mercury. Avoid days when Mars, Saturn, or Neptune are square or opposite the Moon.

Spray and Weed

Spray pests and weeds during the fourth quarter when the Moon is in the barren sign Leo or Aquarius and making favorable aspects to Pluto. Weed during a waning Moon in a barren sign.

Staff (Fire)

Have the Moon in the third or fourth quarter, but not full. The Moon should not be square any planets.

Staff (Hire)

The Moon should be in the first or second quarter, and preferably in the sign of Gemini or Virgo. The Moon should be conjunct, trine, or sextile Mercury or Jupiter.

Stocks (Buy)

The Moon should be in Taurus or Capricorn, and there should be a sextile or trine to Jupiter or Saturn.

Surgical Procedures

Blood flow, like ocean tides, appears to be related to Moon phases. To reduce hemorrhage after a surgery, schedule it within one week before or after a New Moon. Schedule surgery to occur during the increase of the Moon if possible, as wounds heal better and vitality is greater than during the decrease of the Moon. Avoid surgery within one week before or after the Full Moon. Select a date when the Moon is past the sign governing the part of the body involved in the operation. For example, abdominal operations should be done when the Moon is in Sagittarius, Capricorn, or Aquarius. The further removed the Moon sign is from the sign ruling the afflicted part of the body, the better.

For successful operations, avoid times when the Moon is applying to any aspect of Mars. (This tends to promote inflammation and complications.) See the Lunar Aspectarian on odd pages 137–159 to find days with negative Mars aspects and positive Venus and Jupiter aspects. Never operate with the Moon in the same sign as a person's Sun sign or Ascendant. Let the Moon be in a fixed sign and avoid square or opposing aspects. The Moon should not be void-of-course. Cosmetic surgery should be done in the increase of the Moon, when the Moon is not square or in opposition to Mars. Avoid days when the Moon is square or opposing Saturn or the Sun.

Travel (Air)

Start long trips when the Moon is making favorable aspects to the Sun. For enjoyment, aspects to Jupiter are preferable; for visiting, look for favorable aspects to Mercury. To prevent accidents, avoid squares or oppositions to Mars, Saturn, Uranus, or

Pluto. Choose a day when the Moon is in Sagittarius or Gemini and well aspected to Mercury, Jupiter, or Uranus. Avoid adverse aspects of Mars, Saturn, or Uranus.

Visit

On setting out to visit a person, let the Moon be in aspect with any retrograde planet, for this ensures that the person you're visiting will be at home. If you desire to stay a long time in a place, let the Moon be in good aspect to Saturn. If you desire to leave the place quickly, let the Moon be in a cardinal sign.

Wean Children

To wean a child successfully, do so when the Moon is in Sagittarius, Capricorn, Aquarius, or Pisces—signs that do not rule vital human organs. By observing this astrological rule, much trouble for parents and child may be avoided.

Weight (Reduce)

If you want to lose weight, the best time to get started is when the Moon is in the third or fourth quarter and in the barren sign of Virgo. Review the section on How to Use the Moon Tables and Lunar Aspectarian beginning on page 136 to help you select a date that is favorable to begin your weight-loss program.

Wine and Drink Other Than Beer

Start brewing when the Moon is in Pisces or Taurus. Sextiles or trines to Venus are favorable, but avoid aspects to Mars or Saturn.

Write

Write for pleasure or publication when the Moon is in Gemini. Mercury should be making favorable aspects to Uranus and Neptune.

How to Use the Moon Tables and Lunar Aspectarian

Timing activities is one of the most important things you can do to ensure success. In many Eastern countries, timing by the planets is so important that practically no event takes place without first setting up a chart for it. Weddings have occurred in the middle of the night because the influences were best then. You may not want to take it that far, but you can still make use of the influences of the Moon whenever possible. It's easy and it works!

Llewellyn's Moon Sign Book has information to help you plan just about any activity: weddings, fishing, making purchases, cutting your hair, traveling, and more. We provide the guidelines you need to pick the best day out of the several from which you have to choose. The Moon Tables are the *Moon Sign Book's* primary method for choosing dates. Following are instructions, examples, and directions on how to read the Moon Tables. More advanced information on using the tables containing the Lunar Aspectarian and favorable and unfavorable days (found on odd-numbered pages opposite the Moon Tables), Moon void-of-course and retrograde information to choose the dates best for you is also included.

The Five Basic Steps

Step 1: Directions for Choosing Dates

Look up the directions for choosing dates for the activity that you wish to begin, then go to step 2.

Step 2: Check the Moon Tables

You'll find two tables for each month of the year beginning on page 136. The Moon Tables (on the left-hand pages) include the day, date, and sign the Moon is in; the element and nature of the sign; the Moon's phase; and when it changes sign or phase. If there is a time listed after a date, that time is the time when the Moon moves into that zodiac sign. Until then, the Moon is considered to be in the sign for the previous day.

The abbreviation Full signifies Full Moon and New signifies New Moon. The times listed with dates indicate when the Moon changes sign. The times listed after the phase indicate when the Moon changes phase.

Turn to the month you would like to begin your activity. You will be using the Moon's sign and phase information most often when you begin choosing your own dates. Use the Time Zone Map on page 164 and the Time Zone Conversions table on page 165 to convert time to your own time zone.

When you find dates that meet the criteria for the correct Moon phase and sign for your activity, you may have completed the process. For certain simple activities, such as getting a haircut, the phase and sign information is all that is needed. If the directions for your activity include information on certain lunar aspects, however, you should consult the Lunar Aspectarian. An example of this would be if the directions told you not to perform a certain activity when the Moon is square (Q) Jupiter.

Step 3: Check the Lunar Aspectarian

On the pages opposite the Moon Tables you will find tables containing the Lunar Aspectarian and Favorable and Unfavorable Days. The Lunar Aspectarian gives the aspects (or angles) of the Moon to other planets. Some aspects are favorable, while others are not. To use the Lunar Aspectarian, find the planet that the directions list as favorable for your activity, and run down the column to the date desired. For example, you should avoid aspects to Mars if you are planning surgery. So you would look for Mars across the top and then run down that column looking for days where there are no aspects to Mars (as signified by empty boxes). If you want to find a favorable aspect (sextile (X) or trine (T)) to Mercury, run your finger down the column under Mercury until you find an X or T. Adverse aspects to planets are squares (Q) or oppositions (O). A conjunction (C) is sometimes beneficial, sometimes not, depending on the activity or planets involved.

Step 4: Favorable and Unfavorable Days

The tables listing favorable and unfavorable days are helpful when you want to choose your personal best dates because your Sun sign is taken into consideration. The twelve Sun signs are listed on the right side of the tables. Once you have determined which days meet your criteria for phase, sign, and aspects, you can determine whether or not those days are positive for you by checking the favorable and unfavorable days for your Sun sign.

To find out if a day is positive for you, find your Sun sign and then look down the column. If it is marked F, it is very favorable. The Moon is in the same sign as your Sun on a favorable day. If it is marked f, it is slightly favorable; U is very unfavorable; and u means slightly unfavorable. A day marked very unfavorable (U) indicates that the Moon is in the sign opposing your Sun.

Once you have selected good dates for the activity you are about to begin, you can go straight to "Using What You've Learned," beginning on the next page. To learn how to fine-tune your selections even further, read on.

Step 5: Void-of-Course Moon and Retrogrades

This last step is perhaps the most advanced portion of the procedure. It is generally considered poor timing to make decisions, sign important papers, or start special activities during a Moon void-of-course period or during a Mercury retrograde. Once you have chosen the best date for your activity based on steps one through four, you can check the Void-of-Course tables, beginning on page 76, to find out if any of the dates you have chosen have void periods.

The Moon is said to be void-of-course after it has made its last aspect to a planet within a particular sign, but before it has moved into the next sign. Put simply, the Moon is "resting" during the void-of-course period, so activities initiated at this time generally don't come to fruition. You will notice that there are many void periods during the year, and it is nearly impossible to avoid all of them. Some people choose to ignore these altogether and do not take them into consideration when planning activities.

Next, you can check the Retrograde Planets tables on page 160 to see what planets are retrograde during your chosen date(s).

A planet is said to be retrograde when it appears to move backward in the sky as viewed from the Earth. Generally, the farther a planet is away from the Sun, the longer it can stay retrograde. Some planets will retrograde for several months at a time. Avoiding retrogrades is not as important in lunar planning as avoiding the Moon void-of-course, with the exception of the planet Mercury.

Mercury rules thought and communication, so it is advisable not to sign important papers, initiate important business or legal work, or make crucial decisions during these times. As with the Moon void-of-course, it is difficult to avoid all planetary retrogrades when beginning events, and you may choose to ignore this step of the process. Following are some examples using some or all of the steps outlined above.

Using What You've Learned

Let's say it's a new year and you want to have your hair cut. It's thin and you would like it to look fuller, so you find the directions for hair care and you see that for thicker hair you should cut hair while the Moon is Full and in the sign of Taurus, Cancer, or Leo. You should avoid the Moon in Aries, Gemini, or Virgo. Look at the January Moon Table on page 136. You see that the Full Moon is on January 15 at 11:52 pm. The Moon is in Cancer that day and remains in Leo until January 18 at 8:23 pm, so January 15–18 meets both the phase and sign criteria.

Let's move on to a more difficult example using the sign and phase of the Moon. You want to buy a permanent home. After checking the instructions for purchasing a house: "Home (Buy new)" on page 118, you see that you should buy a home when the Moon is in Taurus, Cancer, or Leo. You need to get a loan, so you should also look under "Loan (Ask for)" on page 119. Here it says that the third and fourth quarters favor the borrower (you). You are going to buy the house in October, so go to page 154. The Moon is in the third quarter October 8–15. The Moon is in Cancer from 7:30 pm on October 13 until October 16 at 6:29 am. The best days for obtaining a loan would be October 14–15, while the Moon is in Cancer.

Just match up the best sign and phase (quarter) to come up with the best date. With all activities, be sure to check the favorable and unfavorable days for your Sun sign in the table adjoining the Lunar Aspectarian. If there is a choice between several dates, pick the one most favorable for you. Because buying a home is an important business decision, you may also wish to see if the Moon is void or if Mercury is retrograde during these dates.

Now let's look at an example that uses signs, phases, and aspects. Our example is starting new home construction. We will use the month of April. Look under "Build (Start foundation)" on page 110 and you'll see that the Moon should be in the first quarter of Taurus or Leo. You should select a time when the Moon is not making unfavorable aspects to Saturn. (Conjunctions are usually considered good if they are not to Mars, Saturn, or Neptune.) Look in the April Moon Table. You will see that the Moon is in the first quarter April 1–7. The Moon is in Taurus from 1:20 am on April 1 until April 3 at 7:48 am. Now, look to the April Lunar Aspectarian. We see that there are no squares to Saturn on April 1, 2, or 3, but there is an opposition on April 2. Therefore, April 1 would be the best date to start a foundation.

A Note About Time and Time Zones

All tables in the Moon Sign Book use Eastern Time. You must calculate the difference between your time zone and the Eastern Time Zone. Please refer to the Time Zone Conversions chart on page 165 for help with time conversions. The sign the Moon is in at midnight is the sign shown in the Aspectarian and Favorable and Unfavorable Days tables.

How Does the Time Matter?

Due to the three-hour time difference between the East and West Coasts of the United States, those of you living on the East Coast may be, for example, under the influence of a Virgo Moon, while those of you living on the West Coast will still have a Leo Moon influence.

We follow a commonly held belief among astrologers: whatever sign the Moon is in at the start of a day—12:00 am Eastern

Time—is considered the dominant influence of the day. That sign is indicated in the Moon Tables. If the date you select for an activity shows the Moon changing signs, you can decide how important the sign change may be for your specific election and adjust your election date and time accordingly.

Use Common Sense

Some activities depend on outside factors. Obviously, you can't go out and plant when there is a foot of snow on the ground. You should adjust to the conditions at hand. If the weather was bad during the first quarter, when it was best to plant crops, do it during the second quarter while the Moon is in a fruitful sign. If the Moon is not in a fruitful sign during the first or second quarter, choose a day when it is in a semi-fruitful sign. The best advice is to choose either the sign or phase that is most favorable, when the two don't coincide.

To Summarize

First, look up the activity under the proper heading, then look for the information given in the tables. Choose the best date considering the number of positive factors in effect. If most of the dates are favorable, there is no problem choosing the one that will fit your schedule. However, if there aren't any really good dates, pick the ones with the least number of negative influences. Please keep in mind that the information found here applies in the broadest sense to the events you want to plan or are considering. To be the most effective, when you use electional astrology, you should also consider your own birth chart in relation to a chart drawn for the time or times you have under consideration. The best advice we can offer you is: read the entire introduction to each section.

January Moon Table

Date	Sign	Element	Nature	Phase
1 Wed	Capricorn	Earth	Semi-fruitful	New 6:14 am
2 Thu 12:03 pm	Aquarius	Air	Barren	1st
3 Fri	Aquarius	Air	Barren	1st
4 Sat 11:58 am	Pisces	Water	Fruitful	1st
5 Sun	Pisces	Water	Fruitful	1st
6 Mon 2:45 pm	Aries	Fire	Barren	1st
7 Tue	Aries	Fire	Barren	2nd 10:39 pm
8 Wed 9:24 pm	Taurus	Earth	Semi-fruitful	2nd
9 Thu	Taurus	Earth	Semi-fruitful	2nd
10 Fri	Taurus	Earth	Semi-fruitful	2nd
11 Sat 7:26 am	Gemini	Air	Barren	2nd
12 Sun	Gemini	Air	Barren	2nd
13 Mon 7:25 pm	Cancer	Water	Fruitful	2nd
14 Tue	Cancer	Water	Fruitful	2nd
15 Wed	Cancer	Water	Fruitful	Full 11:52 pm
16 Thu 8:00 am	Leo	Fire	Barren	3rd
17 Fri	Leo	Fire	Barren	3rd
18 Sat 8:23 pm	Virgo	Earth	Barren	3rd
19 Sun	Virgo	Earth	Barren	3rd
20 Mon	Virgo	Earth	Barren	3rd
21 Tue 7:43 am	Libra	Air	Semi-fruitful	3rd
22 Wed	Libra	Air	Semi-fruitful	3rd
23 Thu 4:43 pm	Scorpio	Water	Fruitful	3rd
24 Fri	Scorpio	Water	Fruitful	4th 12:19 am
25 Sat 10:13 pm	Sagittarius	Fire	Barren	4th
26 Sun	Sagittarius	Fire	Barren	4th
27 Mon	Sagittarius	Fire	Barren	4th
28 Tue 12:04 am	Capricorn	Earth	Semi-fruitful	4th
29 Wed 11:33 pm	Aquarius	Air	Barren	4th
30 Thu	Aquarius	Air	Barren	New 4:39 pm
31 Fri 10:45 pm	Pisces	Water	Fruitful	1st

January Aspectarian/Favorable & Unfavorable Days

Date	Sun	Mercury	Venus	Mars	Jupiter	Saturn	Uranus	Neptune	Pluto
1	C	C		Q	O	X	Q		C
2			C						
3				T		Q	X		
4							C		
5	X	X			T	T			X
6			X						
7	Q			O	Q		C		Q
8		Q	Q						
9								X	T
10	T		T			X	O		
11		T						Q	
12				T			X		
13									
14							Q	T	O
15	O		O	Q	C	T			
16									
17		O		X			T		
18						Q			
19				X				O	T
20			T			X			
21	T								
22		T	Q	C	Q		O		Q
23								T	
24	Q		X		T				X
25		Q				C			
26	X						T	Q	
27		X		X					
28			C		O		Q	X	C
29			Q		X				
30	C						X		
31		C		T		Q			

Date	Aries	Taurus	Gemini	Cancer	Leo	Virgo	Libra	Scorpio	Sagittarius	Capricorn	Aquarius	Pisces
1	u	f		U		f	u	f		F		f
2	u	f		U		f	u	f		F		f
3	f	u	f		U		f	u	f		F	
4		f	u	f		U		f	u	f		F
5		f	u	f		U		f	u	f		F
6		f	u	f		U		f	u	f		F
7	F		f	u	f		U		f	u	f	
8	F		f	u	f		U		f	u	f	
9		F		f	u	f		U		f	u	f
10		F		f	u	f		U		f	u	f
11	f		F		f	u	f		U		f	u
12	f		F		f	u	f		U		f	u
13	f		F		f	u	f		U		f	u
14	u	f		F		f	u	f		U		f
15	u	f		F		f	u	f		U		f
16	f	u	f		F		f	u	f		U	
17	f	u	f		F		f	u	f		U	
18	f	u	f		F		f	u	f		U	
19		f	u	f		F		f	u	f		U
20		f	u	f		F		f	u	f		U
21	U		f	u	f		F		f	u	f	
22	U		f	u	f		F		f	u	f	
23	U		f	u	f		F		f	u	f	
24		U		f	u	f		F		f	u	f
25		U		f	u	f		F		f	u	f
26	f		U		f	u	f		F		f	u
27	f		U		f	u	f		F		f	u
28	u	f		U		f	u	f		F		f
29	u	f		U		f	u	f		F		f
30	f	u	f		U		f	u	f		F	
31	f	u	f		U		f	u	f		F	

February Moon Table

Date	Sign	Element	Nature	Phase
1 Sat	Pisces	Water	Fruitful	1st
2 Sun 11:55 pm	Aries	Fire	Barren	1st
3 Mon	Aries	Fire	Barren	1st
4 Tue	Aries	Fire	Barren	1st
5 Wed 4:47 am	Taurus	Earth	Semi-fruitful	1st
6 Thu	Taurus	Earth	Semi-fruitful	2nd 2:22 pm
7 Fri 1:44 pm	Gemini	Air	Barren	2nd
8 Sat	Gemini	Air	Barren	2nd
9 Sun	Gemini	Air	Barren	2nd
10 Mon 1:33 am	Cancer	Water	Fruitful	2nd
11 Tue	Cancer	Water	Fruitful	2nd
12 Wed 2:15 pm	Leo	Fire	Barren	2nd
13 Thu	Leo	Fire	Barren	2nd
14 Fri	Leo	Fire	Barren	Full 6:53 pm
15 Sat 2:26 am	Virgo	Earth	Barren	3rd
16 Sun	Virgo	Earth	Barren	3rd
17 Mon 1:23 pm	Libra	Air	Semi-fruitful	3rd
18 Tue	Libra	Air	Semi-fruitful	3rd
19 Wed 10:33 pm	Scorpio	Water	Fruitful	3rd
20 Thu	Scorpio	Water	Fruitful	3rd
21 Fri	Scorpio	Water	Fruitful	3rd
22 Sat 5:12 am	Sagittarius	Fire	Barren	4th 12:15 pm
23 Sun	Sagittarius	Fire	Barren	4th
24 Mon 8:50 am	Capricorn	Earth	Semi-fruitful	4th
25 Tue	Capricorn	Earth	Semi-fruitful	4th
26 Wed 9:55 am	Aquarius	Air	Barren	4th
27 Thu	Aquarius	Air	Barren	4th
28 Fri 9:53 am	Pisces	Water	Fruitful	4th

February Aspectarian/Favorable & Unfavorable Days

Date	Sun	Mercury	Venus	Mars	Jupiter	Saturn	Uranus	Neptune	Pluto
1			X		T			C	X
2						T			
3			Q		Q		C		Q
4	X			O					
5		X						X	
6	Q		T		X	O			T
7		Q						Q	
8								X	
9	T			T					
10		T					Q	T	
11			O		C				O
12				Q		T			
13							T		
14	O	O		X		Q			
15								O	
16			T		X				T
17						X			
18					Q		O		Q
19		T	Q	C					
20	T				T			T	X
21		Q	X			C			
22	Q						T	Q	
23		X							
24	X			X				X	
25					O	X	Q		C
26			C	Q					
27		C				Q	X		
28				T				C	

Date	Aries	Taurus	Gemini	Cancer	Leo	Virgo	Libra	Scorpio	Sagittarius	Capricorn	Aquarius	Pisces
1		f	u	f		U		f	u	f		F
2		f	u	f		U		f	u	f		F
3	F		f	u	f		U		f	u	f	
4	F		f	u	f		U		f	u	f	
5		F		f	u	f		U		f	u	f
6		F		f	u	f		U		f	u	f
7		F		f	u	f		U		f	u	f
8	f		F		f	u	f		U		f	u
9	f		F		f	u	f		U		f	u
10	u	f		F		f	u	f		U		f
11	u	f		F		f	u	f		U		f
12	u	f		F		f	u	f		U		f
13	f	u	f		F		f	u	f		U	
14	f	u	f		F		f	u	f		U	
15		f	u	f		F		f	u	f		U
16		f	u	f		F		f	u	f		U
17		f	u	f		F		f	u	f		U
18	U		f	u	f		F		f	u	f	
19	U		f	u	f		F		f	u	f	
20		U		f	u	f		F		f	u	f
21		U		f	u	f		F		f	u	f
22	f		U		f	u	f		F		f	u
23	f		U		f	u	f		F		f	u
24	u	f		U		f	u	f		F		f
25	u	f		U		f	u	f		F		f
26	f	u	f		U		f	u	f		F	
27	f	u	f		U		f	u	f		F	
28		f	u	f		U		f	u	f		F

March Moon Table

Date	Sign	Element	Nature	Phase
1 Sat	Pisces	Water	Fruitful	New 3:00 am
2 Sun 10:40 am	Aries	Fire	Barren	1st
3 Mon	Aries	Fire	Barren	1st
4 Tue 2:12 pm	Taurus	Earth	Semi-fruitful	1st
5 Wed	Taurus	Earth	Semi-fruitful	1st
6 Thu 9:37 pm	Gemini	Air	Barren	1st
7 Fri	Gemini	Air	Barren	1st
8 Sat	Gemini	Air	Barren	2nd 8:27 am
9 Sun 9:33 am	Cancer	Water	Fruitful	2nd
10 Mon	Cancer	Water	Fruitful	2nd
11 Tue 10:09 pm	Leo	Fire	Barren	2nd
12 Wed	Leo	Fire	Barren	2nd
13 Thu	Leo	Fire	Barren	2nd
14 Fri 10:17 am	Virgo	Earth	Barren	2nd
15 Sat	Virgo	Earth	Barren	2nd
16 Sun 8:46 pm	Libra	Air	Semi-fruitful	Full 1:08 pm
17 Mon	Libra	Air	Semi-fruitful	3rd
18 Tue	Libra	Air	Semi-fruitful	3rd
19 Wed 5:13 am	Scorpio	Water	Fruitful	3rd
20 Thu	Scorpio	Water	Fruitful	3rd
21 Fri 11:39 am	Sagittarius	Fire	Barren	3rd
22 Sat	Sagittarius	Fire	Barren	3rd
23 Sun 4:03 pm	Capricorn	Earth	Semi-fruitful	4th 9:46 pm
24 Mon	Capricorn	Earth	Semi-fruitful	4th
25 Tue 6:39 pm	Aquarius	Air	Barren	4th
26 Wed	Aquarius	Air	Barren	4th
27 Thu 8:10 pm	Pisces	Water	Fruitful	4th
28 Fri	Pisces	Water	Fruitful	4th
29 Sat 9:54 pm	Aries	Fire	Barren	4th
30 Sun	Aries	Fire	Barren	New 2:45 pm
31 Mon	Aries	Fire	Barren	1st

March Aspectarian/Favorable & Unfavorable Days

Date	Sun	Mercury	Venus	Mars	Jupiter	Saturn	Uranus	Neptune	Pluto
1	C				T	T			X
2			X						
3		X			Q		C		Q
4			Q	O				X	
5	X				X				T
6		Q	T				O		
7							X	Q	
8	Q	T							
9				T				T	
10					C		Q		O
11	T			Q		T			
12			O					T	
13						Q			
14		O		X				O	
15					X				T
16	O					X			
17			T		Q		O		Q
18				C					
19		T						T	
20			Q		T	C			X
21	T	Q						Q	
22			X			T			
23	Q			X					
24		X			O		Q	X	C
25				Q		X			
26	X						X		
27			C	T		Q			
28		C			T			C	X
29						T			
30	C				Q		C		Q
31			X	O					

Date	Aries	Taurus	Gemini	Cancer	Leo	Virgo	Libra	Scorpio	Sagittarius	Capricorn	Aquarius	Pisces
1		f	u	f		U		f	u	f		F
2	F		f	u	f		U		f	u	f	
3	F		f	u	f		U		f	u	f	
4	F		f	u	f		U		f	u	f	
5		F		f	u	f		U		f	u	f
6		F		f	u	f		U		f	u	f
7	f		F		f	u	f		U		f	u
8	f		F		f	u	f		U		f	u
9	u	f		F		f	u	f		U		f
10	u	f		F		f	u	f		U		f
11	u	f		F		f	u	f		U		f
12	f	u	f		F		f	u	f		U	
13	f	u	f		F		f	u	f		U	
14		f	u	f		F		f	u	f		U
15		f	u	f		F		f	u	f		U
16		f	u	f		F		f	u	f		U
17	U		f	u	f		F		f	u	f	
18	U		f	u	f		F		f	u	f	
19		U		f	u	f		F		f	u	f
20		U		f	u	f		F		f	u	f
21	f		U		f	u	f		F		f	u
22	f		U		f	u	f		F		f	u
23	f		U		f	u	f		F		f	u
24	u	f		U		f	u	f		F		f
25	u	f		U		f	u	f		F		f
26	f	u	f		U		f	u	f		F	
27	f	u	f		U		f	u	f		F	
28		f	u	f		U		f	u	f		F
29		f	u	f		U		f	u	f		F
30	F		f	u	f		U		f	u	f	
31	F		f	u	f		U		f	u	f	

April Moon Table

Date	Sign	Element	Nature	Phase
1 Tue 1:20 am	Taurus	Earth	Semi-fruitful	1st
2 Wed	Taurus	Earth	Semi-fruitful	1st
3 Thu 7:48 am	Gemini	Air	Barren	1st
4 Fri	Gemini	Air	Barren	1st
5 Sat 5:40 pm	Cancer	Water	Fruitful	1st
6 Sun	Cancer	Water	Fruitful	1st
7 Mon	Cancer	Water	Fruitful	2nd 4:31 am
8 Tue 5:50 am	Leo	Fire	Barren	2nd
9 Wed	Leo	Fire	Barren	2nd
10 Thu 6:08 pm	Virgo	Earth	Barren	2nd
11 Fri	Virgo	Earth	Barren	2nd
12 Sat	Virgo	Earth	Barren	2nd
13 Sun 4:33 am	Libra	Air	Semi-fruitful	2nd
14 Mon	Libra	Air	Semi-fruitful	2nd
15 Tue 12:20 pm	Scorpio	Water	Fruitful	Full 3:42 am
16 Wed	Scorpio	Water	Fruitful	3rd
17 Thu 5:44 pm	Sagittarius	Fire	Barren	3rd
18 Fri	Sagittarius	Fire	Barren	3rd
19 Sat 9:28 pm	Capricorn	Earth	Semi-fruitful	3rd
20 Sun	Capricorn	Earth	Semi-fruitful	3rd
21 Mon	Capricorn	Earth	Semi-fruitful	3rd
22 Tue 12:18 am	Aquarius	Air	Barren	4th 3:52 am
23 Wed	Aquarius	Air	Barren	4th
24 Thu 2:55 am	Pisces	Water	Fruitful	4th
25 Fri	Pisces	Water	Fruitful	4th
26 Sat 6:01 am	Aries	Fire	Barren	4th
27 Sun	Aries	Fire	Barren	4th
28 Mon 10:23 am	Taurus	Earth	Semi-fruitful	4th
29 Tue	Taurus	Earth	Semi-fruitful	New 2:14 am
30 Wed 4:56 pm	Gemini	Air	Barren	1st

April Aspectarian/Favorable & Unfavorable Days

Date	Sun	Mercury	Venus	Mars	Jupiter	Saturn	Uranus	Neptune	Pluto
1					X			X	
2		X				O			T
3			Q					Q	
4	X			T			X		
5		Q	T						
6					C		Q	T	O
7	Q			Q		T			
8		T							
9	T			X			T		
10						Q			
11			O		X			O	T
12						X			
13									
14		O		C	Q		O		Q
15	O								
16			T		T			T	X
17						C			
18			Q	X			T	Q	
19	T	T							
20				Q	O		Q	X	C
21		Q	X			X			
22	Q			T			X		
23						Q			
24	X	X						C	
25			C		T	T			X
26									
27				O	Q		C		Q
28								X	
29	C	C			X	O			T
30			X						

Date	Aries	Taurus	Gemini	Cancer	Leo	Virgo	Libra	Scorpio	Sagittarus	Capricorn	Aquarius	Pisces
1		F		f	u	f		U		f	u	f
2		F		f	u	f		U		f	u	f
3	f		F		f	u	f		U		f	u
4	f		F		f	u	f		U		f	u
5	f		F		f	u	f		U		f	u
6	u	f		F		f	u	f		U		f
7	u	f		F		f	u	f		U		f
8	f	u	f		F		f	u	f		U	
9	f	u	f		F		f	u	f		U	
10	f	u	f		F		f	u	f		U	
11		f	u	f		F		f	u	f		U
12		f	u	f		F		f	u	f		U
13	U		f	u	f		F		f	u	f	
14	U		f	u	f		F		f	u	f	
15	U		f	u	f		F		f	u	f	
16		U		f	u	f		F		f	u	f
17		U		f	u	f		F		f	u	f
18	f		U		f	u	f		F		f	u
19	f		U		f	u	f		F		f	u
20	u	f		U		f	u	f		F		f
21	u	f		U		f	u	f		F		f
22	f	u	f		U		f	u	f		F	
23	f	u	f		U		f	u	f		F	
24		f	u	f		U		f	u	f		F
25		f	u	f		U		f	u	f		F
26	F		f	u	f		U		f	u	f	
27	F		f	u	f		U		f	u	f	
28		F		f	u	f		U		f	u	f
29		F		f	u	f		U		f	u	f
30		F		f	u	f		U		f	u	f

May Moon Table

Date	Sign	Element	Nature	Phase
1 Thu	Gemini	Air	Barren	1st
2 Fri	Gemini	Air	Barren	1st
3 Sat 2:13 am	Cancer	Water	Fruitful	1st
4 Sun	Cancer	Water	Fruitful	1st
5 Mon 1:55 pm	Leo	Fire	Barren	1st
6 Tue	Leo	Fire	Barren	2nd 11:15 pm
7 Wed	Leo	Fire	Barren	2nd
8 Thu 2:24 am	Virgo	Earth	Barren	2nd
9 Fri	Virgo	Earth	Barren	2nd
10 Sat 1:19 pm	Libra	Air	Semi-fruitful	2nd
11 Sun	Libra	Air	Semi-fruitful	2nd
12 Mon 9:07 pm	Scorpio	Water	Fruitful	2nd
13 Tue	Scorpio	Water	Fruitful	2nd
14 Wed	Scorpio	Water	Fruitful	Full 3:16 pm
15 Thu 1:44 am	Sagittarius	Fire	Barren	3rd
16 Fri	Sagittarius	Fire	Barren	3rd
17 Sat 4:12 am	Capricorn	Earth	Semi-fruitful	3rd
18 Sun	Capricorn	Earth	Semi-fruitful	3rd
19 Mon 5:58 am	Aquarius	Air	Barren	3rd
20 Tue	Aquarius	Air	Barren	3rd
21 Wed 8:18 am	Pisces	Water	Fruitful	4th 8:59 am
22 Thu	Pisces	Water	Fruitful	4th
23 Fri 12:01 pm	Aries	Fire	Barren	4th
24 Sat	Aries	Fire	Barren	4th
25 Sun 5:28 pm	Taurus	Earth	Semi-fruitful	4th
26 Mon	Taurus	Earth	Semi-fruitful	4th
27 Tue	Taurus	Earth	Semi-fruitful	4th
28 Wed 12:47 am	Gemini	Air	Barren	New 2:40 pm
29 Thu	Gemini	Air	Barren	1st
30 Fri 10:13 am	Cancer	Water	Fruitful	1st
31 Sat	Cancer	Water	Fruitful	1st

May Aspectarian/Favorable & Unfavorable Days

Date	Sun	Mercury	Venus	Mars	Jupiter	Saturn	Uranus	Neptune	Pluto
1				T			X	Q	
2									
3			Q	Q				T	
4	X				C	T	Q		O
5		X	T						
6	Q			X			T		
7						Q			
8		Q						O	
9	T				X	X			T
10									
11		T	O	C	Q		O		Q
12									
13								T	X
14	O				T	C			
15				X				Q	
16		O	T				T		
17				Q				X	
18			Q		O	X	Q		C
19	T			T					
20		T	X				Q	X	
21	Q						C		
22					T	T			X
23	X	Q							
24			O	Q			C		Q
25		X	C						
26								X	T
27					X	O			
28	C			T				Q	
29							X		
30		C	X						
31				Q		T	Q	T	O

Date	Aries	Taurus	Gemini	Cancer	Leo	Virgo	Libra	Scorpio	Sagittarius	Capricorn	Aquarius	Pisces
1	f		F		f	u	f		U		f	u
2	f		F		f	u	f		U		f	u
3	u	f		F		f	u	f		U		f
4	u	f		F		f	u	f		U		f
5	u	f		F		f	u	f		U		f
6	f	u	f		F		f	u	f		U	
7	f	u	f		F		f	u	f		U	
8		f	u	f		F		f	u	f		U
9		f	u	f		F		f	u	f		U
10		f	u	f		F		f	u	f		U
11	U		f	u	f		F		f	u	f	
12	U		f	u	f		F		f	u	f	
13		U		f	u	f		F		f	u	f
14		U		f	u	f		F		f	u	f
15	f		U		f	u	f		F		f	u
16	f		U		f	u	f		F		f	u
17	u	f		U		f	u	f		F		f
18	u	f		U		f	u	f		F		f
19	f	u	f		U		f	u	f		F	
20	f	u	f		U		f	u	f		F	
21		f	u	f		U		f	u	f		F
22		f	u	f		U		f	u	f		F
23		f	u	f		U		f	u	f		F
24	F		f	u	f		U		f	u	f	
25	F		f	u	f		U		f	u	f	
26		F		f	u	f		U		f	u	f
27		F		f	u	f		U		f	u	f
28	f		F		f	u	f		U		f	u
29	f		F		f	u	f		U		f	u
30	u	f		F		f	u	f		U		f
31	u	f		F		f	u	f		U		f

June Moon Table

Date	Sign	Element	Nature	Phase
1 Sun 9:43 pm	Leo	Fire	Barren	1st
2 Mon	Leo	Fire	Barren	1st
3 Tue	Leo	Fire	Barren	1st
4 Wed 10:20 am	Virgo	Earth	Barren	1st
5 Thu	Virgo	Earth	Barren	2nd 4:39 pm
6 Fri 10:01 pm	Libra	Air	Semi-fruitful	2nd
7 Sat	Libra	Air	Semi-fruitful	2nd
8 Sun	Libra	Air	Semi-fruitful	2nd
9 Mon 6:38 am	Scorpio	Water	Fruitful	2nd
10 Tue	Scorpio	Water	Fruitful	2nd
11 Wed 11:23 am	Sagittarius	Fire	Barren	2nd
12 Thu	Sagittarius	Fire	Barren	2nd
13 Fri 1:04 pm	Capricorn	Earth	Semi-fruitful	Full 12:11 am
14 Sat	Capricorn	Earth	Semi-fruitful	3rd
15 Sun 1:27 pm	Aquarius	Air	Barren	3rd
16 Mon	Aquarius	Air	Barren	3rd
17 Tue 2:26 pm	Pisces	Water	Fruitful	3rd
18 Wed	Pisces	Water	Fruitful	3rd
19 Thu 5:26 pm	Aries	Fire	Barren	4th 2:39 pm
20 Fri	Aries	Fire	Barren	4th
21 Sat 11:03 pm	Taurus	Earth	Semi-fruitful	4th
22 Sun	Taurus	Earth	Semi-fruitful	4th
23 Mon	Taurus	Earth	Semi-fruitful	4th
24 Tue 7:05 am	Gemini	Air	Barren	4th
25 Wed	Gemini	Air	Barren	4th
26 Thu 5:05 pm	Cancer	Water	Fruitful	4th
27 Fri	Cancer	Water	Fruitful	New 4:08 am
28 Sat	Cancer	Water	Fruitful	1st
29 Sun 4:43 am	Leo	Fire	Barren	1st
30 Mon	Leo	Fire	Barren	1st

June Aspectarian/Favorable & Unfavorable Days

Date	Sun	Mercury	Venus	Mars	Jupiter	Saturn	Uranus	Neptune	Pluto
1					C				
2	X		Q	X					
3						Q	T		
4		X							
5	Q		T			X		O	T
6				X					
7		Q		C					Q
8	T				Q		O		
9		T						T	
10			O		T	C			X
11									
12				X				T	Q
13	O	O							
14			T	Q		X	Q	X	C
15					O				
16				T			Q	X	
17	T	T	Q						
18						T		C	X
19	Q	Q	X		T				
20				O			C		Q
21		X			Q				
22	X							X	T
23					X	O			
24			C					Q	
25				T			X		
26		C							
27	C							T	O
28				Q	C	T	Q		
29			X						
30				X		Q	T		

Date	Aries	Taurus	Gemini	Cancer	Leo	Virgo	Libra	Scorpio	Sagittarius	Capricorn	Aquarius	Pisces
1	u	f		F		f	u	f		U		f
2	f	u	f		F		f	u	f		U	
3	f	u	f		F		f	u	f		U	
4		f	u	f		F		f	u	f		U
5		f	u	f		F		f	u	f		U
6		f	u	f		F		f	u	f		U
7	U		f	u	f		F		f	u	f	
8	U		f	u	f		F		f	u	f	
9		U		f	u	f		F		f	u	f
10		U		f	u	f		F		f	u	f
11	f		U		f	u	f		F		f	u
12	f		U		f	u	f		F		f	u
13	f		U		f	u	f		F		f	u
14	u	f		U		f	u	f		F		f
15	u	f		U		f	u	f		F		f
16	f	u	f		U		f	u	f		F	
17	f	u	f		U		f	u	f		F	
18		f	u	f		U		f	u	f		F
19		f	u	f		U		f	u	f		F
20	F		f	u	f		U		f	u	f	
21	F		f	u	f		U		f	u	f	
22		F		f	u	f		U		f	u	f
23		F		f	u	f		U		f	u	f
24	f		F		f	u	f		U		f	u
25	f		F		f	u	f		U		f	u
26	f		F		f	u	f		U		f	u
27	u	f		F		f	u	f		U		f
28	u	f		F		f	u	f		U		f
29	f	u	f		F		f	u	f		U	
30	f	u	f		F		f	u	f		U	

July Moon Table

Date	Sign	Element	Nature	Phase
1 Tue 5:24 pm	Virgo	Earth	Barren	1st
2 Wed	Virgo	Earth	Barren	1st
3 Thu	Virgo	Earth	Barren	1st
4 Fri 5:43 am	Libra	Air	Semi-fruitful	1st
5 Sat	Libra	Air	Semi-fruitful	2nd 7:59 am
6 Sun 3:33 pm	Scorpio	Water	Fruitful	2nd
7 Mon	Scorpio	Water	Fruitful	2nd
8 Tue 9:24 pm	Sagittarius	Fire	Barren	2nd
9 Wed	Sagittarius	Fire	Barren	2nd
10 Thu 11:24 pm	Capricorn	Earth	Semi-fruitful	2nd
11 Fri	Capricorn	Earth	Semi-fruitful	2nd
12 Sat 11:07 pm	Aquarius	Air	Barren	Full 7:25 am
13 Sun	Aquarius	Air	Barren	3rd
14 Mon 10:40 pm	Pisces	Water	Fruitful	3rd
15 Tue	Pisces	Water	Fruitful	3rd
16 Wed	Pisces	Water	Fruitful	3rd
17 Thu 12:07 am	Aries	Fire	Barren	3rd
18 Fri	Aries	Fire	Barren	4th 10:08 pm
19 Sat 4:43 am	Taurus	Earth	Semi-fruitful	4th
20 Sun	Taurus	Earth	Semi-fruitful	4th
21 Mon 12:36 pm	Gemini	Air	Barren	4th
22 Tue	Gemini	Air	Barren	4th
23 Wed 10:59 pm	Cancer	Water	Fruitful	4th
24 Thu	Cancer	Water	Fruitful	4th
25 Fri	Cancer	Water	Fruitful	4th
26 Sat 10:55 am	Leo	Fire	Barren	New 6:42 pm
27 Sun	Leo	Fire	Barren	1st
28 Mon 11:37 pm	Virgo	Earth	Barren	1st
29 Tue	Virgo	Earth	Barren	1st
30 Wed	Virgo	Earth	Barren	1st
31 Thu 12:09 pm	Libra	Air	Semi-fruitful	1st

July Aspectarian/Favorable & Unfavorable Days

Date	Sun	Mercury	Venus	Mars	Jupiter	Saturn	Uranus	Neptune	Pluto
1		X							
2	X		Q					O	T
3		Q					X		
4					X				
5	Q		T	C				O	Q
6		T			Q				
7	T					C		T	X
8					T				
9								Q	
10		O	O	X			T		
11								X	C
12	O			Q	O	X	Q		
13									
14			T	T		Q	X		
15		T						C	X
16	T		Q			T			
17		Q				T			Q
18	Q			O			C		
19		X	X		Q			X	
20						O			T
21	X				X				
22							X	Q	
23				T					
24			C					T	O
25		C				T	Q		
26	C			Q	C				
27						Q	T		
28									
29				X				O	T
30		X				X			
31		X			X				

Date	Aries	Taurus	Gemini	Cancer	Leo	Virgo	Libra	Scorpio	Sagittarus	Capricorn	Aquarius	Pisces
1	f	u	f		F		f	u	f		U	
2		f	u	f		F		f	u	f		U
3		f	u	f		F		f	u	f		U
4	U		f	u	f		F		f	u	f	
5	U		f	u	f		F		f	u	f	
6	U		f	u	f		F		f	u	f	
7		U		f	u	f		F		f	u	f
8		U		f	u	f		F		f	u	f
9	f		U		f	u	f		F		f	u
10	f		U		f	u	f		F		f	u
11	u	f		U		f	u	f		F		f
12	u	f		U		f	u	f		F		f
13	f	u	f		U		f	u	f		F	
14	f	u	f		U		f	u	f		F	
15		f	u	f		U		f	u	f		F
16		f	u	f		U		f	u	f		F
17	F		f	u	f		U		f	u	f	
18	F		f	u	f		U		f	u	f	
19		F		f	u	f		U		f	u	f
20		F		f	u	f		U		f	u	f
21		F		f	u	f		U		f	u	f
22	f		F		f	u	f		U		f	u
23	f		F		f	u	f		U		f	u
24	u	f		F		f	u	f		U		f
25	u	f		F		f	u	f		U		f
26	f	u	f		F		f	u	f		U	
27	f	u	f		F		f	u	f		U	
28	f	u	f		F		f	u	f		U	
29		f	u	f		F		f	u	f		U
30		f	u	f		F		f	u	f		U
31		f	u	f		F		f	u	f		U

August Moon Table

Date	Sign	Element	Nature	Phase
1 Fri	Libra	Air	Semi-fruitful	1st
2 Sat 10:57 pm	Scorpio	Water	Fruitful	1st
3 Sun	Scorpio	Water	Fruitful	2nd 8:50 pm
4 Mon	Scorpio	Water	Fruitful	2nd
5 Tue 6:19 am	Sagittarius	Fire	Barren	2nd
6 Wed	Sagittarius	Fire	Barren	2nd
7 Thu 9:38 am	Capricorn	Earth	Semi-fruitful	2nd
8 Fri	Capricorn	Earth	Semi-fruitful	2nd
9 Sat 9:52 am	Aquarius	Air	Barren	2nd
10 Sun	Aquarius	Air	Barren	Full 2:09 pm
11 Mon 8:55 am	Pisces	Water	Fruitful	3rd
12 Tue	Pisces	Water	Fruitful	3rd
13 Wed 9:00 am	Aries	Fire	Barren	3rd
14 Thu	Aries	Fire	Barren	3rd
15 Fri 11:58 am	Taurus	Earth	Semi-fruitful	3rd
16 Sat	Taurus	Earth	Semi-fruitful	3rd
17 Sun 6:41 pm	Gemini	Air	Barren	4th 8:26 am
18 Mon	Gemini	Air	Barren	4th
19 Tue	Gemini	Air	Barren	4th
20 Wed 4:45 am	Cancer	Water	Fruitful	4th
21 Thu	Cancer	Water	Fruitful	4th
22 Fri 4:49 pm	Leo	Fire	Barren	4th
23 Sat	Leo	Fire	Barren	4th
24 Sun	Leo	Fire	Barren	4th
25 Mon 5:33 am	Virgo	Earth	Barren	New 10:13 am
26 Tue	Virgo	Earth	Barren	1st
27 Wed 5:54 pm	Libra	Air	Semi-fruitful	1st
28 Thu	Libra	Air	Semi-fruitful	1st
29 Fri	Libra	Air	Semi-fruitful	1st
30 Sat 4:53 am	Scorpio	Water	Fruitful	1st
31 Sun	Scorpio	Water	Fruitful	1st

August Aspectarian/Favorable & Unfavorable Days

Date	Sun	Mercury	Venus	Mars	Jupiter	Saturn	Uranus	Neptune	Pluto
1	X		Q					O	Q
2									
3	Q	Q		C	Q			T	X
4			T			C			
5					T			Q	
6	T	T						T	
7				X				X	
8						X	Q		C
9			O	Q	O				
10	O	O				Q	X		
11			T				C		
12						T			X
13			T		T				
14	T					C		Q	
15		T	Q				X		
16			O	Q	O			T	
17	Q								
18		Q	X		X			Q	
19	X						X		
20							T		
21		X		T		T	Q		O
22									
23			C		C				
24			Q			Q	T		
25	C						O		
26		C		X		X			T
27									
28					X				Q
29			X				O		
30	X						T		
31				C	Q	C			X

Date	Aries	Taurus	Gemini	Cancer	Leo	Virgo	Libra	Scorpio	Sagittarus	Capricorn	Aquarius	Pisces
1	U		f	u	f		F		f	u	f	
2	U		f	u	f		F		f	u	f	
3		U		f	u	f		F		f	u	f
4		U		f	u	f		F		f	u	f
5	f		U		f	u	f		F		f	u
6	f		U		f	u	f		F		f	u
7	u	f		U		f	u	f		F		f
8	u	f		U		f	u	f		F		f
9	f	u	f		U		f	u	f		F	
10	f	u	f		U		f	u	f		F	
11		f	u	f		U		f	u	f		F
12		f	u	f		U		f	u	f		F
13	F		f	u	f		U		f	u	f	
14	F		f	u	f		U		f	u	f	
15		F		f	u	f		U		f	u	f
16		F		f	u	f		U		f	u	f
17		F		f	u	f		U		f	u	f
18	f		F		f	u	f		U		f	u
19	f		F		f	u	f		U		f	u
20	u	f		F		f	u	f		U		f
21	u	f		F		f	u	f		U		f
22	u	f		F		f	u	f		U		f
23	f	u	f		F		f	u	f		U	
24	f	u	f		F		f	u	f		U	
25		f	u	f		F		f	u	f		U
26		f	u	f		F		f	u	f		U
27		f	u	f		F		f	u	f		U
28	U		f	u	f		F		f	u	f	
29	U		f	u	f		F		f	u	f	
30		U		f	u	f		F		f	u	f
31		U		f	u	f		F		f	u	f

September Moon Table

Date	Sign	Element	Nature	Phase
1 Mon 1:17 pm	Sagittarius	Fire	Barren	1st
2 Tue	Sagittarius	Fire	Barren	2nd 7:11 am
3 Wed 6:15 pm	Capricorn	Earth	Semi-fruitful	2nd
4 Thu	Capricorn	Earth	Semi-fruitful	2nd
5 Fri 7:59 pm	Aquarius	Air	Barren	2nd
6 Sat	Aquarius	Air	Barren	2nd
7 Sun 7:47 pm	Pisces	Water	Fruitful	2nd
8 Mon	Pisces	Water	Fruitful	Full 9:38 pm
9 Tue 7:33 pm	Aries	Fire	Barren	3rd
10 Wed	Aries	Fire	Barren	3rd
11 Thu 9:17 pm	Taurus	Earth	Semi-fruitful	3rd
12 Fri	Taurus	Earth	Semi-fruitful	3rd
13 Sat	Taurus	Earth	Semi-fruitful	3rd
14 Sun 2:26 am	Gemini	Air	Barren	3rd
15 Mon	Gemini	Air	Barren	4th 10:05 pm
16 Tue 11:24 am	Cancer	Water	Fruitful	4th
17 Wed	Cancer	Water	Fruitful	4th
18 Thu 11:10 pm	Leo	Fire	Barren	4th
19 Fri	Leo	Fire	Barren	4th
20 Sat	Leo	Fire	Barren	4th
21 Sun 11:54 am	Virgo	Earth	Barren	4th
22 Mon	Virgo	Earth	Barren	4th
23 Tue 11:59 pm	Libra	Air	Semi-fruitful	4th
24 Wed	Libra	Air	Semi-fruitful	New 2:14 am
25 Thu	Libra	Air	Semi-fruitful	1st
26 Fri 10:29 am	Scorpio	Water	Fruitful	1st
27 Sat	Scorpio	Water	Fruitful	1st
28 Sun 6:50 pm	Sagittarius	Fire	Barren	1st
29 Mon	Sagittarius	Fire	Barren	1st
30 Tue	Sagittarius	Fire	Barren	1st

September Aspectarian/Favorable & Unfavorable Days

Date	Sun	Mercury	Venus	Mars	Jupiter	Saturn	Uranus	Neptune	Pluto
1		X	Q						
2	Q				T			T	Q
3		Q	T						
4	T						Q	X	C
5				X		X			
6		T			O		X		
7				Q		Q			
8	O		O					C	X
9				T		T			
10		O			T		C		Q
11									
12			T		Q			X	T
13	T					O			
14				O				Q	
15	Q	T	Q		X		X		
16								T	
17			X				Q		O
18	X	Q				T			
19				T					
20					C	Q	T		
21		X		Q				O	
22									T
23			C			X			
24	C			X					Q
25					X		O		
26		C						T	
27					Q				X
28			X			C			
29	X			C	T			T	Q
30									

Date	Aries	Taurus	Gemini	Cancer	Leo	Virgo	Libra	Scorpio	Sagittarus	Capricorn	Aquarius	Pisces
1		U		f	u	f		F		f	u	f
2	f		U		f	u	f		F		f	u
3	f		U		f	u	f		F		f	u
4	u	f		U		f	u	f		F		f
5	u	f		U		f	u	f		F		f
6	f	u	f		U		f	u	f		F	
7	f	u	f		U		f	u	f		F	
8		f	u	f		U		f	u	f		F
9		f	u	f		U		f	u	f		F
10	F		f	u	f		U		f	u	f	
11	F		f	u	f		U		f	u	f	
12		F		f	u	f		U		f	u	f
13		F		f	u	f		U		f	u	f
14	f		F		f	u	f		U		f	u
15	f		F		f	u	f		U		f	u
16	u	f		F		f	u	f		U		f
17	u	f		F		f	u	f		U		f
18	u	f		F		f	u	f		U		f
19	f	u	f		F		f	u	f		U	
20	f	u	f		F		f	u	f		U	
21		f	u	f		F		f	u	f		U
22		f	u	f		F		f	u	f		U
23		f	u	f		F		f	u	f		U
24	U		f	u	f		F		f	u	f	
25	U		f	u	f		F		f	u	f	
26		U		f	u	f		F		f	u	f
27		U		f	u	f		F		f	u	f
28		U		f	u	f		F		f	u	f
29	f		U		f	u	f		F		f	u
30	f		U		f	u	f		F		f	u

October Moon Table

Date	Sign	Element	Nature	Phase
1 Wed 12:41 am	Capricorn	Earth	Semi-fruitful	2nd 3:33 pm
2 Thu	Capricorn	Earth	Semi-fruitful	2nd
3 Fri 4:00 am	Aquarius	Air	Barren	2nd
4 Sat	Aquarius	Air	Barren	2nd
5 Sun 5:24 am	Pisces	Water	Fruitful	2nd
6 Mon	Pisces	Water	Fruitful	2nd
7 Tue 6:07 am	Aries	Fire	Barren	2nd
8 Wed	Aries	Fire	Barren	Full 6:51 am
9 Thu 7:44 am	Taurus	Earth	Semi-fruitful	3rd
10 Fri	Taurus	Earth	Semi-fruitful	3rd
11 Sat 11:51 am	Gemini	Air	Barren	3rd
12 Sun	Gemini	Air	Barren	3rd
13 Mon 7:30 pm	Cancer	Water	Fruitful	3rd
14 Tue	Cancer	Water	Fruitful	3rd
15 Wed	Cancer	Water	Fruitful	4th 3:12 pm
16 Thu 6:29 am	Leo	Fire	Barren	4th
17 Fri	Leo	Fire	Barren	4th
18 Sat 7:08 pm	Virgo	Earth	Barren	4th
19 Sun	Virgo	Earth	Barren	4th
20 Mon	Virgo	Earth	Barren	4th
21 Tue 7:12 am	Libra	Air	Semi-fruitful	4th
22 Wed	Libra	Air	Semi-fruitful	4th
23 Thu 5:10 pm	Scorpio	Water	Fruitful	New 5:57 pm
24 Fri	Scorpio	Water	Fruitful	1st
25 Sat	Scorpio	Water	Fruitful	1st
26 Sun 12:40 am	Sagittarius	Fire	Barren	1st
27 Mon	Sagittarius	Fire	Barren	1st
28 Tue 6:03 am	Capricorn	Earth	Semi-fruitful	1st
29 Wed	Capricorn	Earth	Semi-fruitful	1st
30 Thu 9:52 am	Aquarius	Air	Barren	2nd 10:48 pm
31 Fri	Aquarius	Air	Barren	2nd

October Aspectarian/Favorable & Unfavorable Days

Date	Sun	Mercury	Venus	Mars	Jupiter	Saturn	Uranus	Neptune	Pluto
1	Q	X	Q					X	C
2							X	Q	
3	T	Q	T						
4				X	O	Q	X		
5		T						C	X
6				Q		T			
7			O						
8	O			T	T			C	Q
9		O					X		
10					Q	O			T
11								Q	
12			T		X		X		
13	T	T		O					
14							Q	T	O
15	Q	Q	Q			T			
16									
17					C		T		
18	X	X	X	T		Q			
19								O	T
20				Q			X		
21									
22		C			X		O		Q
23	C		C	X					
24								T	X
25					Q	C			
26								Q	
27		X			T		T		
28	X		X	C				X	
29		Q				X	Q		C
30	Q								
31		T	Q		O		X		

Date	Aries	Taurus	Gemini	Cancer	Leo	Virgo	Libra	Scorpio	Sagittarus	Capricorn	Aquarius	Pisces
1	u	f		U		f	u	f		F		f
2	u	f		U		f	u	f		F		f
3	f	u	f		U		f	u	f		F	
4	f	u	f		U		f	u	f		F	
5		f	u	f		U		f	u	f		F
6		f	u	f		U		f	u	f		F
7	F		f	u	f		U		f	u	f	
8	F		f	u	f		U		f	u	f	
9		F		f	u	f		U		f	u	f
10		F		f	u	f		U		f	u	f
11	f		F		f	u	f		U		f	u
12	f		F		f	u	f		U		f	u
13	f		F		f	u	f		U		f	u
14	u	f		F		f	u	f		U		f
15	u	f		F		f	u	f		U		f
16	f	u	f		F		f	u	f		U	
17	f	u	f		F		f	u	f		U	
18	f	u	f		F		f	u	f		U	
19		f	u	f		F		f	u	f		U
20		f	u	f		F		f	u	f		U
21	U		f	u	f		F		f	u	f	
22	U		f	u	f		F		f	u	f	
23	U		f	u	f		F		f	u	f	
24		U		f	u	f		F		f	u	f
25		U		f	u	f		F		f	u	f
26	f		U		f	u	f		F		f	u
27	f		U		f	u	f		F		f	u
28	u	f		U		f	u	f		F		f
29	u	f		U		f	u	f		F		f
30	f	u	f		U		f	u	f		F	
31	f	u	f		U		f	u	f		F	

November Moon Table

Date	Sign	Element	Nature	Phase
1 Sat 12:37 pm	Pisces	Water	Fruitful	2nd
2 Sun	Pisces	Water	Fruitful	2nd
3 Mon 1:53 pm	Aries	Fire	Barren	2nd
4 Tue	Aries	Fire	Barren	2nd
5 Wed 4:33 pm	Taurus	Earth	Semi-fruitful	2nd
6 Thu	Taurus	Earth	Semi-fruitful	Full 5:23 pm
7 Fri 8:45 pm	Gemini	Air	Barren	3rd
8 Sat	Gemini	Air	Barren	3rd
9 Sun	Gemini	Air	Barren	3rd
10 Mon 3:38 am	Cancer	Water	Fruitful	3rd
11 Tue	Cancer	Water	Fruitful	3rd
12 Wed 1:44 pm	Leo	Fire	Barren	3rd
13 Thu	Leo	Fire	Barren	3rd
14 Fri	Leo	Fire	Barren	4th 10:16 am
15 Sat 2:08 am	Virgo	Earth	Barren	4th
16 Sun	Virgo	Earth	Barren	4th
17 Mon 2:30 pm	Libra	Air	Semi-fruitful	4th
18 Tue	Libra	Air	Semi-fruitful	4th
19 Wed	Libra	Air	Semi-fruitful	4th
20 Thu 12:31 am	Scorpio	Water	Fruitful	4th
21 Fri	Scorpio	Water	Fruitful	4th
22 Sat 7:19 am	Sagittarius	Fire	Barren	New 7:32 am
23 Sun	Sagittarius	Fire	Barren	1st
24 Mon 11:31 am	Capricorn	Earth	Semi-fruitful	1st
25 Tue	Capricorn	Earth	Semi-fruitful	1st
26 Wed 2:23 pm	Aquarius	Air	Barren	1st
27 Thu	Aquarius	Air	Barren	1st
28 Fri 5:03 pm	Pisces	Water	Fruitful	1st
29 Sat	Pisces	Water	Fruitful	2nd 5:06 am
30 Sun 8:14 pm	Aries	Fire	Barren	2nd

November Aspectarian/Favorable & Unfavorable Days

Date	Sun	Mercury	Venus	Mars	Jupiter	Saturn	Uranus	Neptune	Pluto
1				X		Q		C	
2	T		T						X
3						T			
4				Q			C		Q
5		O			T				
6	O		O	T				X	T
7					Q	O			
8							X	Q	
9					X				
10		T						T	
11	T			O			Q		O
12			T			T			
13		Q					T		
14	Q		Q		C	Q			
15								O	
16		X		T					T
17	X		X			X			
18							O		Q
19				Q	X				
20								T	X
21		C		X	Q				
22	C		C			C		Q	
23					T		T		
24								X	
25						Q			C
26	X	X		C		X			
27			X				X		
28		Q			O	Q			
29	Q		Q					C	X
30				X		T			

Date	Aries	Taurus	Gemini	Cancer	Leo	Virgo	Libra	Scorpio	Sagittarus	Capricorn	Aquarius	Pisces
1	f	u	f		U		f	u	f		F	
2		f	u	f		U		f	u	f		F
3		f	u	f		U		f	u	f		F
4	F		f	u	f		U		f	u	f	
5	F		f	u	f		U		f	u	f	
6		F		f	u	f		U		f	u	f
7		F		f	u	f		U		f	u	f
8	f		F		f	u	f		U		f	u
9	f		F		f	u	f		U		f	u
10	u	f		F		f	u	f		U		f
11	u	f		F		f	u	f		U		f
12	u	f		F		f	u	f		U		f
13	f	u	f		F		f	u	f		U	
14	f	u	f		F		f	u	f		U	
15		f	u	f		F		f	u	f		U
16		f	u	f		F		f	u	f		U
17		f	u	f		F		f	u	f		U
18	U		f	u	f		F		f	u	f	
19	U		f	u	f		F		f	u	f	
20		U		f	u	f		F		f	u	f
21		U		f	u	f		F		f	u	f
22	f		U		f	u	f		F		f	u
23	f		U		f	u	f		F		f	u
24	u	f		U		f	u	f		F		f
25	u	f		U		f	u	f		F		f
26	u	f		U		f	u	f		F		f
27	f	u	f		U		f	u	f		F	
28	f	u	f		U		f	u	f		F	
29		f	u	f		U		f	u	f		F
30		f	u	f		U		f	u	f		F

December Moon Table

Date	Sign	Element	Nature	Phase
1 Mon	Aries	Fire	Barren	2nd
2 Tue	Aries	Fire	Barren	2nd
3 Wed 12:15 am	Taurus	Earth	Semi-fruitful	2nd
4 Thu	Taurus	Earth	Semi-fruitful	2nd
5 Fri 5:28 am	Gemini	Air	Barren	2nd
6 Sat	Gemini	Air	Barren	Full 7:27 am
7 Sun 12:34 pm	Cancer	Water	Fruitful	3rd
8 Mon	Cancer	Water	Fruitful	3rd
9 Tue 10:14 pm	Leo	Fire	Barren	3rd
10 Wed	Leo	Fire	Barren	3rd
11 Thu	Leo	Fire	Barren	3rd
12 Fri 10:19 am	Virgo	Earth	Barren	3rd
13 Sat	Virgo	Earth	Barren	3rd
14 Sun 11:05 pm	Libra	Air	Semi-fruitful	4th 7:51 am
15 Mon	Libra	Air	Semi-fruitful	4th
16 Tue	Libra	Air	Semi-fruitful	4th
17 Wed 9:52 am	Scorpio	Water	Fruitful	4th
18 Thu	Scorpio	Water	Fruitful	4th
19 Fri 4:55 pm	Sagittarius	Fire	Barren	4th
20 Sat	Sagittarius	Fire	Barren	4th
21 Sun 8:25 pm	Capricorn	Earth	Semi-fruitful	New 8:36 pm
22 Mon	Capricorn	Earth	Semi-fruitful	1st
23 Tue 9:52 pm	Aquarius	Air	Barren	1st
24 Wed	Aquarius	Air	Barren	1st
25 Thu 11:07 pm	Pisces	Water	Fruitful	1st
26 Fri	Pisces	Water	Fruitful	1st
27 Sat	Pisces	Water	Fruitful	1st
28 Sun 1:35 am	Aries	Fire	Barren	2nd 1:31 pm
29 Mon	Aries	Fire	Barren	2nd
30 Tue 5:56 am	Taurus	Earth	Semi-fruitful	2nd
31 Wed	Taurus	Earth	Semi-fruitful	2nd

December Aspectarian/Favorable & Unfavorable Days

Date	Sun	Mercury	Venus	Mars	Jupiter	Saturn	Uranus	Neptune	Pluto
1	T	T						C	Q
2			T	Q	T				
3								X	T
4					Q				
5				T			O		Q
6	O	O			X		X		
7			O					T	
8							Q		O
9						T			
10			O				T		
11	T	T			C				
12			T			Q		O	
13									T
14	Q	Q				X			
15			Q	T					
16					X		O		Q
17	X	X						T	
18			X	Q					X
19				Q	C				
20				X			T	Q	
21	C				T				
22		C	C				Q	X	C
23					X				
24				C		X			
25					O	Q			
26	X							C	X
27		X	X						
28	Q					T	C		
29		Q	Q	X	T				Q
30	T							X	
31				Q	Q				T

Date	Aries	Taurus	Gemini	Cancer	Leo	Virgo	Libra	Scorpio	Sagittarius	Capricorn	Aquarius	Pisces
1	F		f	u	f		U		f	u	f	
2	F		f	u	f		U		f	u	f	
3		F		f	u	f		U		f	u	f
4		F		f	u	f		U		f	u	f
5	f		F		f	u	f		U		f	u
6	f		F		f	u	f		U		f	u
7	f		F		f	u	f		U		f	u
8	u	f		F		f	u	f		U		f
9	u	f		F		f	u	f		U		f
10	f	u	f		F		f	u	f		U	
11	f	u	f		F		f	u	f		U	
12		f	u	f		F		f	u	f		U
13		f	u	f		F		f	u	f		U
14		f	u	f		F		f	u	f		U
15	U		f	u	f		F		f	u	f	
16	U		f	u	f		F		f	u	f	
17		U		f	u	f		F		f	u	f
18		U		f	u	f		F		f	u	f
19		U		f	u	f		F		f	u	f
20	f		U		f	u	f		F		f	u
21	f		U		f	u	f		F		f	u
22	u	f		U		f	u	f		F		f
23	u	f		U		f	u	f		F		f
24	f	u	f		U		f	u	f		F	
25	f	u	f		U		f	u	f		F	
26		f	u	f		U		f	u	f		F
27		f	u	f		U		f	u	f		F
28	F		f	u	f		U		f	u	f	
29	F		f	u	f		U		f	u	f	
30		F		f	u	f		U		f	u	f
31		F		f	u	f		U		f	u	f

2014 Retrograde Planets

Planet	Begin	Eastern	Pacific	End	Eastern	Pacific
Jupiter	11/6/13		**9:03 pm**	3/6/14	5:42 am	**2:42 am**
	11/7/13	12:03 am				
Venus	12/21/13	4:53 pm	**1:53 pm**	1/31/14	3:49 pm	**12:49 pm**
Mercury	2/6/14	4:43 pm	**1:43 pm**	2/28/14	9:00 am	**6:00 am**
Mars	3/1/14	11:23 am	**8:23 am**	5/19/14	9:31 pm	**6:31 pm**
Saturn	3/2/14	11:20 am	**8:20 am**	7/20/14	4:35 pm	**1:35 pm**
Pluto	4/14/14	7:47 pm	**4:47 pm**	9/22/14	8:36 pm	**5:36 pm**
Mercury	6/7/14	7:56 am	**4:56 am**	7/1/14	8:50 am	**5:50 am**
Neptune	6/9/14	3:51 pm	**12:51 pm**	11/15/14		**11:04 pm**
				11/16/14	2:04 am	
Uranus	7/21/14	10:53 pm	**7:53 pm**	12/21/14	5:45 pm	**2:45 pm**
Mercury	10/4/14	1:02 pm	**10:02 am**	10/25/14	3:17 pm	**12:17 pm**
Jupiter	12/8/14	3:41 pm	**12:41 pm**	4/8/15	12:57 pm	**9:57 am**

Eastern Time in plain type, **Pacific Time in bold type**

	Dec 13	Jan 14	Feb	Mar	Apr	May	Jun	Jul	Aug	Sep	Oct	Nov	Dec	Jan 15
☿			▨				▨				▨			
♀		▨												
♂				▨	▨									
♃	▨	▨											▨	▨
♄				▨	▨	▨								
♅						▨	▨	▨	▨	▨				
♆							▨	▨	▨	▨	▨			
♇				▨	▨	▨	▨	▨	▨					

Egg-Setting Dates

To Have Eggs by this Date	Sign	Qtr.	Date to Set Eggs
Jan 4, 11:58 am–Jan 6, 2:45 pm	Pisces	1st	Dec 14, 2013
Jan 8, 9:24 pm–Jan 11, 7:26 am	Taurus	2nd	Dec 18, 2013
Jan 13, 7:25 pm–Jan 15, 11:52 pm	Cancer	2nd	Dec 23, 2013
Jan 31, 10:45 pm–Feb 2, 11:55 pm	Pisces	1st	Jan 10, 2014
Feb 5, 4:47 am–Feb 7, 1:44 pm	Taurus	1st	Jan 15
Feb 10, 1:33 am–Feb 12, 2:15 pm	Cancer	2nd	Jan 20
Mar 1, 3:00 am–Mar 2, 10:40 am	Pisces	1st	Feb 08
Mar 4, 2:12 pm–Mar 6, 9:37 pm	Taurus	1st	Feb 11
Mar 9, 9:33 am–Mar 11, 10:09 pm	Cancer	2nd	Feb 16
Apr 1, 1:20 am–Apr 3, 7:48 am	Taurus	1st	Mar 11
Apr 5, 5:40 pm–Apr 8, 5:50 am	Cancer	1st	Mar 15
Apr 13, 4:33 am–Apr 15, 3:42 am	Libra	2nd	Mar 23
Apr 29, 2:14 am–Apr 30, 4:56 pm	Taurus	1st	Apr 08
May 3, 2:13 am–May 5, 1:55 pm	Cancer	1st	Apr 12
May 10, 1:19 pm–May 12, 9:07 pm	Libra	2nd	Apr 19
May 30, 10:13 am–Jun 1, 9:43 pm	Cancer	1st	May 09
Jun 6, 10:01 pm–Jun 9, 6:38 am	Libra	2nd	May 16
Jun 27, 4:08 am–Jun 29, 4:43 am	Cancer	1st	Jun 06
Jul 4, 5:43 am–Jul 6, 3:33 pm	Libra	1st	Jun 13
Jul 31, 12:09 pm–Aug 2, 10:57 pm	Libra	1st	Jul 10
Aug 27, 5:54 pm–Aug 30, 4:53 am	Libra	1st	Aug 06
Sep 7, 7:47 pm–Sep 8, 9:38 pm	Pisces	2nd	Aug 17
Sep 24, 2:14 am–Sep 26, 10:29 am	Libra	1st	Sep 03
Oct 5, 5:24 am–Oct 7, 6:07 am	Pisces	2nd	Sep 14
Nov 1, 12:37 pm–Nov 3, 1:53 pm	Pisces	2nd	Oct 11
Nov 5, 4:33 pm–Nov 6, 5:23 pm	Taurus	2nd	Oct 15
Nov 28, 5:03 pm–Nov 30, 8:14 pm	Pisces	1st	Nov 07
Dec 3, 12:15 am–Dec 5, 5:28 am	Taurus	2nd	Nov 12
Dec 25, 11:07 pm–Dec 28, 1:35 am	Pisces	1st	Dec 04

Dates to Hunt and Fish

Date	Quarter	Sign
Jan 4, 11:58 am–Jan 6, 2:45 pm	1st	Pisces
Jan 13, 7:25 pm–Jan 16, 8:00 am	2nd	Cancer
Jan 23, 4:43 pm–Jan 25, 10:13 pm	3rd	Scorpio
Jan 31, 10:45 pm–Feb 2, 11:55 pm	1st	Pisces
Feb 10, 1:33 am–Feb 12, 2:15 pm	2nd	Cancer
Feb 19, 10:33 pm–Feb 22, 5:12 am	3rd	Scorpio
Feb 22, 5:12 am–Feb 24, 8:50 am	3rd	Sagittarius
Feb 28, 9:53 am–Mar 2, 10:40 am	4th	Pisces
Mar 9, 9:33 am–Mar 11, 10:09 pm	2nd	Cancer
Mar 19, 5:13 am–Mar 21, 11:39 am	3rd	Scorpio
Mar 21, 11:39 am–Mar 23, 4:03 pm	3rd	Sagittarius
Mar 27, 8:10 pm–Mar 29, 9:54 pm	4th	Pisces
Apr 5, 5:40 am–Apr 8, 5:50 am	1st	Cancer
Apr 15, 12:20 pm–Apr 17, 5:44 pm	3rd	Scorpio
Apr 17, 5:44 pm–Apr 19, 9:28 pm	3rd	Sagittarius
Apr 24, 2:55 am–Apr 26, 6:01 am	4th	Pisces
May 3, 2:13 am–May 5, 1:55 pm	1st	Cancer
May 12, 9:07 pm–May 15, 1:44 am	2nd	Scorpio
May 15, 1:44 am–May 17, 4:12 am	3rd	Sagittarius
May 21, 8:18 am–May 23, 12:01 pm	3rd	Pisces
May 30, 10:13 am–Jun 1, 9:43 pm	1st	Cancer
Jun 9, 6:38 am–Jun 11, 11:23 am	2nd	Scorpio
Jun 11, 11:23 am–Jun 13, 1:04 pm	2nd	Sagittarius
Jun 17, 2:26 pm–Jun 19, 5:26 pm	3rd	Pisces
Jun 26, 5:05 pm–Jun 29, 4:43 am	4th	Cancer
Jul 6, 3:33 pm–Jul 8, 9:24 pm	2nd	Scorpio
Jul 8, 9:24 pm–Jul 10, 11:24 pm	2nd	Sagittarius
Jul 14, 10:40 pm–Jul 17, 12:07 am	3rd	Pisces
Jul 17, 12:07 am–Jul 19, 4:43 am	3rd	Aries
Jul 23, 10:59 pm–Jul 26, 10:55 am	4th	Cancer
Aug 2, 10:57 pm–Aug 5, 6:19 am	1st	Scorpio
Aug 5, 6:19 am–Aug 7, 9:38 am	2nd	Sagittarius
Aug 11, 8:55 am–Aug 13, 9:00 am	3rd	Pisces
Aug 13, 9:00 am–Aug 15, 11:58 am	3rd	Aries
Aug 20, 4:45 am–Aug 22, 4:49 pm	4th	Cancer
Aug 30, 4:53 am–Sep 1, 1:17 pm	1st	Scorpio
Sep 7, 7:47 pm–Sep 9, 7:33 pm	2nd	Pisces
Sep 9, 7:33 pm–Sep 11, 9:17 pm	3rd	Aries
Sep 16, 11:24 am–Sep 18, 11:10 pm	4th	Cancer
Sep 26, 10:29 am–Sep 28, 6:50 pm	1st	Scorpio
Oct 5, 5:24 am–Oct 7, 6:07 am	2nd	Pisces
Oct 7, 6:07 am–Oct 9, 7:44 am	2nd	Aries
Oct 13, 7:30 pm–Oct 16, 6:29 am	3rd	Cancer
Oct 23, 5:10 pm–Oct 26, 12:40 am	4th	Scorpio
Nov 1, 12:37 pm–Nov 3, 1:53 pm	2nd	Pisces
Nov 3, 1:53 pm–Nov 5, 4:33 pm	2nd	Aries
Nov 10, 3:38 am–Nov 12, 1:44 pm	3rd	Cancer
Nov 20, 12:31 am–Nov 22, 7:19 am	4th	Scorpio
Nov 28, 5:03 pm–Nov 30, 8:14 pm	1st	Pisces
Nov 30, 8:14 pm–Dec 3, 12:15 am	2nd	Aries
Dec 7, 12:34 pm–Dec 9, 10:14 pm	3rd	Cancer
Dec 17, 9:52 am–Dec 19, 4:55 pm	4th	Scorpio
Dec 25, 11:07 pm–Dec 28, 1:35 am	1st	Pisces

Dates to Destroy Weeds and Pests

Date	Sign	Qtr.
Jan 16, 8:00 am–Jan 18, 8:23 pm	Leo	3rd
Jan 18, 8:23 pm–Jan 21, 7:43 am	Virgo	3rd
Jan 25, 10:13 pm–Jan 28, 12:04 am	Sagittarius	4th
Jan 29, 11:33 pm–Jan 30, 4:39 pm	Aquarius	4th
Feb 14, 6:53 pm–Feb 15, 2:26 am	Leo	3rd
Feb 15, 2:26 am–Feb 17, 1:23 pm	Virgo	3rd
Feb 22, 5:12 am–Feb 22, 12:15 pm	Sagittarius	3rd
Feb 22, 12:15 pm–Feb 24, 8:50 am	Sagittarius	4th
Feb 26, 9:55 am–Feb 28 ,9:53 am	Aquarius	4th
Mar 16, 1:08 pm–Mar 16 ,8:46 pm	Virgo	3rd
Mar 21, 11:39 am–Mar 23, 4:03 pm	Sagittarius	3rd
Mar 25, 6:39 pm–Mar 27, 8:10 pm	Aquarius	4th
Mar 29, 9:54 pm–Mar 30, 2:45 pm	Aries	4th
Apr 17, 5:44 pm–Apr 19, 9:28 pm	Sagittarius	3rd
Apr 22, 12:18 am–Apr 22, 3:52 am	Aquarius	3rd
Apr 22, 3:52 am–Apr 24, 2:55 am	Aquarius	4th
Apr 26, 6:01 am–Apr 28, 10:23 am	Aries	4th
May 15, 1:44 am–May 17, 4:12 am	Sagittarius	3rd
May 19, 5:58 am–May 21, 8:18 am	Aquarius	3rd
May 23, 12:01 pm–May 25, 5:28 pm	Aries	4th
May 28, 12:47 am–May 28, 2:40 am	Gemini	4th
Jun 13, 12:11 am–Jun 13, 1:04 pm	Sagittarius	3rd
Jun 15, 1:27 pm–Jun 17, 2:26 pm	Aquarius	3rd
Jun 19, 5:26 pm–Jun 21, 11:03 pm	Aries	4th
Jun 24, 7:05 am–Jun 26, 5:05 pm	Gemini	4th
Jul 12, 11:07 pm–Jul 14, 10:40 pm	Aquarius	3rd
Jul 17, 12:07 am–Jul 18, 10:08 pm	Aries	3rd
Jul 18, 10:08 pm–Jul 19, 4:43 am	Aries	4th
Jul 21, 12:36 pm–Jul 23, 10:59 pm	Gemini	4th
Jul 26, 10:55 am–Jul 26, 6:42 pm	Leo	4th
Aug 10, 2:09 pm–Aug 11, 8:55 am	Aquarius	3rd
Aug 13, 9:00 am–Aug 15, 11:58 am	Aries	3rd
Aug 17, 6:41 pm–Aug 20, 4:45 am	Gemini	4th
Aug 22, 4:49 am–Aug 25, 5:33 am	Leo	4th
Aug 25, 5:33 am–Aug 25, 10:13 am	Virgo	4th
Sep 9, 7:33 pm–Sep 11, 9:17 pm	Aries	3rd
Sep 14, 2:26 am–Sep 15, 10:05 pm	Gemini	3rd
Sep 15, 10:05 pm–Sep 16, 11:24 am	Gemini	4th
Sep 18, 11:10 pm–Sep 21, 11:54 am	Leo	4th
Sep 21, 11:54 am–Sep 23, 11:59 pm	Virgo	4th
Oct 8, 6:51 am–Oct 9, 7:44 am	Aries	3rd
Oct 11, 11:51 am–Oct 13, 7:30 pm	Gemini	3rd
Oct 16, 6:29 am–Oct 18, 7:08 pm	Leo	4th
Oct 18, 7:08 pm–Oct 21, 7:12 am	Virgo	4th
Nov 7, 8:45 pm–Nov 10, 3:38 am	Gemini	3rd
Nov 12, 1:44 pm–Nov 14, 10:16 am	Leo	3rd
Nov 14, 10:16 am–Nov 15, 2:08 am	Leo	4th
Nov 15, 2:08 am–Nov 17, 2:30 pm	Virgo	4th
Nov 22, 7:19 am–Nov 22, 7:32 am	Sagittarius	4th
Dec 6, 7:27 am–Dec 7, 12:34 pm	Gemini	3rd
Dec 9, 10:14 am–Dec 12, 10:19 am	Leo	3rd
Dec 12, 10:19 am–Dec 14, 7:51 am	Virgo	3rd
Dec 14, 7:51 am–Dec 14, 11:05 pm	Virgo	4th
Dec 19, 4:55 pm–Dec 21, 8:25 pm	Sagittarius	4th

Time Zone Map

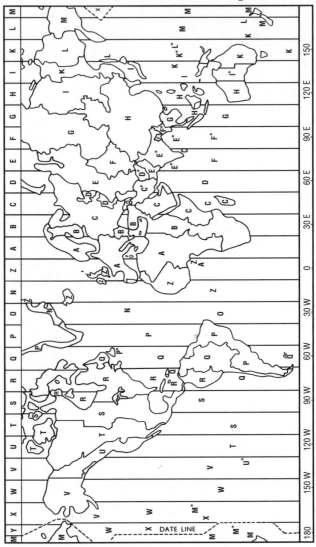

Time Zone Conversions

(R) EST—Used in book
(S) CST—Subtract 1 hour
(T) MST—Subtract 2 hours
(U) PST—Subtract 3 hours
(V) Subtract 4 hours
(V*) Subtract 4½ hours
(U*) Subtract 3½ hours
(W) Subtract 5 hours
(X) Subtract 6 hours
(Y) Subtract 7 hours
(Q) Add 1 hour
(P) Add 2 hours
(P*) Add 2½ hours
(O) Add 3 hours
(N) Add 4 hours
(Z) Add 5 hours
(A) Add 6 hours
(B) Add 7 hours
(C) Add 8 hours
(C*) Add 8½ hours

(D) Add 9 hours
(D*) Add 9½ hours
(E) Add 10 hours
(E*) Add 10½ hours
(F) Add 11 hours
(F*) Add 11½ hours
(G) Add 12 hours
(H) Add 13 hours
(I) Add 14 hours
(I*) Add 14½ hours
(K) Add 15 hours
(K*) Add 15½ hours
(L) Add 16 hours
(L*) Add 16½ hours
(M) Add 17 hours
(M*) Add 18 hours
(P*) Add 2½ hours

Important!

All times given in the *Moon Sign Book* are set in Eastern Time. The conversions shown here are for standard times only. Use the time zone conversions map and table to calculate the difference in your time zone. You must make the adjustment for your time zone and adjust for Daylight Saving Time where applicable.

Weather,
Economic
& Lunar
Forecasts

Forecasting the Weather

by Kris Brandt Riske

Astrometeorology—astrological weather forecasting—reveals seasonal and weekly weather trends based on the cardinal ingresses (Summer and Winter Solstices, and Spring and Autumn Equinoxes) and the four monthly lunar phases. The planetary alignments and the longitudes and latitudes they influence have the strongest effect, but the zodiacal signs are also involved in creating weather conditions.

The components of a thunderstorm, for example, are heat, wind, and electricity. A Mars-Jupiter configuration generates the necessary heat and Mercury adds wind and electricity. A severe thunderstorm, and those that produce tornados, usually involve Mercury, Mars, Uranus, or Neptune. The zodiacal signs add their energy to the planetary mix to increase or decrease the chance of weather phenomena and their severity.

In general, the fire signs (Aries, Leo, Sagittarius) indicate heat and dryness, both of which peak when Mars, the planet with a similar nature, is in these signs. Water signs (Cancer, Scorpio, Pisces) are conducive to precipitation, and air signs (Gemini, Libra, Aquarius) to cool temperatures and wind. Earth signs (Taurus, Virgo, Capricorn) vary from wet to dry, heat to cold. The signs and their prevailing weather conditions are listed here:

Aries: Heat, dry, wind
Taurus: Moderate temperatures, precipitation
Gemini: Cool temperatures, wind, dry
Cancer: Cold, steady precipitation
Leo: Heat, dry, lightning
Virgo: Cold, dry, windy
Libra: Cool, windy, fair
Scorpio: Extreme temperatures, abundant precipitation
Sagittarius: Warm, fair, moderate wind
Capricorn: Cold, wet, damp
Aquarius: Cold, dry, high pressure, lightning
Pisces: Wet, cool, low pressure

Take note of the Moon's sign at each lunar phase. It reveals the prevailing weather conditions for the next six to seven days. The same is true of Mercury and Venus. These two influential weather planets transit the entire zodiac each year, unless retrograde patterns add their influence.

Planetary Influences

People relied on astrology to forecast weather for thousands of years. They were able to predict drought, floods, and temperature variations through interpreting planetary alignments. In recent years there has been a renewed interest in astrometeorology. A weather forecast can be composed for any date—tomorrow, next week, or a thousand years in the future. According to astrometeorology, each planet governs certain weather phenomena. When certain planets are aligned with other planets, weather—precipitation, cloudy or clear skies, tornados, hurricanes, and other conditions—are generated.

Sun and Moon

The Sun governs the constitution of the weather and, like the Moon, it serves as a trigger for other planetary configurations that result in weather events. When the Sun is prominent in a cardinal ingress or lunar phase chart, the area is often warm and sunny. The Moon can bring or withhold moisture, depending upon its sign placement.

Mercury

Mercury is also a triggering planet, but its main influence is wind direction and velocity. In its stationary periods, Mercury reflects high winds, and its influence is always prominent in major weather events, such as hurricanes and tornadoes, when it tends to lower the temperature.

Venus

Venus governs moisture, clouds, and humidity. It brings warming trends that produce sunny, pleasant weather if in positive aspect to other planets. In some signs—Libra, Virgo, Gemini, Sagittarius—Venus is drier. It is at its wettest when placed in Cancer, Scorpio, Pisces, or Taurus.

Mars

Mars is associated with heat, drought, and wind, and can raise the temperature to record-setting levels when in a fire sign (Aries, Leo, Sagittarius). Mars is also the planet that provides the spark that generates thunderstorms and is prominent in tornado and hurricane configurations.

Jupiter

Jupiter, a fair-weather planet, tends toward higher temperatures when in Aries, Leo, or Sagittarius. It is associated with high-pressure systems and is a contributing factor at times to dryness. Storms are often amplified by Jupiter.

Saturn

Saturn is associated with low-pressure systems, cloudy to over-cast skies, and excessive precipitation. Temperatures drop when Saturn is involved. Major winter storms always have a strong Saturn influence, as do storms that produce a slow, steady downpour for hours or days.

Uranus

Like Jupiter, Uranus indicates high-pressure systems. It reflects descending cold air and, when prominent, is responsible for a jet stream that extends far south. Uranus can bring drought in winter, and it is involved in thunderstorms, tornados, and hurricanes.

Neptune

Neptune is the wettest planet. It signals low-pressure systems and is dominant when hurricanes are in the forecast. When Neptune is strongly placed, flood danger is high. It's often associated with winter thaws. Temperatures, humidity, and cloudiness increase where Neptune influences weather.

Pluto

Pluto is associated with weather extremes, as well as unseasonably warm temperatures and drought. It reflects the high winds involved in major hurricanes, storms, and tornadoes.

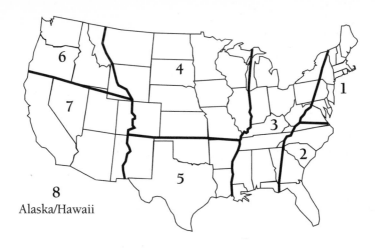

6

4

1

7

3

2

5

8
Alaska/Hawaii

Weather Forecast for 2014

by Kris Brandt Riske

Winter 2014

Zone 1 will see wind more often than usual, along with major storms and temperatures that are generally below average, sometimes significantly so. In zone 2, temperatures will be average to below across the zone with stormy conditions centering primarily in northern and central coastal areas. Inland and southern areas will be more temperate with average precipitation; thunderstorms with tornado potential are possible. In zone 3, precipitation will be average to below with seasonal temperatures. Wind, however, will be a factor.

Zone 4 temperatures will range from average to below, and the zone will see some major storms with high winds and significant precipitation in western areas. Low-pressure systems will form in the western and eastern parts of the zone. Central parts of zone 5 will see the most precipitation. Central and eastern areas will be seasonal, while western areas will be colder and wetter. Zone 6 can expect significant precipitation in western and eastern areas and cooler-than-average temperatures west and central. Eastern areas will be generally more seasonal and cloudy. Western parts of zone 7 will see average to above-average precipitation, and major storms with high winds will occur in the central mountains. Temperatures will range from seasonal to below.

Temperatures in central and western Alaska will be cold, along with a higher-than-average storm potential, while eastern areas of the state will be more seasonal, with precipitation that ranges from average to above. Temperatures in Hawaii will range from seasonal to below; precipitation will be average to below.

New Moon, January 1–6

Zone 1: Some southern areas see abundant precipitation, and much of the zone is cloudy with seasonal temperatures.

Zone 2: The zone could see a major storm with sleet or strong thunderstorms with tornado potential in central and southern areas; temperatures are seasonal.

Zone 3: Temperatures range from seasonal to below, and skies are variably cloudy; central and eastern areas have storm potential with sleet or strong thunderstorms and tornado potential in southern areas.

Zone 4: The zone is variably cloudy and seasonal to below, with precipitation west as a front moves into the western Plains; eastern areas see scattered precipitation.

Zone 5: Scattered precipitation and cloudy skies accompany temperatures seasonal to below; eastern areas could be stormy.

Zone 6: Much of the zone is cloudy with precipitation, some locally heavy, and temperatures range from seasonal to below; a major winter storm is possible.

Zone 7: Western and central parts of the zone, especially northern areas, see precipitation, possibly from a major winter storm; temperatures are seasonal.

Zone 8: Western and central Alaska are windy, stormy, and cold with abundant downfall in some areas, while eastern parts of the state are mostly fair and seasonal. Eastern Hawaii sees precipitation, central areas are fair to partly cloudy, and zonal temperatures are seasonal.

2nd Quarter Moon, January 7–14

Zone 1: Temperatures ranging from seasonal to below accompany windy, fair-to-partly-cloudy skies.

Zone 2: The zone is seasonal and partly cloudy with scattered precipitation.

Zone 3: Skies are windy and variably cloudy with scattered precipitation, and temperatures are seasonal.

Zone 4: The zone is windy as a front advances east from the central Plains; western areas see scattered precipitation under variably cloudy skies; temperatures are seasonal to below.

Zone 5: Variably cloudy skies and seasonal temperatures accompany precipitation across much of the zone, some locally heavy in central and western areas; strong thunderstorms with tornado potential are possible in southern areas.

Zone 6: The zone is windy and cloudy with precipitation that is heaviest east; temperatures are seasonal to below.

Zone 7: Temperatures are seasonal to below; and conditions are windy in northern areas with abundant precipitation in the mountains moving east, while central and eastern southern areas are fair to partly cloudy with temperatures seasonal to above.

Zone 8: Alaska is mostly cloudy with temperatures seasonal to below; central and eastern areas see precipitation, some abundant. Hawaii is windy, seasonal, and variably cloudy with scattered precipitation.

Full Moon, January 15–23

Zone 1: Northern areas are fair to partly cloudy, temperatures are seasonal, and southern parts of the zone see precipitation.

Zone 2: The zone is windy with temperatures seasonal to below, central and southern areas could see strong thunderstorms with tornado potential and stormy sleet, and northern parts of the zone see precipitation—some locally heavy.

Zone 3: Much of the zone sees precipitation, with a chance for thunderstorms or stormy sleet in southern areas; temperatures are seasonal to below.

Zone 4: The zone is variably cloudy with scattered precipitation in central areas, storm potential in eastern parts of the zone, and temperatures seasonal to below.

Zone 5: Western parts of the zone see scattered precipitation, eastern and western areas are partly cloudy, central areas are mostly fair, and temperatures are seasonal.

Zone 6: Skies are cloudy with precipitation in western parts of the zone, central and eastern areas are windy and variably cloudy with precipitation, and temperatures are seasonal.

Zone 7: The zone is variably cloudy with precipitation in northern coastal areas and scattered precipitation in much of the rest of the zone; temperatures are seasonal.

Zone 8: Alaska is windy, partly cloudy, and seasonal with scattered precipitation. Hawaiian temperatures are seasonal under variably cloudy and windy skies with scattered precipitation.

4th Quarter Moon, January 24–29

Zone 1: Temperatures range from seasonal to below, and skies are fair to partly cloudy.

Zone 2: Seasonal temperatures accompany mostly fair skies.

Zone 3: Western areas are windy with precipitation, central and eastern areas are variably cloudy with scattered precipitation east, temperatures are seasonal, and southern areas could see strong thunderstorms with tornado potential.

Zone 4: Much of the zone sees precipitation; stormy conditions develop in some areas along with high winds and abundant downfall under cloudy skies; temperatures are seasonal to below.

Zone 5: Temperatures range from seasonal to below with precipitation, cloudy skies, and heavy downfall in eastern areas; strong thunderstorms with tornado potential are possible east.

Zone 6: Western and central parts of the zone are partly cloudy, eastern areas see scattered precipitation with more clouds, and temperatures are seasonal.

Zone 7: Northern coastal areas are windy with precipitation, temperatures are seasonal, and the rest of the zone is fair to partly cloudy with a chance for precipitation.

Zone 8: Central Alaska is overcast and stormy with abundant precipitation, western and eastern areas are fair to partly cloudy, and temperatures are seasonal. Hawaii is windy with variable cloudiness, precipitation in eastern areas, and seasonal temperatures.

New Moon, January 30–February 5

Zone 1: The zone is seasonal, windy, and partly cloudy with scattered precipitation.

Zone 2: Northern areas are windy with scattered precipitation, central and southern parts of the zone could see abundant precipitation with high winds and possible thunderstorms, and temperatures are seasonal to below.

Zone 3: Much of the zone sees precipitation and cloudy skies, with the heaviest in central areas, and temperatures are seasonal to below.

Zone 4: Central areas are fair to partly cloudy, eastern areas are cloudy with scattered precipitation, western areas are cloudy with precipitation, and temperatures are seasonal.

Zone 5: The zone is variably cloudy and windy with precipitation and temperatures ranging from seasonal to below.

Zone 6: Eastern areas are cloudy with precipitation, western and central areas see scattered precipitation, eastern areas are windy, and temperatures are seasonal.

Zone 7: The zone is windy with precipitation in central areas—some abundant—and skies are variably cloudy with temperatures seasonal to above.

Zone 8: Western Alaska is windy, central parts of the state see precipitation, skies are mostly fair to partly cloudy, and temperatures are seasonal to below. Hawaii is partly cloudy, windy, and seasonal with scattered precipitation.

2nd Quarter Moon, February 6–13

Zone 1: Seasonal temperatures accompany scattered precipitation under skies that are generally fair to partly cloudy.

Zone 2: Central and southern areas see scattered precipitation, northern areas see precipitation later in the week, skies are variably cloudy, and temperatures are seasonal.

Zone 3: Some western areas see abundant precipitation and strong thunderstorms with tornado potential, central areas are windy with precipitation, and eastern parts of the zone could see abundant precipitation later in the week; temperatures range from seasonal to below.

Zone 4: Much of the zone could see increasing clouds and precipitation (abundant in western areas) throughout the week, along with seasonal temperatures.

Zone 5: The zone is generally cloudy and windy with precipitation (some abundant) and seasonal temperatures; strong thunderstorms with tornado potential are possible east.

Zone 6: The zone is partly cloudy and seasonal with precipitation later in the week in central and eastern areas.

Zone 7: Western parts of the zone are partly cloudy with scattered precipitation, eastern areas see more clouds with precipitation (some abundant), and temperatures are seasonal.

Zone 8: Alaska is variably cloudy and seasonal with precipitation in central areas. Hawaii is seasonal and partly cloudy with scattered precipitation.

Full Moon, February 14–21

Zone 1: The zone is fair to partly cloudy and seasonal with a chance for precipitation in northern areas and scattered precipitation south.

Zone 2: Temperatures are seasonal, northern areas are windy with scattered precipitation, and central southern parts of the zone see precipitation, some locally heavy.

Zone 3: Western areas are overcast and windy with potential for abundant precipitation, central and eastern areas see precipitation (some abundant with flood potential), and temperatures are seasonal.

Zone 4: Skies are fair to partly cloudy with scattered precipitation west; increasing clouds in eastern areas bring abundant downfall and stormy conditions; and temperatures are seasonal to below.

Zone 5: Western skies are mostly fair, central areas are partly cloudy with scattered precipitation, eastern parts of the zone could see abundant downfall later in the week along with stormy conditions, and temperatures are seasonal to below.

Zone 6: Skies become partly cloudy in western parts of the zone with scattered precipitation later in the week, central and eastern areas are fair to partly cloudy, and temperatures are seasonal.

Zone 7: The zone is generally fair to partly cloudy with windy conditions in western and central parts of the zone, a chance for precipitation in central areas, and temperatures seasonal to above.

Zone 8: Central Alaska is mostly fair, eastern and western parts of the state are windy with abundant precipitation, and temperatures are seasonal. Hawaii is fair to partly cloudy and seasonal with scattered precipitation.

4th Quarter Moon, February 22–28

Zone 1: Much of the zone is windy and cloudy with precipitation, some abundant with flood potential; temperatures are seasonal.

Zone 2: Precipitation across the zone is accompanied by seasonal to below temperatures, and coastal areas see the heaviest precipitation, with flood potential.

Zone 3: Eastern areas are mostly fair, temperatures are seasonal, and cloudy skies bring precipitation to western and central parts of the zone.

Zone 4: The zone is variably cloudy with more cloudiness in central areas, and much of the zone sees precipitation, with potential for abundant downfall and high winds east; temperatures are seasonal to below.

Zone 5: Temperatures are seasonal to below with increasing cloudiness as central and eastern areas see precipitation, some locally heavy.

Zone 6: Much of the zone is windy and cloudy with precipitation, heaviest in central areas, and temperatures are seasonal.

Zone 7: The zone is windy, cloudy, and seasonal with precipitation, some locally heavy, in western and central areas, advancing into eastern parts of the zone.

Zone 8: Alaskan temperatures are seasonal to below with precipitation across the state as a front advances, bringing abundant downfall to western areas. Hawaii is windy, partly cloudy, and seasonal, with precipitation in eastern areas.

New Moon, March 1–7

Zone 1: The zone is windy, seasonal, and partly cloudy to cloudy with precipitation.

Zone 2: Northern areas are cloudy with precipitation, central and southern areas are fair to partly cloudy, and temperatures are seasonal.

Zone 3: Western and central parts of the zone are variably cloudy with scattered precipitation, some eastern areas see abundant precipitation with flood potential, and temperatures are seasonal.

Zone 4: The zone is variably cloudy, windy west and central, and seasonal to below; more cloudiness and precipitation moves into eastern areas.

Zone 5: Skies are partly cloudy and windy with a chance for precipitation, and temperatures are seasonal.

Zone 6: Western and central parts of the zone are cloudy with precipitation (some abundant), temperatures are seasonal, and eastern areas are partly cloudy to cloudy with a chance for precipitation.

Zone 7: Eastern areas are partly cloudy, some western and central parts of the zone see abundant precipitation, and temperatures are seasonal.

Zone 8: Central and western Alaska are cloudy with precipitation, eastern areas are windy and mostly fair, and temperatures are seasonal. Hawaii is windy, variably cloudy, and seasonal to above with thunderstorms in western areas.

2nd Quarter Moon, March 8–15

Zone 1: Southern areas are partly cloudy, northern areas are windy with more cloudiness and precipitation, and temperatures are seasonal.

Zone 2: Temperatures are seasonal to below, northern areas are windy with scattered precipitation, and central and southern areas could see strong thunderstorms with tornado potential.

Zone 3: Some western areas see abundant precipitation that moves into central parts of the zone, with high winds and abundant downfall in some locations; strong storms with tornado potential are possible; and temperatures are seasonal to below.

Zone 4: Much of the zone is windy with a chance for precipitation under variably cloudy skies, temperatures are seasonal, and eastern areas have a greater chance for precipitation.

Zone 5: Central areas are windy, temperatures are seasonal, and much of the zone has a chance for precipitation under variably cloudy skies.

Zone 6: Western areas see abundant precipitation that moves into central and eastern areas accompanied by stormy conditions, much cloudiness, and seasonal temperatures.

Zone 7: Eastern parts of the zone are fair to partly cloudy with a chance for precipitation, western and central areas are cloudy, northern coastal areas see precipitation, and temperatures are seasonal to above in the desert.

Zone 8: Alaska is windy and seasonal with precipitation, some locally heavy. Much of Hawaii sees precipitation, and temperatures are seasonal.

Full Moon, March 16–22

Zone 1: The zone is windy, seasonal, and variably cloudy with scattered precipitation.

Zone 2: Central and southern areas are mostly fair, northern areas are partly cloudy to cloudy with precipitation, and temperatures are seasonal.

Zone 3: Western and central parts of the zone are windy and cloudy with locally heavy precipitation, eastern areas are partly cloudy, and temperatures are seasonal.

Zone 4: Much of the zone is cloudy with precipitation, and strong thunderstorms with tornado potential are possible in eastern areas; temperatures are seasonal.

Zone 5: Western and central parts of the zone are cloudy with precipitation, temperatures are seasonal, and eastern areas could see strong thunderstorms with tornado potential.

Zone 6: Western and central parts of the zone are windy and overcast with locally heavy precipitation that moves into eastern areas later in the week, and temperatures are seasonal to below.

Zone 7: Much of the zone is seasonal and cloudy with precipitation, and eastern areas are fair to partly cloudy.

Zone 8: Much of Alaska sees precipitation with locally heavy downfall in central parts of the state, and temperatures are seasonal. Hawaii is partly cloudy to cloudy with precipitation in western areas and seasonal temperatures.

Spring 2014

Zone 1 will have an above-average number of storms and low-pressure systems, along with abundant precipitation and wind at times; temperatures will be mostly seasonal. In zone 2, precipitation will be normal to above and temperatures will be seasonal. Central areas will see an above-average number of strong thunderstorms with tornado potential, and southern parts of the zone will see more cloudiness. Zone 3 temperatures will be above normal with drier conditions in western areas. Central areas will see above-average thunderstorm activity with tornado potential along with heavy precipitation at times and temperatures seasonal to below, and eastern areas will be generally seasonal but with more cloudiness.

Zone 4 will see significant storms and low-pressure systems with abundant downfall in some areas, along with high flood potential in the eastern Plains; central areas will be drier and warmer than western parts of the zone, but they will also see strong storms. Zone 5 will tend toward dryness and warmth, but eastern areas will see abundant precipitation at times along with an increased risk for flooding. Temperatures will range from seasonal to below in much of zone 6, and central and eastern areas can expect precipitation from normal to above, while western parts of the zone will drier than normal. Western parts of zone 7 will be windy and seasonal to below, eastern areas will be seasonal with average precipitation, and central areas will be cooler with significant downfall in some locations, primarily mountain areas.

Temperatures in Alaska will range from seasonal to above in western areas and seasonal to below in central and eastern parts of the state. Fair weather and dryness will accompany temperatures ranging from normal to above in Hawaii; eastern areas could see strong thunderstorms with high winds.

4th Quarter Moon, March 23–29

Zone 1: Skies are variably cloudy with precipitation north, scattered precipitation south, and seasonal temperatures.

Zone 2: The zone is windy, fair to partly cloudy, and seasonal.

Zone 3: Windy conditions and clouds in western areas bring precipitation and possibly strong thunderstorms, central and eastern areas are fair to partly cloudy, and temperatures are seasonal.

Zone 4: Much of the zone is windy with storm potential and abundant precipitation in some areas under variably cloudy skies; thunderstorms with tornado potential are possible in the eastern Plains; and temperatures are seasonal to below.

Zone 5: Eastern and western parts of the zone are cloudy with precipitation, eastern areas could see strong thunderstorms with tornado potential, temperatures are seasonal to below, and the zone is windy.

Zone 6: Much of the zone sees precipitation under variably cloudy skies and seasonal temperatures, with the heaviest downfall and cloudiness in eastern areas.

Zone 7: Northern coastal areas see precipitation, southern coastal and central parts of the zone have a chance for precipitation, and eastern areas are cloudy with precipitation; temperatures are seasonal to below.

Zone 8: Much of Alaska is cloudy and windy with precipitation that advances eastward, and temperatures are seasonal to below. Western and central Hawaii are cloudy with precipitation, eastern areas are partly cloudy, and temperatures are seasonal.

New Moon, March 30–April 6

Zone 1: Northern areas see clouds and scattered precipitation, and southern areas are partly cloudy; temperatures are seasonal across the zone.

Zone 2: The zone is fair to partly cloudy and seasonal with a chance for precipitation.

Zone 3: Western areas could see strong thunderstorms with tornado potential, central and eastern parts of the zone are fair to partly cloudy, and temperatures are seasonal.

Zone 4: Western areas and the western Plains are windy and cloudy, central and eastern areas see precipitation under partly cloudy to cloudy skies, and temperatures are seasonal to below; strong thunderstorms with tornado potential are possible.

Zone 5: Much of the zone is cloudy with precipitation and temperatures ranging from seasonal to below; thunderstorms with tornado potential are possible.

Zone 6: The zone is windy under variably cloudy skies with precipitation and temperatures ranging from seasonal to below.

Zone 7: Western and central parts of the zone see precipitation under variably cloudy skies, eastern areas are mostly fair, and temperatures range from seasonal to above.

Zone 8: Eastern Alaska sees abundant precipitation under overcast skies, central and western parts of the state are fair to partly cloudy with a chance for precipitation, and temperatures are seasonal. Hawaii is partly cloudy, windy, and seasonal with scattered precipitation.

2nd Quarter Moon, April 7–14

Zone 1: Temperatures ranging from seasonal to below accompany variably cloudy skies and precipitation later in the week.

Zone 2: Much of the zone sees precipitation later in the week, with strong thunderstorms possible; skies are variably cloudy and temperatures are seasonal.

Zone 3: Locally heavy precipitation is possible across much of the zone under overcast skies and strong thunderstorms; temperatures are seasonal.

Zone 4: Western and central parts of the zone are windy with scattered precipitation and partly cloudy to cloudy skies, and eastern areas could see abundant precipitation under overcast skies; temperatures are seasonal, and strong storms are possible.

Zone 5: Temperatures are seasonal and much of the zone is windy with precipitation later in the week as skies become increasingly cloudy; western areas see scattered precipitation.

Zone 6: Western parts of the zone are windy with precipitation that moves into central areas, and temperatures are seasonal; eastern areas have a chance for precipitation.

Zone 7: Northern coastal areas see precipitation, and the rest of the zone is fair to partly cloudy with temperatures ranging from seasonal to above; eastern areas are windy.

Zone 8: Eastern and western Alaska are windy with abundant precipitation later in the week, central areas are cloudy with scattered precipitation, and temperatures are seasonal to below. Hawaii is variably cloudy with a chance for precipitation and temperatures seasonal to above.

Full Moon, April 15–21

Zone 1: The zone is cloudy with precipitation, especially in northern areas; temperatures are seasonal.

Zone 2: Seasonal temperatures accompany windy skies with scattered precipitation north and the potential for strong thunderstorms with tornadoes in central and southern areas.

Zone 3: Much of the zone is cloudy with precipitation; abundant downfall is possible in eastern areas, with strong thunderstorms with tornado potential in central parts of the zone; temperatures are seasonal to below.

Zone 4: The zone is partly cloudy to cloudy and windy with scattered precipitation and the potential for strong thunderstorms and tornadoes; eastern areas could see abundant precipitation under overcast skies; temperatures are seasonal to below.

Zone 5: Variably cloudy skies, with more cloudiness central and east, accompany scattered precipitation and seasonal temperatures; strong thunderstorms with tornado potential are possible.

Zone 6: Stormy conditions in western parts of the zone move into central areas, bringing locally heavy precipitation, while eastern areas are partly cloudy to cloudy with scattered precipitation; temperatures are seasonal to below.

Zone 7: Locally heavy precipitation is possible in northern areas of western and central parts of the zone, which are variably cloudy; southern areas are fair to partly cloudy; and temperatures are seasonal to above.

Zone 8: Much of Alaska sees precipitation, with the most abundant in western areas, along with windy conditions east as a front advances; skies are variably cloudy, and temperatures are seasonal. Hawaii is cloudy and seasonal with precipitation across much of the state, locally heavy in western areas.

4th Quarter Moon, April 22–28

Zone 1: The zone is windy, seasonal, and cloudy with precipitation.

Zone 2: Northern areas of the zone see precipitation, and increasing cloudiness in central and southern areas later in the week could bring strong thunderstorms with tornado potential; temperatures are seasonal.

Zone 3: The zone is variably cloudy with strong thunderstorms and tornadoes possible in western areas, while eastern skies have more cloudiness with precipitation; temperatures are seasonal.

Zone 4: Variably cloudy skies across the zone bring a chance for precipitation west and central and strong thunderstorms with tornado potential in eastern areas; temperatures are seasonal.

Zone 5: The zone is seasonal, windy, and variably cloudy with a chance for precipitation and strong thunderstorms with tornado potential in eastern areas.

Zone 6: Windy conditions and precipitation in western areas move across the zone as a front advances, bringing scattered precipitation; eastern areas are windy; temperatures are seasonal.

Zone 7: The zone is variably cloudy and windy with chance for showers west and central; temperatures are seasonal to above.

Zone 8: Central and western Alaska are cloudy with precipitation, eastern areas are fair to partly cloudy, and temperatures are seasonal. Much of Hawaii sees showers under variably cloudy skies with seasonal temperatures.

New Moon, April 29–May 5

Zone 1: The zone is partly cloudy and seasonal with a chance for precipitation south.

Zone 2: Skies are partly cloudy with a chance for scattered thunderstorms in northern and coastal areas, inland parts of the zone see more cloudiness with potential for significant precipitation later in the week, and temperatures are seasonal.

Zone 3: The zone is variably cloudy and seasonal with scattered precipitation possible in western areas and abundant precipitation in eastern areas later in the week.

Zone 4: Western and central parts of the zone are fair to partly cloudy with a chance for thunderstorms, and strong thunderstorms with tornado potential are possible in central and eastern areas as a front advances; temperatures are seasonal.

Zone 5: The zone is seasonal and fair to partly cloudy with a chance for scattered thunderstorms and showers in central and eastern areas.

Zone 6: Western parts of the zone are partly cloudy, strong thunderstorms are possible in central areas along with showers, eastern areas see precipitation later in the week, and temperatures are seasonal.

Zone 7: Showers and strong thunderstorms accompany seasonal temperatures in western and central parts of the zone, and eastern areas are partly cloudy.

Zone 8: Western Alaska is windy and stormy, central areas are fair to partly cloudy, and temperatures are seasonal. Hawaiian temperatures are seasonal, central and eastern parts of the state are mostly fair, and western areas see thunderstorms.

2nd Quarter Moon, May 6–13

Zone 1: Skies are windy and fair to partly cloudy with precipitation later in the week; temperatures are seasonal.

Zone 2: Much of the zone sees scattered thunderstorms, some strong with tornado potential, along with wind and temperatures seasonal to above.

Zone 3: The zone is mostly seasonal with scattered precipitation.

Zone 4: The zone is partly cloudy and seasonal, with precipitation east and possible strong thunderstorms.

Zone 5: Skies are fair to partly cloudy, and the zone is seasonal with a chance for precipitation.

Zone 6: The zone is windy with increasing cloudiness as a front advances through the area, bringing precipitation across much of the zone, with the heaviest in central and eastern areas; temperatures are seasonal.

Zone 7: Northern parts of western and central areas are windy with precipitation, desert areas are mostly fair, temperatures are seasonal to above, and skies are variably cloudy.

Zone 8: Western and central Alaska see precipitation (some abundant), and eastern areas are fair; temperatures are seasonal. Hawaii is windy, fair to partly cloudy, and seasonal, with locally heavy precipitation later in the week.

Full Moon, May 14–20

Zone 1: The zone is fair to partly cloudy and seasonal.

Zone 2: Seasonal temperatures and fair to partly cloudy skies accompany a chance for showers.

Zone 3: Western and central areas are windy with potential for strong thunderstorms and tornadoes, eastern areas are fair to partly cloudy, and temperatures are seasonal.

Zone 4: Western skies are partly cloudy with scattered precipitation; central and eastern parts of the zone see scattered thunderstorms, some strong with tornado potential and locally heavy precipitation; central and eastern areas are windy; and temperatures are seasonal.

Zone 5: Much of the zone sees precipitation under cloudy skies, with possibly strong thunderstorms and tornado potential in central and eastern areas, along with significant precipitation; temperatures are seasonal.

Zone 6: Western parts of the zone are partly cloudy with scattered precipitation, central and eastern areas are overcast with potential for abundant precipitation in higher elevations, and temperatures are seasonal to below.

Zone 7: Much of the zone sees precipitation under cloudy skies, especially northern areas; eastern and southern areas are variably cloudy with scattered showers; and temperatures are seasonal to above in desert areas.

Zone 8: Much of Alaska is cloudy with precipitation, central areas are windy and stormy, and temperatures are seasonal. Hawaiian temperatures are seasonal to above, eastern areas are windy, and much of the state sees scattered showers and thunderstorms.

4th Quarter Moon, May 21–27

Zone 1: Much of the zone is cloudy and windy with precipitation and seasonal temperatures.

Zone 2: Skies are partly cloudy, temperatures are seasonal, and the zone sees scattered showers and thunderstorms.

Zone 3: Western areas are fair to partly cloudy, eastern areas see more cloudiness, temperatures are seasonal, and much of the zone has a chance for precipitation.

Zone 4: The zone is windy, eastern areas see more cloudiness with possible strong thunderstorms with tornado potential, and temperatures are seasonal.

Zone 5: Seasonal temperatures accompany cloudy skies.

Zone 6: Western parts of the zone are windy with scattered precipitation, eastern areas see precipitation under cloudy skies, central areas are mostly fair, and temperatures are seasonal.

Zone 7: Northern coastal areas see precipitation, and the rest of the zone is fair to partly cloudy and windy; temperatures range from seasonal to above.

Zone 8: Much of Alaska is seasonal and fair to partly cloudy, central areas are windy, and eastern parts of the state see precipitation. Hawaii is windy with scattered precipitation, variable cloudiness, and temperatures seasonal to above.

New Moon, May 28–June 4

Zone 1: The zone is mostly cloudy and windy with scattered showers and thunderstorms, and temperatures are seasonal.

Zone 2: Northern areas see scattered showers, central and southern parts of the zone are mostly fair, and temperatures are seasonal to above.

Zone 3: Variably cloudy skies accompany scattered showers and thunderstorms in western areas, central and eastern areas have a chance for precipitation, and temperatures are seasonal.

Zone 4: The zone is windy, partly cloudy, and seasonal with scattered showers and thunderstorms.

Zone 5: Western parts of the zone are partly cloudy, and central and eastern areas see more cloudiness with potential for locally heavy precipitation from scattered thunderstorms, some strong with tornado potential; temperatures are seasonal.

Zone 6: Temperatures range from seasonal to below, and the zone is variably cloudy with scattered showers and thunderstorms.

Zone 7: Northern coastal and northern central areas of the zone are cloudy with showers, southern and eastern areas are fair to partly cloudy with a chance for thunderstorms east, and temperatures are seasonal to above.

Zone 8: Central Alaska is windy with storm potential and abundant precipitation, western and eastern areas are fair to partly cloudy with precipitation moving into eastern areas later in the week, and temperatures are seasonal to below. Central and eastern Hawaii are windy with showers and precipitation, western parts of the state are fair to partly cloudy, and temperatures are seasonal.

2nd Quarter Moon, June 5–12

Zone 1: The zone is cloudy and windy with showers and seasonal temperatures.

Zone 2: Skies are fair to partly cloudy; temperatures are seasonal.

Zone 3: Temperatures and humidity ranging from seasonal to above accompany fair to partly cloudy skies.

Zone 4: The zone is variably cloudy with temperatures and humidity seasonal to above along with scattered showers and thunderstorms, some strong in central areas.

Zone 5: Western areas of the zone are windy with scattered showers and thunderstorms, central and eastern areas see strong thunderstorms with tornado potential, and temperatures are seasonal to above.

Zone 6: Much of the zone is partly cloudy to cloudy and seasonal with scattered precipitation; eastern areas see more precipitation and windy conditions.

Zone 7: Eastern areas are windy and cloudy with scattered precipitation, western and central parts of the zone are fair to partly cloudy with scattered precipitation in northern coastal areas, and temperatures are seasonal to below.

Zone 8: Western Alaska's skies are overcast with abundant precipitation and high winds later in the week, central and eastern parts of the state are fair to partly cloudy, and temperatures are seasonal. Hawaii is variably cloudy and windy with showers in western and central areas and seasonal temperatures.

Full Moon, June 13–18

Zone 1: The zone is generally fair to partly cloudy and humid with temperatures seasonal to above and scattered showers and thunderstorms, some with locally heavy precipitation.

Zone 2: Temperatures ranging from seasonal to above accompany humidity and thunderstorms, some strong with tornado potential and heavy precipitation.

Zone 3: Western and central areas see scattered thunderstorms, some strong with tornado potential; eastern areas see scattered storms with locally heavy precipitation; and the zone is variably cloudy, humid, with temperatures seasonal to above.

Zone 4: The western Plains see showers and more cloudiness, while the rest of the zone is generally fair to partly cloudy with scattered thunderstorms, some strong with tornado potential in eastern areas; temperatures range from seasonal to above.

Zone 5: Conditions are humid with temperatures seasonal to above, western areas see scattered thunderstorms, and central and eastern areas are cloudy with potential for locally heavy downfall.

Zone 6: Western areas are cloudy with scattered precipitation, central and eastern areas are windy and partly cloudy with a chance for precipitation, and temperatures are seasonal.

Zone 7: The zone is fair to partly cloudy with a chance for showers, and eastern areas are humid and windy with temperatures seasonal to above.

Zone 8: In Alaska, locally heavy precipitation accompanies cloudy skies and wind in western and eastern parts of the state, temperatures are seasonal, and central areas are partly cloudy with scattered precipitation. Hawaii is fair to partly cloudy and seasonal.

Summer 2014

Zone 1 temperatures will be above average and conditions dry in northern areas, and southern areas will see closer to average precipitation and seasonal temperatures along with severe thunderstorms with tornado potential. Precipitation will be average across zone 2 with temperatures seasonal to above. Much of zone 3 will experience temperatures ranging from seasonal to below along with average precipitation and more cloudiness.

Temperatures across zone 4 will be seasonal to above; central areas and the eastern Plains can expect an above-average number of severe thunderstorms with tornado potential along with abundant precipitation at times; and western areas will see low-pressure storm systems with high winds and precipitation average to below. Central parts of zone 5 will see an above-average number of severe thunderstorms with tornado potential, precipitation in western and eastern areas will be average to below, and temperatures will be seasonal to above. The western Gulf is the most likely region to see tropical storm and hurricane activity. In zone 6, dryness will prevail, with eastern areas seeing more precipitation, and temperatures will be seasonal. Northern coastal areas of zone 7 will see above-average precipitation, and the rest of the zone will tend toward dryness and above-average temperatures.

Western Alaska will be windy with below-average precipitation, central parts of the state can expect average precipitation, eastern areas will see strong storms, and temperatures will range from seasonal to below. Hawaii will be generally fair and seasonal with below-average precipitation.

4th Quarter Moon, June 19–26

Zone 1: Temperatures range from seasonal to above, and the zone is fair to partly cloudy and humid with a chance for precipitation.

Zone 2: Above-normal temperatures could trigger severe thunderstorms with tornado potential.

Zone 3: Western areas are partly cloudy and humid, and central and eastern parts of the zone see thunderstorms, some strong with tornado potential; temperatures are seasonal to above.

Zone 4: Western areas are mostly fair and windy with a chance for precipitation, central and eastern Plains see more cloudiness and precipitation, and eastern parts of the zone are humid with a chance for precipitation; temperatures are seasonal to above.

Zone 5: The zone is variably cloudy and seasonal, mostly fair west, and scattered showers central and east.

Zone 6: The zone is seasonal and partly cloudy with a chance for scattered showers and thunderstorms.

Zone 7: Temperatures range from seasonal to above under partly cloudy to cloudy skies with scattered showers and storms.

Zone 8: Alaska is mostly fair to partly cloudy and seasonal, with more cloudiness and precipitation in eastern areas. Hawaii is humid, seasonal, and fair to partly cloudy.

New Moon, June 27–July 4

Zone 1: The zone is fair to partly cloudy with temperatures seasonal to above.

Zone 2: Variably cloudy skies accompany a chance for showers and temperatures seasonal to above.

Zone 3: Much of the zone is partly cloudy, and eastern areas see more cloudiness with locally heavy precipitation; temperatures are seasonal to above.

Zone 4: Western parts of the zone are partly cloudy to cloudy with showers and thunderstorms, central and eastern areas are fair to partly cloudy, and temperatures are seasonal to above.

Zone 5: The zone is partly cloudy and humid with temperatures seasonal to above, and western and central areas see scattered showers.

Zone 6: Western and central areas are partly cloudy with a chance for showers, eastern areas are windy with thunderstorms, some strong; temperatures are seasonal to above.

Zone 7: Northern coastal areas are partly cloudy with scattered precipitation, southern coastal and central parts of the zone are fair to partly cloudy, eastern areas see strong thunderstorms, and temperatures are seasonal to above.

Zone 8: Abundant precipitation and stormy conditions in central Alaska move into eastern parts of the state, western areas are mostly fair, and temperatures are seasonal. Central and eastern Hawaii see locally heavy precipitation, western areas are fair and windy, and temperatures are seasonal.

2nd Quarter Moon, July 5–11

Zone 1: The zone is partly cloudy and seasonal.

Zone 2: Northern areas are partly cloudy, and central and southern areas see thunderstorms, some strong with tornado potential; high humidity accompanies temperatures seasonal to above.

Zone 3: Temperatures are seasonal to above with scattered showers and thunderstorms, some strong with tornado potential in western and central parts of the zone.

Zone 4: Much of the zone is windy with scattered showers and storms, some strong with tornado potential; skies are generally fair to partly cloudy, and temperatures seasonal to above.

Zone 5: Western areas are windy with more cloudiness, central and eastern parts of the zone could see strong thunderstorms, and high humidity accompanies temperatures seasonal to above.

Zone 6: Western and central parts of the zone see showers, some locally heavy, and temperatures are seasonal.

Zone 7: The zone is variably cloudy with locally heavy precipitation in northern coastal areas, scattered precipitation west and central, and windy with a chance for thunderstorms east; temperatures are seasonal.

Zone 8: Western and central Alaska see precipitation, skies are variably cloudy, and temperatures seasonal. Hawaii is fair to partly cloudy and seasonal.

Full Moon, July 12–17

Zone 1: The zone is humid with temperatures seasonal to above and fair to partly cloudy skies.

Zone 2: Humidity and temperatures seasonal to above accompany scattered thunderstorms and fair to partly cloudy skies.

Zone 3: Much of the zone sees scattered thunderstorms, some strong with tornado potential; temperatures are seasonal to above.

Zone 4: Western areas see showers and scattered thunderstorms, some strong, and the rest of the zone is variably cloudy; high humidity accompanies temperatures seasonal to above.

Zone 5: The zone is humid with temperatures seasonal to above, and western and central areas see scattered showers and storms.

Zone 6: Western areas are windy with precipitation, central parts of the zone are fair, eastern areas see showers, and temperatures are seasonal.

Zone 7: Northern coastal areas see locally heavy precipitation, southern coastal and central parts of the zone are fair to partly cloudy with a chance for showers, and eastern areas are humid; temperatures are seasonal to above.

Zone 8: Alaska is variably cloudy with precipitation central and eastern with seasonal temperatures. Hawaii is fair and seasonal.

4th Quarter Moon, July 18–25

Zone 1: The zone is partly cloudy and seasonal.

Zone 2: Variably cloudy skies accompany scattered showers and storms (some strong), and temperatures are seasonal to above.

Zone 3: Skies are variably cloudy, temperatures seasonal to above, and much of the zone could see thunderstorms, some strong with tornado potential.

Zone 4: The zone is variably cloudy with showers west, scattered showers central and east, and seasonal to above temperatures.

Zone 5: Central and eastern skies are mostly fair with a chance for precipitation later in the week, western areas see showers, and temperatures are seasonal to above.

Zone 6: Temperatures are seasonal to above and skies are fair to partly cloudy with a chance for precipitation.

Zone 7: Eastern areas are humid, temperatures are seasonal to above, and the zone is mostly fair.

Zone 8: Western Alaska is windy, and the state is mostly fair and seasonal. Hawaii is fair to partly cloudy with temperatures ranging from seasonal to above.

New Moon, July 26–August 2

Zone 1: The zone is seasonal, humid, and fair to partly cloudy with scattered showers south.

Zone 2: High humidity and temperatures seasonal to above accompany showers and thunderstorms, some strong with tornado potential and locally heavy precipitation.

Zone 3: Strong thunderstorms with tornado potential are possible across much of the zone, which is humid and seasonal.

Zone 4: Western and central areas have a chance for thunderstorms, and eastern parts of the zone see showers and scattered thunderstorms, some strong with tornado potential; skies are variably cloudy, and temperatures are seasonal.

Zone 5: Temperatures are seasonal to above, humidity is high, skies are variably cloudy, and much of the zone sees scattered showers and thunderstorms, with more precipitation east along with potential for strong thunderstorms and tornadoes.

Zone 6: Locally heavy precipitation in western areas moves into central parts of the zone, eastern skies are mostly fair, and conditions are windy and seasonal.

Zone 7: Northern coastal areas see locally heavy precipitation, southern coastal and central areas see showers and thunderstorms, skies are windy, and temperatures are seasonal.

Zone 8: Western and central Alaska are windy with precipitation, eastern areas are fair and windy, and temperatures are seasonal. Hawaii is fair and windy with temperatures seasonal to above.

2nd Quarter Moon, August 3–9

Zone 1: Temperatures are seasonal, northern areas see scattered showers, and southern parts of the zone are fair to partly cloudy.

Zone 2: The zone could see locally heavy precipitation—possibly from strong thunderstorms and a tropical storm—along with high humidity and seasonal temperatures.

Zone 3: Western and central skies are variably cloudy, eastern areas see scattered showers and thunderstorms (some with locally heavy precipitation), and temperatures are seasonal to above.

Zone 4: Much of the zone has a chance for showers, with strong thunderstorms possibly in eastern areas; skies are generally fair to partly cloudy with high humidity and temperatures seasonal to above.

Zone 5: Central and eastern parts of the zone see showers and thunderstorms later in the week, western areas are fair, eastern areas are windy, and high humidity accompanies temperatures seasonal to above.

Zone 6: Western areas see precipitation, central parts of the zone are mostly fair with showers later in the week, and eastern areas see scattered thunderstorms, some strong; skies are variably cloudy with seasonal temperatures.

Zone 7: Northern coastal areas see showers, southern coastal and central parts of the zone are fair, eastern areas are humid with showers and thunderstorms and temperatures seasonal to above.

Zone 8: Central Alaska is windy with precipitation that advances into eastern areas, western parts of the state see precipitation, skies are variably cloudy, and temperatures are seasonal to below.

Hawaii is mostly fair to partly cloudy and seasonal with windy conditions and scattered showers and thunderstorms east.

Full Moon, August 10–16

Zone 1: High humidity accompanies temperatures ranging from seasonal to above under partly cloudy to cloudy skies with a chance for scattered showers and thunderstorms, some with locally heavy downfall.

Zone 2: The zone is mostly fair with temperatures seasonal to above, along with a chance for strong thunderstorms with tornado potential later in the week.

Zone 3: Western areas are windy, the zone is fair to partly cloudy with temperatures seasonal to above, and eastern areas see scattered thunderstorms later in the week.

Zone 4: The zone is variably cloudy with humidity and temperatures ranging from seasonal to above; central and eastern areas could see strong thunderstorms with tornado potential.

Zone 5: Western parts of the zone are fair, central areas see storms with tornado potential, eastern areas are fair to partly cloudy, and temperatures are seasonal to above with high humidity.

Zone 6: Western areas are windy with precipitation later in the week, central parts of the zone are partly cloudy with scattered precipitation, eastern areas are cloudy with precipitation, and temperatures are seasonal.

Zone 7: Northern coastal areas are windy with precipitation later in the week, southern coastal and central parts of the zone are partly cloudy, eastern areas are cloudy with showers, and temperatures are seasonal.

Zone 8: Central Alaska is windy with precipitation, western and eastern areas are mostly fair, and temperatures are seasonal. Hawaii is seasonal with partly cloudy to cloudy skies and showers.

4th Quarter Moon, August 17–24

Zone 1: The zone is fair to partly cloudy with a chance for precipitation and temperatures ranging from seasonal to above.

Zone 2: Temperatures range from seasonal to above, and skies are fair to partly cloudy.

Zone 3: Western and central areas could see abundant precipitation with thunderstorms with tornado potential, possibly from a tropical storm; eastern areas are fair to partly cloudy with a chance for showers.

Zone 4: Increasing cloudiness later in the week brings showers to western areas; central and eastern parts of the zone are windy with precipitation (some locally heavy), as well as thunderstorms with tornado potential, possibly from a tropical storm.

Zone 5: The zone is variably cloudy with scattered showers and thunderstorms later in the week.

Zone 6: Western skies are fair, precipitation in central areas moves east under windy conditions, and temperatures are seasonal.

Zone 7: Much of the zone has a chance for scattered showers, eastern areas see more cloudiness, and temperatures are seasonal to above.

Zone 8: Alaska is windy and seasonal with variable cloudiness and scattered precipitation in central areas. Hawaii is fair to partly cloudy and seasonal with scattered showers.

New Moon, August 25–September 1

Zone 1: Northern parts of the zone are fair, temperatures are seasonal to above, and southern areas see precipitation, some locally heavy, possibly from a tropical storm.

Zone 2: The zone is seasonal to above and windy with locally heavy precipitation, possibly from a tropical storm.

Zone 3: Western and central areas are fair to partly cloudy, central areas have a chance for showers, and eastern areas see more cloudiness with showers and thunderstorms, some producing locally heavy precipitation; temperatures are seasonal to above.

Zone 4: Eastern and western areas are mostly fair to partly cloudy, while central parts of the zone see scattered showers and thunderstorms; temperatures range from seasonal to above.

Zone 5: Eastern areas see more clouds and scattered showers and thunderstorms than western and central parts of the zone, which are fair to partly cloudy; temperatures are seasonal to above.

Zone 6: Western areas are cloudy with abundant precipitation in some locations, central parts of the zone are fair, eastern areas are partly cloudy with scattered showers, and temperatures are seasonal to above.

Zone 7: Northern coastal areas see precipitation, some abundant, and the rest of the zone is variably cloudy with a chance for showers and thunderstorms in eastern areas; temperatures are seasonal to above.

Zone 8: Central Alaska is windy and stormy with precipitation that moves into eastern areas of the state, western locations are fair, and temperatures range from seasonal to below. Hawaii is windy, humid, seasonal, and fair to partly cloudy.

2nd Quarter Moon, September 2–7

Zone 1: The zone is fair to partly cloudy with temperatures ranging from seasonal to below.

Zone 2: Skies are variably cloudy, conditions are humid, and temperatures are seasonal to above.

Zone 3: Much of the zone is windy with scattered showers and thunderstorms, some strong with tornado potential, and temperatures range from seasonal to above.

Zone 4: Central parts of the zone see scattered showers and thunderstorms, eastern areas see showers, western skies are cloudy and windy with precipitation, and temperatures are seasonal.

Zone 5: The zone is variably cloudy and windy with precipitation and seasonal temperatures.

Zone 6: Temperatures are seasonal to above under mostly fair skies.

Zone 7: Skies are fair to partly cloudy, and temperatures range from seasonal to above.

Zone 8: Central Alaska is windy with precipitation that moves into eastern areas, western parts of the state are fair, and temperatures are seasonal to below. Hawaii is mostly windy and seasonal.

Full Moon, September 8–14

Zone 1: Northern areas are windy, and the zone is fair to partly cloudy with scattered showers and thunderstorms; temperatures are seasonal to above.

Zone 2: Central and southern areas see thunderstorms (some with tornado potential), northern areas are partly cloudy with a chance for showers, and the zone is windy and seasonal to above.

Zone 3: The zone is windy and variably cloudy with showers and thunderstorms (some strong with tornado potential), and temperatures are seasonal to above.

Zone 4: Western skies are fair to partly cloudy, and strong thunderstorms with tornado potential are possible in central and eastern locations along with locally heavy precipitation and windy conditions; humidity and temperatures are seasonal to above.

Zone 5: Skies are variably cloudy with temperatures and humidity seasonal to above; strong thunderstorms with tornado potential are possible in eastern locations.

Zone 6: Much of the zone is fair to partly cloudy and seasonal, with showers in western areas later in the week.

Zone 7: The zone is partly cloudy with more clouds and precipitation in northern coastal areas and a chance for showers in southern coastal and central areas; temperatures are seasonal.

Zone 8: Eastern Alaska is windy and cloudy with precipitation, western and central areas are partly cloudy with scattered precipitation, and temperatures are seasonal. Hawaii is fair to partly cloudy and seasonal with scattered showers.

4th Quarter Moon, September 15–23

Zone 1: The zone is partly cloudy and seasonal with scattered precipitation.

2013 © Viktoriia Khorzhevska Image from BigStockPhoto.com

Zone 2: Skies are variably cloudy, central and southern areas see showers and thunderstorms, and temperatures are seasonal.

Zone 3: Western and central parts of the zone see scattered precipitation, skies are partly cloudy to cloudy and windy, and temperatures are seasonal.

Zone 4: Western areas are partly cloudy, stormy conditions are possible in central and eastern areas with potential for strong storms and tornadoes, and temperatures are seasonal to above.

Zone 5: Strong storms with tornado potential are possible in central and eastern areas, western parts of the zone are windy with scattered precipitation, and temperatures are seasonal to above.

Zone 6: Skies are fair to partly cloudy, temperatures are seasonal, and western areas see scattered precipitation.

Zone 7: The zone is fair to partly cloudy with a chance for precipitation in eastern areas; temperatures are seasonal to above.

Zone 8: Western and central Alaska see precipitation, eastern areas are windy with precipitation later in the week (some locally heavy), skies are variably cloudy with seasonal temperatures. Western Hawaii is cloudy, central and eastern areas see scattered precipitation, and temperatures are seasonal.

Autumn 2014

Cooler temperatures and dryness will prevail across much of zone 1. Central parts of zone 2 will see more precipitation than other areas, and temperatures will be seasonal to above; central areas may see a tropical storm or hurricane along with severe thunderstorms with tornado potential. In zone 3, temperatures will range from seasonal to above, and central and eastern areas will see severe thunderstorms with tornado potential and possible tropical storm activity in the central Gulf.

Western and central parts of zone 4 will see an above-average number of low-pressure storm systems and more cloudiness alternating with the above-normal temperatures that will be the norm in eastern areas; precipitation will be average. In zone 5, precipitation will be average to below, with central areas seeing the greatest downfall; temperatures will be seasonal to above. Zone 6 will tend toward dryness with temperatures seasonal to above, but the zone will also see some significant storms. Fire weather will be a concern in western and southern parts of zone 7, along with dryness. Precipitation will be average in central mountain areas, eastern areas will see average precipitation, and temperatures will be seasonal to above.

Alaskan temperatures will range from seasonal to above and precipitation average to below except in central parts of the state, which will see more and abundant downfall at times. Temperatures will be above average in Hawaii and precipitation below the norm; however, the state may experience a hurricane this season.

New Moon, September 24–30

Zone 1: The zone is windy with precipitation in southern areas, variable cloudiness, and temperatures and humidity seasonal to above.

Zone 2: Skies are fair to partly cloudy, and the zone is humid with temperatures seasonal to above and a chance for precipitation in northern areas.

Zone 3: Temperatures and humidity are seasonal to above under windy, fair to partly cloudy skies, with a chance for precipitation.

Zone 4: Western and central areas could see scattered precipitation, and the zone is variably cloudy and windy with temperatures seasonal to above.

Zone 5: The zone is humid with seasonal temperatures and variably cloudy skies with a chance for scattered showers.

Zone 6: Windy and variably cloudy skies with seasonal temperatures accompany precipitation in central and eastern areas.

Zone 7: Southern coastal and central areas see scattered precipitation, eastern areas have a chance for precipitation, and the zone is variably cloudy and windy with temperatures ranging from seasonal to above.

Zone 8: Western and central Alaska are windy, eastern areas see locally heavy precipitation, and temperatures are seasonal to below. Western and central Hawaii are windy, eastern areas see scattered precipitation, skies are fair to partly cloudy, and temperatures are seasonal.

2nd Quarter Moon, October 1–7

Zone 1: The zone is cloudy with precipitation and temperatures ranging from seasonal to below.

Zone 2: Northern areas see more cloudiness with precipitation, central and southern areas are windy and variably cloudy with precipitation, and temperatures are seasonal.

Zone 3: The zone is fair to partly cloudy with more cloudiness and precipitation in eastern areas; temperatures are seasonal.

Zone 4: Partly cloudy skies prevail with a chance for precipitation, and temperatures are seasonal.

Zone 5: Western and central areas are partly cloudy, eastern areas see more cloudiness and wind with precipitation, and temperatures are seasonal.

Zone 6: Much of the zone is windy with precipitation under partly cloudy to cloudy skies; temperatures are seasonal to below.

Zone 7: Western and central areas see precipitation, eastern areas are fair to partly cloudy, and the zone is windy with temperatures seasonal to below.

Zone 8: Western and central Alaska are cloudy with precipitation, eastern areas are fair, and the state is windy and seasonal. Western and central Hawaii are cloudy with precipitation, eastern areas are fair, and temperatures are seasonal.

Full Moon, October 8–14

Zone 1: The zone is cloudy, windy, and stormy with temperatures seasonal to below, possibly as a result of a tropical storm.

Zone 2: Northern, central, and southern coastal areas see abundant downfall under cloudy skies, possibly from a tropical storm.

Zone 3: Western and central parts of the zone are fair to partly cloudy, and eastern areas are cloudy and stormy with abundant precipitation, possibly from a tropical storm; temperatures are seasonal to below.

Zone 4: Windy and variably cloudy skies along with scattered precipitation prevail in western and central areas of the zone, eastern areas are partly cloudy, and temperatures are seasonal.

Zone 5: Western and central areas are cloudy and windy, eastern areas are fair to partly cloudy, and temperatures are seasonal.

Zone 6: Much of the zone is partly cloudy to cloudy, western and central areas see precipitation, and temperatures are seasonal.

Zone 7: Precipitation (some locally heavy) and cloudy skies in western areas move into central parts of the zone, eastern areas are fair, and temperatures are seasonal.

Zone 8: Central Alaska is stormy and cloudy, western and eastern areas are fair to partly cloudy, and temperatures are seasonal to below. Hawaii is mostly fair and seasonal; eastern areas are windy.

4th Quarter Moon, October 15–22

Zone 1: The zone is windy and variably cloudy with precipitation (some abundant in northern areas); temperatures are seasonal.

Zone 2: Northern skies are fair to partly cloudy, central and southern areas are cloudy with precipitation, and temperatures are seasonal to below.

Zone 3: Much of the zone is windy and seasonal, with a chance for precipitation in western and central areas.

Zone 4: Most of the zone is fair to partly cloudy, eastern areas are windy with a chance for precipitation, and temperatures are seasonal.

Zone 5: Western areas are fair, with central and eastern parts of the zone seeing more cloudiness and a chance for precipitation; temperatures are seasonal.

Zone 6: Western and central skies are partly cloudy, eastern areas see precipitation with potential for a major low-pressure storm, and temperatures are seasonal to below.

Zone 7: Much of the zone is fair to partly cloudy, eastern areas are windy with more cloudiness and precipitation, and temperatures are seasonal.

Zone 8: Abundant precipitation in central Alaska moves into eastern parts of the state, skies are fair to partly cloudy west, and temperatures are seasonal. Hawaii sees locally heavy precipitation under mostly cloudy skies and seasonal temperatures.

New Moon, October 23–29

Zone 1: Temperatures are seasonal to below under fair to partly cloudy and windy skies with scattered precipitation.

Zone 2: The zone is fair to partly cloudy and windy with temperatures seasonal to below.

Zone 3: Western areas see precipitation and possibly thunderstorms, eastern areas are windy, and the zone is partly cloudy to cloudy with temperatures seasonal to below.

Zone 4: The zone is partly cloudy to cloudy and windy with seasonal temperatures and precipitation in central and eastern areas.

Zone 5: Skies are mostly fair to partly cloudy, eastern areas see precipitation with a chance for thunderstorms, and temperatures are seasonal.

Zone 6: The zone is seasonal with variable cloudiness and a chance for precipitation, eastern areas see more cloudiness, and central parts of the zone see scattered precipitation.

Zone 7: Western and central areas are variably cloudy with a chance for precipitation, eastern areas are partly cloudy with scattered precipitation, and temperatures are seasonal.

Zone 8: Western and central Alaska are windy with precipitation, eastern areas are mostly fair, and temperatures are seasonal. Eastern Hawaii sees precipitation and cloudy skies, western and central areas are fair to partly cloudy, and temperatures are seasonal.

2nd Quarter Moon, October 30–November 5

Zone 1: The zone is cloudy with precipitation and temperatures ranging from seasonal to below.

Zone 2: Northern areas are cloudy, thunderstorms are possible in central and southern areas under variably cloudy skies, and temperatures are seasonal to below.

Zone 3: Much of the zone sees precipitation under variably cloudy skies and seasonal temperatures.

Zone 4: Some western areas see abundant precipitation, central and eastern areas are partly cloudy to cloudy with precipitation, and temperatures are seasonal.

Zone 5: Western areas are windy with precipitation, central and eastern areas are windy with a chance for showers and thunderstorms, skies are variably cloudy, and temperatures are seasonal.

Zone 6: Western skies are mostly fair, central and eastern areas are cloudy and windy with scattered precipitation, and temperatures are seasonal.

Zone 7: Much of the zone sees precipitation with temperatures ranging from seasonal to below, western and central areas are cloudy, and eastern parts of the zone are fair to partly cloudy.

Zone 8: Western Alaska is windy with precipitation that moves into central areas, eastern parts of the state are mostly fair, and temperatures are seasonal to below. Hawaii is mostly fair and windy with seasonal temperatures.

Full Moon, November 6–13

Zone 1: Temperatures are seasonal to below, and the zone is windy and partly cloudy.

Zone 2: Northern areas see scattered precipitation, central and southern areas are windy, skies are partly cloudy to cloudy, and temperatures are seasonal.

Zone 3: The zone is seasonal and partly cloudy with a chance for precipitation.

Zone 4: Stormy conditions develop in western areas later in the week and move into central parts of the zone, bringing abundant downfall to some areas; eastern areas are partly cloudy with scattered precipitation; temperatures are seasonal to below.

Zone 5: Western areas are windy with scattered precipitation, temperatures are seasonal to below, and central areas are stormy, possibly with sleet and abundant downfall moving east.

Zone 6: The zone is variably cloudy, seasonal, and windy with a chance for precipitation east.

Zone 7: Seasonal temperatures accompany windy and fair to partly cloudy skies.

Zone 8: Much of Alaska sees precipitation (some abundant) under variably cloudy skies with temperatures seasonal to below. Hawaii is cloudy with precipitation and temperatures seasonal to below.

4th Quarter Moon, November 14–21

Zone 1: The zone is windy and partly cloudy with scattered precipitation.

Zone 2: Northern areas see scattered precipitation, and central and southern parts of the zone see precipitation (some abundant) later in the week; partly cloudy to cloudy skies accompany seasonal temperatures.

Zone 3: Western and central parts of the zone see precipitation with possible thunderstorms and tornado potential in southern areas, eastern areas are partly cloudy and windy, and temperatures are seasonal.

Zone 4: Western skies are partly cloudy, central eastern areas see more cloudiness along with stormy conditions and possibly sleet, and temperatures are seasonal to below.

Zone 5: Eastern areas are windy with precipitation (some locally heavy), western and central skies are partly cloudy, and temperatures are seasonal to below.

Zone 6: Western areas are cloudy with abundant precipitation later in the week, central and eastern parts of the zone are variably cloudy with scattered precipitation, and temperatures are seasonal.

Zone 7: The zone is seasonal, partly cloudy east, windy west with abundant precipitation in northern coastal areas, and scattered precipitation central.

Zone 8: Alaska is partly cloudy and windy west with seasonal temperatures. Hawaii is mostly fair and seasonal.

New Moon, November 22–28

Zone 1: Seasonal temperatures accompany partly cloudy to cloudy skies with precipitation.

Zone 2: The zone is variably cloudy with precipitation in northern areas, central and southern parts of the zone could see strong thunderstorms with locally heavy precipitation, and temperatures are seasonal.

Zone 3: Partly cloudy to cloudy skies accompany precipitation in western and central parts of the zone and scattered precipitation east; conditions are windy and temperatures seasonal.

Zone 4: Much of the zone is windy with precipitation, and central and eastern areas could see stormy conditions with abundant downfall; temperatures are seasonal to below.

Zone 5: Western parts of the zone are windy with scattered precipitation and variably cloudy skies, central and eastern areas are windy with precipitation (some abundant), and temperatures are seasonal to below.

Zone 6: The zone is fair to partly cloudy and seasonal.

Zone 7: Western skies are partly cloudy, central and eastern areas are fair, and temperatures are seasonal.

Zone 8: Central and eastern Alaska are windy with abundant precipitation, western parts of the state are mostly fair, and temperatures are seasonal to below. Hawaii is seasonal and fair to partly cloudy with scattered showers.

2nd Quarter Moon, November 29–December 5

Zone 1: Northern parts of the zone are cloudy and cold, while southern areas are fair to partly cloudy and seasonal.

Zone 2: The zone is fair to partly cloudy with temperatures ranging from seasonal to below.

Zone 3: Temperatures range from seasonal to below, skies are generally fair to partly cloudy, and western and central areas see precipitation later in the week.

Zone 4: Much of the zone is windy and cloudy with precipitation as the week unfolds, and temperatures are seasonal.

Zone 5: Western and central parts of the zone are windy and partly cloudy, eastern areas see precipitation, central areas could see thunderstorms, and temperatures are seasonal.

Zone 6: The zone is variably cloudy with more cloudiness central and east and precipitation in eastern areas (some abundant); conditions are windy and seasonal to below.

Zone 7: Western areas are partly cloudy, central and eastern parts of the zone see more cloudiness with precipitation, and the zone is windy and seasonal to below.

Zone 8: Mostly cloudy skies bring precipitation across much of Alaska, some abundant, and temperatures are seasonal. Hawaii is fair to partly cloudy, seasonal, and windy with abundant precipitation later in the week and possibly stormy conditions.

Full Moon, December 6–13

Zone 1: Northern areas are cloudy with precipitation, central and southern areas are partly cloudy, and temperatures are seasonal to below.

Zone 2: The zone is variably cloudy and seasonal with scattered precipitation.

Zone 3: Much of the zone sees precipitation under variably cloudy skies and seasonal temperatures.

Zone 4: Temperatures range from seasonal to below, and central and eastern areas are cloudy with precipitation, some abundant.

Zone 5: The zone is variably cloudy and seasonal with precipitation, some abundant, in eastern areas.

Zone 6: Western and central parts of the zone see scattered precipitation under variably cloudy skies, eastern areas are cloudy with precipitation, and temperatures are seasonal to below.

Zone 7: The zone is fair to partly cloudy with more cloudiness, wind, and precipitation east; temperatures are seasonal to below.

Zone 8: Central Alaska is windy, central and eastern areas see precipitation, and temperatures are seasonal to below. Hawaii is very windy and cloudy with precipitation and temperatures seasonal to below.

4th Quarter Moon, December 14–20

Zone 1: The zone is partly cloudy and seasonal.

Zone 2: Skies are cloudy and precipitation abundant in central and southern areas, northern parts of the zone are partly cloudy, and temperatures are seasonal to below.

Zone 3: Much of the zone sees precipitation, some abundant in eastern and central areas, and skies are windy; temperatures are seasonal to below.

Zone 4: Variable cloudiness brings scattered precipitation across the zone, with more precipitation east; temperatures are seasonal.

Zone 5: Western skies are fair, central and eastern areas are variably cloudy with precipitation, and temperatures are seasonal.

Zone 6: Much of the zone is cloudy and seasonal, western areas see precipitation at week's end, and eastern areas have a chance for precipitation.

Zone 7: Cloudy skies across much of the zone bring scattered precipitation in northern areas and locally heavy downfall in central parts of the zone, temperatures are seasonal, and eastern areas are mostly fair.

Zone 8: Alaska is variably cloudy and seasonal with precipitation and wind in eastern areas. Hawaii is fair to partly cloudy and seasonal.

New Moon, December 21–27

Zone 1: The zone is seasonal with below-average temperatures and windy with scattered precipitation.

Zone 2: Northern areas are windy with scattered precipitation, central and southern parts of the zone are partly cloudy, and temperatures are seasonal.

Zone 3: The zone is seasonal and partly cloudy with scattered precipitation east.

Zone 4: Storm potential could bring abundant precipitation to western and central areas, eastern parts of the zone are partly cloudy, and temperatures are seasonal to below.

Zone 5: Much of the zone sees precipitation, some abundant in western areas, and temperatures are seasonal to below.

Zone 6: Variable cloudiness across the zone accompanies scattered precipitation and seasonal temperatures.

Zone 7: The zone is variably cloudy with precipitation in northern areas and a chance for precipitation in other locations; temperatures are seasonal to below.

Zone 8: Western parts of Alaska are windy, central and eastern areas see abundant precipitation, and temperatures are seasonal. Hawaii is mostly fair, seasonal, and windy.

2nd Quarter Moon, December 28–January 4, 2015

Zone 1: The zone is partly cloudy and seasonal with precipitation at week's end.

Zone 2: Much of the zone is cloudy with precipitation, and temperatures are seasonal.

Zone 3: Western areas could be stormy later in the week, central and eastern parts of the zone see precipitation, skies are variably cloudy, and temperatures are seasonal to below.

Zone 4: Stormy conditions in eastern areas could bring abundant downfall to some areas under cloudy skies and temperatures that range from seasonal to below across the zone.

Zone 5: Western and central areas are partly cloudy with possible thunderstorms, and eastern areas are stormy under cloudy skies later in the week; temperatures range from seasonal to above in western and central areas, and seasonal to below to the east.

Zone 6: Most of the zone is fair to partly cloudy with a chance for precipitation in central areas and temperatures ranging from seasonal to above.

Zone 7: Zonal temperatures are seasonal to above, and skies are fair to partly cloudy with a chance for precipitation.

Zone 8: Western and central Alaska see precipitation under variably cloudy skies and seasonal temperatures. Hawaii is fair and seasonal.

About the Author

Kris Brandt Riske is the executive director and a professional member of the American Federation of Astrologers (AFA), the oldest U.S. astrological organization, founded in 1938; and a member of the National Council for Geocosmic Research (NCGR). She has a master's degree in journalism and a certificate of achievement in weather forecasting from Penn State. Kris is the author of several books, including Llewellyn's Complete Book of Astrology: The Easy Way to Learn Astrology; Mapping Your Money; *and* Mapping Your Future; *and she is coauthor of* Mapping Your Travels and Relocation *and* Astro-meteorology: Planetary Powers in Weather Forecasting. *Her newest* book is Llewellyn's Complete Book of Predictive Astrology. *She also writes for astrology publications and does the annual weather forecast for* Llewellyn's Moon Sign Book.

In addition to astrometeorology, she specializes in predictive astrology. Kris is an avid NASCAR fan, although she'd rather be a driver than a spectator. In 2011 she fulfilled her dream when she drove a stock car for twelve fast laps. She posts a weather forecast for each of the thirty-six race weekends (qualifying and race day) for NASCAR drivers and fans. Visit her at www.pitstopforecasting.com. Kris also enjoys gardening, reading, jazz, and her three cats.

Economic Forecast for 2014

by Christeen Skinner

Solar Power

Everything starts and finishes with our special star, the Sun. Without its output, life here would be unsustainable. Yet solar output is inconstant even if there does appear to be some kind of rhythm or pulse at work. Forecasting techniques with regard to terrestrial weather using the positions of the planets and Moon is improving, but without greater understanding and observation of what is happening within the Sun itself, determining probable crop yields and food prices is still far short of the accuracy economic traders would hope for.

The most basic solar rhythm comes from sunspots. These powerful areas of explosion on the Sun's surface seem to have a rhythm of a little over twenty-two years, which is divided into two halves; the polarity of the sunspots changes at the midpoint. No two cycles are the same. In some, the number of sunspots reaches several hundred in a year, while others might have only sixty spots.

What is clear is that each cycle includes a period of maxima and minima. The present solar cycle (Number 24) began in 2008. This was a period of unusually low solar activity: for over two hundred days, no sunspots appeared at all. Without doubt this impacted terrestrial weather and Earth's crop cycles. Harvests during solar minima (2008–2010) were poor, either due to drought or excess rain and flooding. The harvests of 2011 and 2012 were expected to be better. The pattern of sunspots was not quite as anticipated, however, and the harvests in these years were not as abundant as had been hoped. Once again, terrestrial weather patterns—dictated by those on the Sun—resulted in poor yields.

In "good" years, excess grains are stored and food-mountains are created, which are then used to offset poor harvests in other years. This is helpful in holding prices steady and generally results in a two-year lag between a year of poor harvests and higher food prices. As stated, harvests from 2008 onward have not been good. In 2012 it was clear that food prices were indeed rising. Given the poor harvest that year, and allowing for that two-year lag, food prices may be expected to be high at least through the early part of 2014. This could even give rise to "food riots" in some parts of the world.

If 2013–2014 does indeed bring the expected solar maxima, harvests should improve and eventually food prices should fall—though not, perhaps, until 2016. Investors take note: the time to invest in food commodities may have passed.

Challenges

Uranus's journey around the Sun takes approximately eighty-four years, while Pluto's takes nearly a quarter of a millennium. Years in which either planet moves from one sign of the zodiac to another herald social, political, and economic change. In 2008,

Pluto began its Capricorn journey, and in 2010, Uranus moved into Aries. Both Aries and Capricorn are cardinal signs of the zodiac, having in common a need for action. This has certainly been the case in the global markets. The disintegration of many conglomerates and major banks has shocked many. Big has not been beautiful, and downsizing has become the norm. The austerity faced by many countries will no doubt continue until Uranus moves on into the next sign in 2017.

Uranus and Pluto together are often seen as a revolutionary combination. They demand change and upheaval. Together they seem to have the ability to kick over anything whose foundations are in any way insecure. Thus many businesses (and countries) with weak capital bases have already found themselves vulnerable and liable to annihilation. Throughout 2014, the exact right angle (square aspect) between these two planets continues. This is indicative of even more pain to come.

Uranus is often thought of as the planet of technology, and it is entirely possible that this sector will be strapped for cash through 2014. A further possibility is that fast-paced developments—mini-revolutions, if you will—will render certain technologies obsolete. Those firms and businesses whose research and development departments have been underfunded in recent years may find they are unable to compete.

On a positive note, however, those who make it their business to re-invigorate should do well. Waste disposal firms should find growing demand for their services. It is probable too that those who are willing to invest in small and family-based enterprises will see the much-talked-about "green shoots" emerging and will realize rewards as the aspect wanes (in 2015).

In September 2014, the Uranus-Pluto midpoint aligns first with the Jupiter-Chiron midpoint (September 6) and then with Saturn-Neptune (September 30). It might help to view this sequence as two hinges, both of which bring loud creaks. This could be the final "get real" moment when sovereign debts have to be faced and managed.

As we will see later, September 2014 promises to be the most critical financial month of the year. Developments are likely to affect foreign exchange (forex) markets as well as equities. Yet this could also mark the low of the year. Indices should rise from this, although it will come after a few weeks of turbulence. It will be interesting to see which currencies emerge relatively unscathed from this period.

Geodetics, New York, and History

The studious astro-investor takes account of the geographical areas likely to be sensitive to planetary activity. There are numerous ways of doing this, but a common approach is to use the Greenwich Meridian to mark the beginning zodiac degree (0 Aries) and, working eastward, allow each degree to mark succeeding degrees of the zodiac. This system places New York and Wall Street (over 270 degrees away from the Meridian) under the influence of Capricorn—the exact area of the zodiac through which Pluto makes its passage in 2014.

Pluto, god of the underworld, has a track record of being present at moments of great crisis, though it should also be pointed out that this is the planet of re-potting prior to eventual re-growth. Pluto's dominant presence coincides with periods of upheaval— even catastrophe—before a time of rebuilding. The very foundations of the Dow Jones, NASDAQ, and S&P indices could be affected in 2014, as may be the great city of New York itself as Pluto makes its geodetic passage over New York's meridian.

The position of Pluto in 2014 has particular relevance for the US, whose July 4 birthdate positions the Sun at 14 degrees Cancer in its chart. In 2014, Jupiter passes this degree as Pluto opposes it. Meanwhile Mars and Uranus take up positions at right angles to this opposition, creating what is known as a Cardinal Grand

Cross. The cosmos doesn't "do" exact repeats; that said, an earlier and similar lineup of planets occurred in December 1835 and coincided with the Great Fire of New York, when several hundred houses and homes were destroyed.

On its own, the Jupiter-Pluto position suggests financial misfortune, perhaps an extreme "gamble." This particular alignment is often visible in the charts of those experiencing bankruptcy. The history of American banking and government shows it to have experienced financial difficulties when these two planets have formed hard aspects in the past. It may be that this is part of the cellular memory of the nation, and that this experience is repeated again in 2014. Coupled with a Mars-Uranus alignment in May, this suggests sudden events could shake the foundations of the US government.

This particular planetary formation occurs just weeks before Jupiter and Saturn reach the final third phase of their cycle. Throughout the twentieth century, this phase marked significant stock market lows.

It seems probable then that 2014 will witness significantly negative financial activity in the US particularly, although for those with cash, this will surely present a buying opportunity. Remember: the planets do move on from significant lows, so there will eventually be a high.

Eclipses

Another celestial phenomenon of interest to astro-investors is the eclipse cycle. In any year there will be a minimum of two solar eclipses and as many as five. In 2014 there are just two: April 29 and October 23. Both are accompanied by lunar eclipses occurring at the Full Moon just two weeks before these solar eclipses.

The first eclipse of 2014 on April 15 is lunar. This Full Moon will then be conjunct the asteroid Ceres. Unsurprisingly, as one of the goddesses of crops, this asteroid is usually prominent in the charts of those financial moments when food prices have hit the headlines. It is reasonable to expect this to be the case again in 2014. This could prove a peak before prices fall.

Eclipses can be viewed as cosmic punctuation marks. A lunar eclipse *before* a solar eclipse offers a different kind of cosmic grammar. The fact that the two solar eclipses of 2014 are preceded by lunar eclipses is indicative of high drama—as though the cosmic punctuation marks were underlined for further emphasis.

The astro-investor also has interest in the zodiac placement of each eclipse. The solar eclipses are at 8 degrees Taurus and 0 degrees Scorpio, both fixed signs of the zodiac, while their accompanying lunar eclipses are in Libra and Aries, both cardinal signs.

Cardinal signs tend to bring dramatic activity, whereas fixed signs bring "full stops." It is probable that the two lunar eclipses (April 15 and October 8) will coincide with short, sharp, and negative shocks across various indices, with markets recovering only after the accompanying solar eclipses on April 29 and October 23.

The lunar eclipse on October 8 could be particularly dramatic, since this Full Moon aligns with Uranus. One need go back no further than the Full Moon in September 2008 for an example, when a similar Moon-Uranus conjunction marked a significant moment in the financial crisis of that year. Substantial market "earthquakes" in October 2014 may be very similar to that earlier period.

Interestingly, the April eclipse signs (Libra and Taurus) are both ruled by Venus and the October ones by Mars (Aries and Scorpio, traditional). Venus is associated with the beauty sector and Mars with engineering. The cosmetics industry could feel the brunt of the April eclipses, when the collapse of a proposed merger may be another factor in falling markets. In October, engineering, military, and financial sectors are most likely to be in headlines accompanying news of falling share prices.

Solar eclipses are like "sophisticated" New Moons with their own special power. The Sun and Moon meet and begin a new cycle every month, with each of these cycles carrying economic significance. It is not at all unusual to find increased volume around the Full Moon, which occurs roughly two weeks after the New Moon. A Full Moon that is also a lunar eclipse can see that volume increase to the point at which it is recognized as panic selling. October 8 may eventually be described as a Black Wednesday.

Mercury Combust

The Sun also holds regular "meetings" or conjunctions with Mercury, the planet of commerce. Perhaps unsurprisingly, these dates usually mark turning points, especially in the commodity markets. Obviously the sign in which the conjunction takes place is important: this extra information points to *which* commodities might experience the more exaggerated moves.

The actual conjunction is formed when the Sun and Mercury share longitude, yet the effect of combustion (as Mercury appears to travel into the Sun's rays and is apparently "burnt" by the Sun) occurs before the exactitude. Some astrologers determine Mercury's combustion period as occurring when the planet is within 8 degrees either side of the Sun.

Stocks associated with the signs involved get "burned" and lose value during such periods; they then regain value as the distance between the two widens. An astro-investing approach would be to sell these stocks prior to combustion and to buy again before the period ends and while prices are low.

Sun-Mercury conjunctions in 2014 are as follows:

Feb 15 at 27 Aquarius; combustion Feb 12–19

Apr 25 at 5 Taurus; combustion Apr 18–May 3

Jun 19 at 28 Gemini; combustion Jun 14–25

Aug 8 at 16 Leo; combustion Aug 1–17

Oct 16 at 23 Libra; combustion Oct 13–20

Dec 8 at 16 Sagittarius; combustion Nov 24–Dec 23

Of these dates, June 19 is particular interesting in that this is close to the summer solstice—another marker for change of economic pace. The actual degree (28 Gemini) is within the orb of an opposition to the Galactic Center, suggesting that any movement will be felt worldwide. Gemini is one of the key signs associated with telecommunications, so it may be that it is this sector affected by developments in the commodity markets. Note too that this is one of the longer periods of combustion. The astro-trader would observe all the aspects taking place over those weeks and the dates when other planets change signs (again affecting price) and would then likely plan various buying and selling entry points.

It is reasonable to assume that the sector most likely to be affected by the February combustion will be high-tech (Aquarius) but also media including the Internet (as Mercury will move into Pisces). We should see a drop in these shares from mid-February to early March.

The accent in April (the Taurus conjunction) covers both Taurus and Aries stocks. This suggests loss of value in engineering and beauty sectors. Ordinarily we might expect these share prices to rise after mid-April; there is a lunar eclipse waiting in the wings, however, and so these stocks might not rally until May.

The June date has already been identified as potentially affecting telecommunications and, perhaps, travel stocks. These should recover from mid-July onward.

August's combustion should affect leisure stocks, with these losing value at the start of the month but gaining before the end of August.

Recall that October offers a lunar and solar eclipse, which could result in exaggerated moves. Sun-Mercury combustion in the sign of Libra suggests difficulties for the cosmetics and fashion industries as well, perhaps for those companies specializing in mergers and acquisitions.

The final Sun-Mercury combustion of the year occurs in December and is Sagittarian. This one should affect travel and airline stocks especially.

Venus Combust

Mercury is, of course, not the only planet than can be rendered combust by the Sun. Each planet experiences such periods. Venus is conjunct the Sun on January 11 but combust from January 7 to 16. Venus's next solar conjunction is on October 25, but its combust period is far longer than at the start of the year. Combustion begins in late September and does not conclude until November 19 as the Sun moves from Scorpio into Sagittarius.

During both periods, we should expect poor figures from the retail sector. With both signs involved associated with finance and banking, and Venus linked to money itself, we should anticipate severe cash flow difficulties in many areas. It is probable too that banking and insurance stocks will be subject to negative activity in October. From late September through November 19, those with cash seem likely to be offered an array of investment opportunities bringing fast return, since indices are likely to rise from late November onward.

Currencies, Forex, and West/East Commerce

Though the Sun opposes both Jupiter and Saturn every year, Mars opposes the Sun only every twenty-five or twenty-six months. In 2014, Mars will be retrograde in Libra and opposed to the Sun on April 8. This is part of two more complicated patterns: one of fifteen years and one of seventy-nine years.

As we know, the cosmos never repeat exactly. Yet research into cycles often provides clues as to the probable events of a period as a cycle recurs, although the position of *other* planets will differ from that earlier time. The planetary conditions in 2014 have similarities with 1935 (the longer cycle mentioned above).

On Tuesday, March 12, 1935, the Dow Jones Index hit bottom and then began to rise, bringing to an end the Great Depression. In March 1935, Mars was, as in 2014, retrograde in the sign of Libra. From spring 1935 onward, the Dow Jones Index rose, and several new companies had joined the index by November. Among these were steelmakers and Chrysler: high-quality engineering firms whose stock rose after Mars completed its retrograde motion.

It is unlikely that 2014 will see the latter replicated exactly, since the solar eclipse patterns are markedly different. Yet by the very end of the year, there could be more than a glimmer of light on the world's financial stage.

Having opposed the Sun in April, Mars appears to pick up speed; by September it moves more quickly through the zodiac. On September 13, it begins its passage through Sagittarius before moving on into Capricorn on October 26. Mars's journey through Sagittarius encompasses the lunar and solar eclipses of October that year. It is not abnormal for the price of gold and other precious metals to rise as Mars moves through this sign. It may be that those attuned to market movements sense the probability of an October crisis in the days around the Full Moon on September 8, and that fissures in market prices apparent around this time lead to gold price moves a day or so later.

The September 8 Full Moon is interesting for several reasons. First, the Moon aligns with Chiron in Pisces. From the financial perspective, this suggests difficulties for those companies working in health (and chemicals particularly) and media (with emphasis on the Internet). One possibility is a computer viral attack.

We should also note that this same chart includes a conjunction of the asteroid Vesta with Saturn in Scorpio, with Mars not too far away. One of the many images for Scorpio is that of a Great Eagle—one of the symbols appearing on the US dollar. Vesta is often prominent when there are major movements in foreign exchange prices. It may be that the US dollar comes under pressure during September 2014, which could be a key factor in pushing gold prices higher.

There are, of course, many currencies operating across the globe. A stellium (group) of planets and the asteroid Vesta in this Full Moon chart may be indicative of problems with implications for all forex trading. It might not be just the US dollar that is affected; we should also consider Asiatic monies and the effect of the long Neptune-Pluto cycle of 496 years.

With each conjunction of Neptune and Pluto, there is a shift in commercial emphasis from the Eastern to the Western Hemisphere and back again. The present cycle began in the 1890s and started the shift from Western to Eastern dominance. It is now clear that the Asian region is thriving in a way that the West is not. The currencies of this region offer fascinating study for those seeking a correlation between planet cycles and commercial activity on Earth.

As some Asiatic currencies have a known "birth date," those charts can be closely assessed. Where the data is unknown (e.g., sterling), considerable research has to be employed to determine which planet phases correlate most closely with fluctuations in the value of the currency concerned. Research to date suggests that both the Singapore dollar and the Thai baht could be markedly affected in September 2014. It may be that both gain stature throughout what could be a tricky few weeks of trading for Western Hemisphere countries.

Another distinct possibility is that one of the very old currencies of the Middle East will be resurrected in the last quarter of 2014. Those who choose to take a chance on the Iraqi dinar, for example, may not be disappointed. Two dates stand out: October 30 and November 28. On both days, we should expect major movements across currency exchanges.

Both dates occur close to second-quarter Moons, with the October date also falling close to Mercury's direct station. We know that there is a sequence to lunations and that in the case of a second-quarter Moon, if we look back roughly nine months, we will find a New Moon at roughly the same degree. This offers insight. The astro-investor takes note of which currency pairs make the greatest moves at the New Moon; he or she can then be reasonably sure that this same pair will be highlighted again at the subsequent second-quarter Moon in the same degree. In this instance, careful observation of forex movements around January 30 should give clues as to which pairs are likely to be headline news around October 30.

The same formula can be used for the March 1 New Moon, which shares the same degree as the November 29 second-quarter Moon. Moves in this instance should be less dramatic than the October move, which is also affected by Mercury's station. Whenever Mercury is involved, fluctuations tend to be greater than usual. With this planet holding retrograde status for part of October, stability in the forex markets seems unlikely. The astro-investor who takes careful notes in both late January and February will surely have useful information to add to his or her trading toolbox.

Jupiter

As Jupiter moves from one sign to the next on its twelve-year journey around the Sun, there is potential for growth in a different sector of the marketplace. In 2014, Jupiter moves from Cancer into Leo on July 16, neatly dividing the year into almost exactly two halves.

For the first half of the year, growth should be obvious in all areas associated with the sign of Cancer. This includes home building and furnishings, including kitchen wares, home fabrics, household cleaning systems, storage, products for gardens, home security, containers, management systems, services and products to improve animal husbandry, roofing systems, water management, and silver mining.

Companies working in each of these areas and whose shares were first listed as the Sun moved through Cancer should experience growth. Yes, the birthdates of companies have relevance! You will need to do this research yourself to ascertain the incorporation date of a company and draw its natal chart. Jupiter does not begin the year in the first degree of Cancer, so some of these companies may have shone most brightly toward the end of 2013. Those which were listed or first traded with their Sun position later than 9 degrees of Cancer are set to benefit most before July 2014. (This list includes McDonalds, Old Mutual, Invitrogen, and Helen of Troy.)

Note that restaurants have not been included in the list for Cancer. Although Cancer would seem to rule this sector, the correlation doesn't hold here. With food prices high, many of these establishments will surely struggle to achieve adequate profit. The next time Jupiter moves through Cancer, the sunspot cycle will be at a different phase. With food prices then lower, this sector should *then* experience the usual expansion and profit rewards as Jupiter travels through this sign.

Jupiter's Leo transit brings potential for growth to the luxury sector. Jupiter will be in Leo from July 16 through the early months of 2015. As it is, food prices should fall from the end of 2014 onward, hopefully increasing the amount of cash available for other items. Then the luxury sector should experience real growth.

The leisure sector should see expansion from July onward, and not just for high-end products, which is more likely to start gently and build to crescendo later in the year. There is overlap between leisure and sports. There's a high probability that the sports industry will expand after July. Leisure also includes the arts. On the day of Jupiter's Leo ingress, accent is on the sign of Libra (Mars, Ceres, Vesta, and the North Node all occupy it). This suggests a new boost to the arts—theatre especially—and also to the cosmetics and beauty sectors.

Another area that should benefit from this important transit is the film industry. This will be the first time in its history that Jupiter will be in Leo while Neptune is in Pisces. This combination suggests great advance in "fun and imagination." Given the amazing media developments of recent years, it is highly likely that many of the films launched after July 2014 will exceed all known box-office figures, with some headed toward the financial stratosphere. We can narrow the time frame for this by building a planetary picture that includes Jupiter and Neptune and adding Uranus, the planet of the unexpected. One such picture occurs in early September. Films launched around September 4, 2014, could exceed all their financial expectations.

2014 First Quarter

It is often said by astrologers that there is no such thing as a "good" date to launch a business, since every date carries with it the potential for pitfall. The positions of Mercury, Venus, and Mars throughout this first quarter of the year are notable for all the "wrong" commercial reasons; finding a "good" date within this time frame may be akin to finding a needle in the haystack.

The year begins with Venus retrograde, which is rarely a good time to launch a new business, particularly if it involves a partnership. It could be argued that it would be better to wait until early March, when Venus revisits the degree at which the planet stationed on December 21, 2013. Yet early March is problematic in that Mars, Vesta, and Saturn each station prior to retrograde motion. Furthermore, Venus forms a square aspect to Mars on March 2. The early part of March promises to be highly volatile as the lunar node underlines the planetary picture. However, if the early days of the month do indeed prove negative, markets could turn upward after March 4 as those aspects diminish in energy. If a business is to be launched then, it may be possible to find an appropriate date after March 5. While the first three months of the year present real difficulties for start-up companies, the same is unlikely to be true of established ones—or for certain sectors.

Jupiter accelerates through Cancer, forming a trine to Chiron on February 5. The great investor W. D. Gann noted the importance of the solstice and equinoctial dates as well as the halfway points between each. February 5 is very close to one of these points. To have a major planetary phase coincide with this date suggests it is a date of some market significance. It is reasonable to assume that since the signs involved are water ones, and since Jupiter and Chiron are involved, this could be a boon day for the health sector.

Just two days earlier (February 3), the asteroid Ceres will move into Scorpio. Recall from the notes on solar activity that there is an expectation of high food prices at least for the first half of the year. This date could indicate a peak for cereal crop prices. It might also be a positive indicator for those companies whose task is to store and secure food for distribution. These share prices could rise in early February. Further, developments in the health industry and in areas where it is shown that "food is the best medicine" can expect to hear a new superfood being lauded, and for these prices to soar. Investors should still have time to buy into companies harvesting and delivering in this area, since prices should continue on their upward trajectory for some months.

2014 Second Quarter

From our geocentric perspective, a major planetary picture forms as the Sun moves from Aries to Taurus. You will recall that Uranus and Pluto have been at right angles for a few years and that this has coincided with sweeping changes—socially, politically, and economically.

There is high probability that the lunar eclipse of April 15 will coincide with negative market activity. Just a week later—and within the eclipse window (between lunar and solar eclipse when the geomagnetic field is altered)—Mars, Jupiter, Uranus, *and* Pluto form a Grand Cross in the cardinal signs. This rare alignment suggests unusual and harsh vibrations at work, probably resulting in tumbling indices. Increasing bitterness and anger toward those governing the banks of nations could lead to public disorder and political challenge. All the indicators are that this will be a time of military tension and great fiscal pressure.

Added to this, the important Jupiter-Saturn cycle reaches the last 120 degrees of its cycle on May 24. Throughout the twentieth century, this angle coincided with a low in the business cycle. The last week of May may mark the financial low point of the year; the weeks following the lunar eclipse and through late May might see many equity markets fall.

That said, it is worth mentioning that the day before the New York Stock Exchange's "birthday" (May 17), Venus and Uranus form a conjunction. Market reaction to this aspect could be particularly volatile and might even mark a short and sharply positive spike. If markets do indeed fall as expected around the lunar eclipse of April 15, experienced investors could take a short profit by buying in at a low and selling on this May 17 spike. This, though, is a strategy to discuss with your financial advisor before adoption!

A near-vertical rise after this date is unlikely; it's likely that market levels will stay low until at least the solstice on June 21.

Some sectors could take many months to recover. In particular, transport and media sectors may be badly affected. Again, it would be wise to discuss moves with your financial advisor—these shares may reach a low and be considered a "buy."

2014 Third Quarter

If the past does indeed repeat, there are several dates in this quarter when planetary alignments could coincide with significant financial eventfulness here on Earth. Several low points are probable between April and late October, but June 27 stands out most. This should be followed by a little progress from Mercury's direct station on July 1, paving the way for a flurry of positive activity on July 14—most probably affecting European indices and the Euro. Jupiter makes its geocentric Leo ingress on July 16. As noted earlier, this ingress is indicative of advances for leisure industry companies particularly. Given a probable wariness where equities are concerned, you may have time to invest in these even in the last few days of July, when there may still be some bargain-priced stocks available.

Mars joins Saturn in Scorpio in the last week of July, indicating a potential turning point in precious metal and jewel prices. These two planets conjunct on August 25. In the past, this configuration has coincided with mining difficulties. Investors should take note that although the price of these shares may rise after late July, they could fall at the end of August should there be either industrial dispute or calamity. This date could mark a low in both the mining and engineering sectors.

As mentioned earlier in this article, the film and media industry should benefit from planetary configurations in mid-August. Films and similar enterprises launched at this point might see quick and stellar rewards within weeks—even by end of September—despite deep and growing disquiet on the world's financial stage. This wouldn't be the first time this sector has done well while other sectors experienced crisis: similar resonance occurred in the 1920s and '30s.

Saturn conjoins with the asteroid Vesta on September 13 as Mars makes its Sagittarius ingress. This will likely bring difficulties in the currency sectors—most probably affecting the US dollar—and a rise in the price of gold or other hard commodities.

The equinoctial points (roughly March 21 and September 21) often bring days of high volatility, and September 2014 is unlikely to be an exception. This period should be approached very warily indeed. Foreign exchange rates are likely to fluctuate wildly, bringing headaches to both small and large companies and demanding yet again that there is recognition that the world really is a global village.

2014 Fourth Quarter

Throughout 2014 and into early 2015, Uranus and Pluto (from the geocentric perspective) hold an apparent 90-degree angle, which is exact in late 2013. Heliocentrically, this is exact on November 1, 2013. The latter date will be observed closely by astro-traders, since it is recognized that heliocentric aspects often offer hints of things to come.

Planetary positions are not the only technique used by astro-traders. Noting values on significant dates and factoring this information together with favored technical analysis can yield excellent results. There may well be links between November 2013 and December 2014 from the technical as well as the astro-trading perspective.

Since the alignment gained strength in 2010, the vibration of Uranus in Aries with Pluto in another of the cardinal signs, Capricorn, has brought considerable social and economic upheaval—notably the Arab uprising. It is reasonable to assume that these themes will continue into this quarter, with accompanying financial mayhem. A strong possibility is that issues of sovereign debt and government bonds will command attention. It may well be that some countries have no choice but to default on payments. Though this has been suggested in recent years, the clamor for debt to be written off is likely to grow in the second half of 2014.

This last quarter of the year will surely be an uncomfortable period for currency traders, as volatility in this sector demands that traders deal with many unknowns: determining actual value and forecasting the probable action to be taken by governments as they attempt to avert widespread chaos. Key dates are September 27/28, October 6 to the lunar eclipse on October 8, and the solar eclipse on October 23.

The Uranus-Pluto aspect demands that fresh approaches to challenges be taken. Just as attitudes to investment changed when the two planets conjoined in the mid-1960s, it is probable that a new breed of investor will emerge as the right angle between the two planets dissolves. By the close of 2014, the number of people investing in local businesses and family enterprises will surely have increased.

The close of 2014 offers exciting possibilities for those not turned off by trading due to the negative aspects of earlier in the year. Those who choose to invest in local producers and service providers and in those goods and services which they themselves would use are unlikely to be disappointed. The future should show that that many investors "got in at the ground floor" in late 2014 and found rewards within a relatively short time frame.

About the Author

Christeen Skinner is the author of Financial Universe *(2004), in which she forecast the banking crisis. She works in London, UK, and has a broad clientele—from City traders to entrepreneurs to private investors. She taught for the Faculty of Astrological Studies for a half-nodal cycle, was chair of the Astrological Association of Great Britain, and is a trustee of Urania Trust.*

2013 © Victoria Purdie Image from BigStockPhoto.com

New and Full Moon Forecasts for 2014

by Sally Cragin

The first question I ask when presenting an astrology workshop is always, "What is the Moon doing this week? Is it getting bigger, or smaller?" Usually a couple of people get the answer right, and before long we're talking about the planetary influence easiest to explain: the phases of the Moon.

A lunar month is very close to a calendar month: 29.5 days, versus 30 or 31 (not counting February). So each phase takes about a week. That means about six or seven days after the New Moon, you see the second quarter. A week after that, you see the Full Moon, and a week later, the fourth quarter. The final days of the waning Moon are easy to overlook—the Moon is as slim as an open parenthesis in the sky. By understanding its phases, our appreciation of the Moon will only deepen, and the following almanac of New and Full Moons includes other celestial objects to look for (planets, meteor showers, and star clusters).

Between the **New Moon** and Full Moon comes the **second quarter**. Overall, this two-week waxing phase is useful for starting projects. Folklorical customs that accompany the New Moon include jingling the change in your pocket when you first see it for good luck. Between that second quarter and the Full Moon, action gets more intense. A project or relationship that has begun could accelerate quickly. The **gibbous Moon** occurs when the Moon is well past second quarter and close to the Full Moon phase. As more of the Moon is revealed, the pace gets hectic. This is when lots of folks ask the question: is it a Full Moon or what?

Between the **Full Moon** and the New Moon comes the **fourth-quarter Moon**. I have clients who are born at the time of the Full Moon who are sensation seekers, craving excitement and activity. (Those born around the time of the New Moon are more reticent, guarded, and even vulnerable.) Just after the Moon is Full, the waning period begins. You will see the shadow of the Earth crossing the Moon from right to left. This waning phase is about getting results, but it's also a time when you may lose interest in a project or decide that a relationship isn't working. Are your phone calls not being returned? If you're trying to make a meeting happen with multiple groups of people, aim for the phase between second and fourth quarter. After the fourth quarter, when the Moon is in its **balsamic** stage and near New, new projects won't fly. This time is helpful for cleaning or removing items. The day before the New Moon is the "dark of the Moon"—definitely hold off on decisions until after the New Moon!

January

For the last two weeks of the month, Venus (attraction), Mars (taking action), and Jupiter (good fortune) are in an astrological position called a T-Square (yes, like the carpentry tool). This may make for intolerance among loved ones and potential over-indulgence in regard to emotions. After the Yuletide hullabaloo, some folks may need more love and attention than they're getting, particularly cardinal Sun signs Aries, Cancer, Libra, and Capricorn (usually so independent).

Wednesday, January 1, New Moon in Capricorn. The sign of the goat rules structures, building, lessons learned, and instruction. I vacillate about having New Year's resolutions, but this January 1 looks tremendously positive for making—and keeping—vows. Scorpio, Sagittarius, Capricorn, Aquarius, Pisces, Taurus, and Virgo may have bold new ideas to get organized, get in shape, or get solvent. Aries, Libra, and Cancer could feel vexed or at odds with others, while Leo and Gemini could be persuadable. These last folks may be overwhelmed by someone with a more dynamic or decisive personality.

Wednesday, January 15, Full Moon in Cancer. Jupiter and Mars are in harmony right now, so bakers and cooks should be creative in the kitchen. This is the Winter Moon, also known as the Holiday Moon for the Chinese. Playing with clay, getting a massage, and soothing your stomach with rich baked goods will all be enjoyable activities. Taurus, Gemini, Cancer, Leo, Virgo, Scorpio, and Pisces have deep insights into loved ones and their own domestic environment. Aries, Libra, and Capricorn may not be acting on all the information available (be aware of acting impulsively—it's easy to go over the top). Aquarius and Sagittarius could surprise themselves by being sentimental or emotional.

Thursday, January 30, New Moon in Aquarius. Innovation rules and going by the book is old school. Eccentric friends beat a path to your door. Escapism makes long winter days shorter—when is the last time you indulged in a multi-part fantasy novel, film, or TV series? This is a superb time for making travel plans with faraway friends. Sagittarius, Capricorn, Aquarius, Pisces, Aries, Gemini, Libra, Cancer, and Virgo: don't be satisfied with the same old, same old. You're crying out for something novel, and you'll settle for nothing less. Taurus, Leo, and Scorpio: unreliable folks could irritate you more than usual. You're happy with predictability from others, though you reserve the right to be intermittently reliable.

February

Mercury retrogrades from February 6 through 27. Mercury retrograde generally creates (or increases) chaos relating to miscommunication, misdirection, or information that's corrupted. If your electronic devices get compromised, hold on to any receipts you may have obtained in the course of repairs. This month, Venus (love) and Mars (passion) are increasingly at odds with each other, so by the end of February, some friendships may be frayed. However, with Jupiter and Uranus opposing each other, you may make some interesting, even quirky, new friends.

Friday, February 14, Full Moon in Leo. Happy Valentine's Day! Childlike interests, pursuits, or preoccupations could dominate. Deploy chocolate and flowers where necessary in the workplace or in your personal life. Leo Moons are all about performance, advertising, and partying, so if you have a Valentine's Day gala in the works, you're sure to have a jolly time. Gemini, Cancer, Leo, Virgo, Libra, Sagittarius, Aries, Pisces, and Capricorn: do something fun with your hair! Taurus, Scorpio, and Aquarius: you could misread the motives or actions of others. Before you take offense, check in with a more rational friend.

March

Mars (being proactive) retrogrades this month, which could delay forward momentum for Libra folks, as well as Capricorn, Aries, and Cancer. From March 27 forward, Venus (friend-making) and Saturn (teaching) make a difficult angle to each other. If you are female, and you have an older male mentor—or you have a difficult father—problems may emerge that find you wanting to press the escape button and disappear! Neptune and Mercury are in harmony and conjunct around March 22–25 in Pisces, the sign of Neptune's rulership. Those are super days for making art, hearing secrets, or standing up for those who can't speak for themselves.

Saturday, March 1, New Moon in Pisces. When the Moon is in the sign of the fish, artistic pursuits are favored, particularly photography, and working backstage. If you're someone who's always quietly pulling the strings behind the curtain, this New Moon gives you an opportunity to assess your own usefulness—and also evaluate whether it's time for *you* to step out on center stage. Capricorn, Aquarius, Pisces, Aries, Taurus, Cancer, Scorpio, Leo, and Libra: this lunar phase is bringing out your sentimental side. Is this a good thing? If you're usually "hardcore" about your relationships and interactions, so you may enjoy being less intense. Virgo, Gemini, and Sagittarius: you may feel overly sensitive or easily irritated by the follies of others, especially those who don't do what they say they'll do. Now that you know, you should be able to handle this more suavely.

Sunday, March 16, Full Moon in Virgo. Dealing with your health, renewing vows to exercise, or getting involved with a charity are all wise activities that feed your body and soul. Virgo concerns itself with work matters also, and if you've been in your present job for a while (particularly 19 months, 3.5 years, 7 years, 10.5 years, 14 years, 17.5 years), this is a promising weekend for perusing the classified ads to see what's out there. This is doubly true if your current job is stressing you out to the point of illness! Super-perceptiveness could be the story for Cancer, Leo, Virgo, Libra, Scorpio, Capricorn, Taurus, Aries, and Aquarius. Gemini, Sagittarius, and Pisces: watch your reactions to others, particularly if you are hearing information that (a) doesn't give you full credit; or (b) seems super critical. This cuts both ways, and you three signs could also be highly picky right now.

Sunday, March 30, New Moon in Aries. The spring equinox is behind us, and this Full Moon in Aries heralds the beginning of the zodiacal year. Aries Moons are about completing tasks quickly or getting in touch with your own impulses. Figure that spring fever is definitely on the menu. If you've been mired in procrastination or other delays, taking flight comes easily, particularly for Aquarius, Pisces, Aries, Taurus, Gemini, Leo, Sagittarius, Scorpio, and Virgo. Impatience could make life difficult for Libra, Capricorn, and Cancer. You three may find that others don't take projects as seriously as you do.

April

April brings the sweet spring showers and a burst of renewed energy for all. Now that days are getting longer, even Mars (argumentativeness) retrograding in Libra won't keep anyone down for long. Astrologically, a difficult angle combining Mars, Jupiter (indulgence), and Uranus (freedom) suggests that forward momentum will be compromised. On a global scale, some eccentric new character may emerge on the world scene to delight (or dismay) us all.

Tuesday, April 15, Full Moon in Libra. Tax day craziness! The Moon in Libra brings out a spirit of sociability, although some folks (Cancer, Capricorn, and Aries) could feel touchy or indecisive. If you're having difficulties with people with those birthdays, give them some space. Leo, Virgo, Libra, Scorpio, Sagittarius, Gemini, Aquarius, Taurus, and Pisces: look for opportunities to bring harmony, particularly in the workplace or with a partnership. This lunar phase is also helpful for home decor or buying some lovely new spring outfit to lift your winter-worn spirits.

Tuesday, April 29, New Moon in Taurus. The Taurus New Moon could awaken a desire to redecorate your home or to review your financial papers (now that taxes are behind you). Have you looked at your investments recently? This is also a tremendous week for spring cleaning—get rid of items that are broken, bruised, worn, or ignored. Pisces, Aries, Taurus, Gemini, Cancer, Virgo, Capricorn, Libra, and Sagittarius are in a sociable mood and may be drawn to gatherings of new folks or events where they can network. Leo, Scorpio, and Aquarius: clean up, but be patient with others. This Moon could find you irritable.

May

Mars (taking action) now finishes retrograde and moves forward in Libra. May also finds Jupiter (enthusiasm) and Uranus (insights) making an awkward angle. Being a spendthrift could come easily to Capricorn and Libra (who are usually pretty sensible with their money). Mother's Day favors everyone but particularly fire-sign moms (Aries, Leo, and Sagittarius), who will be dynamic with their loved ones and able to communicate more clearly than usual.

Wednesday, May 14, Full Moon in Scorpio. Feel the heat? Spring fever should be at a peak during this Full Moon, particularly for Scorpio, Pisces, Cancer, Gemini, Libra, Virgo, Sagittarius, Capricorn, and Aries. Scorpio Moons are also sensual, so even though it's the middle of the week, you may need to put on those red shoes or form-flattering garment and strut your stuff. Taurus, Leo, and Aquarius: make sure you do a lengthy mirror-check before heading out—this Moon could be awkward for you. Cutting to the chase or getting to the heart of a matter comes easily. You may find the most simple question elicits true confessions from sensitive people in your circle.

Wednesday, May 28, New Moon in Gemini. Gemini Moons encourage and bring out communication skills, so if you like to write, email, text, or just plain yak, you'll have plenty to say to others. Gemini Moons can also make people better at communicating, so if you're shopping with a friend, you should have useful conversations about items you're attracted to. Aries, Taurus,

Gemini, Cancer, Leo, Libra, Aquarius, Scorpio, and Capricorn: reach out to new people. This Moon sign encourages new friendships, particularly with people in your peer group. Virgo, Pisces, and Sagittarius: indecision could delay or derail your plans. Are you being consistent about taking care of the important items first? (For example, making sure the rent is paid before putting down that money for plane fare.) You may find that everyone has a strong opinion during this Moon phase—a strong opinion that changes a moment later.

June

The halfway point of the year finds another Mercury retrograde (May 7–July 1). Double-check directions, since summer months are when people travel most. Is there anything more frustrating than embarking on an excursion and finding that your map or the instructions you received are all wrong? June 12–16 finds Venus (friend-making) and Saturn (commitment) opposing each other. If you're looking to get a "whole new look," you may want to think twice before hopping into the salon chair.

Friday, June 13, Full Moon in Sagittarius. Despite Mercury retrograde, this is a promising period to get more information in a variety of arenas, including justice, summer school, or travel (this is the famous Honey Moon). Some folks find Friday the 13th gives them the willies, but look at it this way: it's Friday. Isn't that better than Wednesday? Libra, Scorpio, Sagittarius, Capricorn, Aquarius, Aries, Leo, Taurus, and Cancer: you could be dynamic and attractive to everyone, especially when you keep your sense of humor. Pisces, Virgo, and Gemini could be accident-prone—move slowly and deliberately.

Friday, June 27, New Moon in Cancer. This New Moon could find everyone slightly over-sensitive (and not just because of Mercury retrograde). If you're feeling vulnerable and just want to cocoon, give yourself a gold star, because that's the message Lady Moon is sending. This lunar phase also puts you in the mood for baking, getting a massage, or working with your hands. Some folks—particularly water signs Cancer, Scorpio, and Pisces—could be feeling "psychic" right now, and you three as well as Taurus, Gemini, Leo, Virgo, Sagittarius, and Aquarius have the ability to see deeply into others' vulnerabilities. Capricorn, Libra, and Aries could be feeling confused or low-energy and shouldn't make decisions if they can help it.

July

The month in which the Crab takes center stage is also the month in which the Lion takes over from the Crab in Jupiter (generosity, lucky breaks). For the next twelve months or so, Leos will have opportunities galore: job offers, lucky breaks, and romantic indulgence. Look back to 2002 if you want to get a sense of the "good stuff" heading in your direction. However, the other eleven signs have some harmonious planetary alignments as well. With Venus (attraction) and Mars (action) making helpful angles to one another in air signs, having clarity in your romantic and personal relationships will come easily.

Saturday, July 12, Full Moon in Capricorn. Take another look at the structure in your life, such as routines or habits, as well as details in your abode. Do you have squeaky hinges or broken fixtures? This Full Moon nurtures practicality, and you may find that just identifying a problem (a leaky faucet) and taking a trip to the hardware store makes for an easy fix. If you look further and examine your career or your educational level, you can see whether you need to make substantive change in your skills set. The worldwide recession may be over for some, but if that's not the case for you, consider training that will make you more desirable. (Yes, everyone else is thinking vacation, but you can be the smart one thinking long-term advantages.) Scorpio, Sagittarius, Capricorn, Aquarius, Pisces, Taurus, Virgo, Leo, and Gemini will want to simplify their life and perhaps be a little bit miserly. Normally accommodating Aries, Libra, and Cancer could be skeptical or even rude to others.

Saturday, July 26, New Moon in Leo. Some New Moons (like the wintertime New Moon in Capricorn, or the springtime New Moon in Pisces) can make life slow or bring out the procrastinating urge. Not so for fire-sign New Moons, which can put the "can do" into relationships or other projects, especially those just beginning. A Leo New Moon can bring out your childish, pleasure-seeking side—which can be lots of fun and should be enjoyed by Gemini, Cancer, Leo, Virgo, Libra, Capricorn, Pisces, Aries, and Sagittarius. The planets are telling you to be social and get a new toy! Taurus, Scorpio, and Aquarius may find they feel highly sensitive, especially around folks who may not understand how complex or self-conscious they are.

August

With the Sun in merry, fun-seeking Leo, it's easy to have a good time, especially since this month Jupiter (good fortune) has joined Mercury (communication) and Venus (affection). August 23 to the end of the month finds Venus and Mars making difficult angles to each other—this could find you attracted to someone who's usually not your type, or it could create those May/December romances that others like to talk about.

Sunday, August 10, Full Moon in Aquarius. Escape to fantasy island—wouldn't that be nice? If you're on vacation right now, you'll be drawn to the eccentrics in your environment, or the folks who deliberately upset the applecart. And if you're not on vacation, you may want to listen to crazy theories or get in touch with faraway friends. For Sagittarius, Capricorn, Aquarius, Pisces, Aries, Gemini, Libra, Virgo, and Cancer, being a rebel comes easily and feels pretty good. Taurus, Leo, and Scorpio may temporarily admire those who buck the system, but it's not recommended that you follow in their path—some folks get away with mischief, while others are destined to be caught.

Monday, August 25, New Moon in Virgo. Being touchy or critical comes with this Moon. So does working in a garden or taking a good look at your health plan or medical practitioners. This New Moon may bring a desire to explore non-conventional health remedies as well as charitable impulses. Are you helping a friend who really doesn't need it? Be smart about your resources, even if you feel like you can afford to take a chance. Cancer, Leo, Virgo, Libra, Scorpio, Capricorn, Taurus, Aquarius, and Sagittarius: you've got great instincts and work ethic (even though it's still those "lazy crazy days of summer"). Pisces, Gemini, and Sagittarius: being profligate with your talents or funds may feel good (especially if you're feeling a guilt trip from others), but it's not the best long-term move.

September

In the Northern Hemisphere, the days are shortening, but not as so most of us would notice, and September brings a snap to the air. There are some recommended weekends for parties coming up, including Labor Day weekend and September 19/20. Mars (assertiveness) and Saturn (lessons learned) are in introspective Scorpio for the first half of the month, which could put the brakes on romances that were going just great earlier in the summer. This month most of the Western world gets back to business—and that's not a bad thing, although Sagittarius, Pisces, Virgo, and Gemini could be restless and looking for a change of job.

Monday, September 8, Full Moon in Pisces. Do you like the arts? Do you make a point of getting theater or concert tickets? Make that effort now, as this lunar phase is promising for enjoying performance, music, or visual arts. It's also a good time for you to create your own masterpiece. Make the time and you will shine. You can explore places that would otherwise be inaccessible to you.

Since Pisces rules prisons, photography, x-rays, and subconscious motives, you shouldn't take anything at face value, but don't tip your hand if you need to ask questions or not accept the status quo. Capricorn, Aquarius, Pisces, Aries, Taurus, Cancer, Scorpio, Libra, and Leo will be curious about others' motives and may discover a sympathy for the downtrodden. Gemini, Sagittarius, and Virgo: you're easily swayed right now. Retreat rather than advance.

Wednesday, September 24, New Moon in Libra. Joni Mitchell's song "Both Sides Now" has some guidance for all this month: looking at both sides doesn't mean you'll see anything clearly, but you may enjoy the activity anyway. Partnership is a preoccupation for some, and strengthening friendships or work alliances is a smart move, particularly for Leo, Virgo, Libra, Scorpio, Sagittarius, Gemini, Aquarius, Pisces, and Taurus. Exaggeration could be a danger for Capricorn, Aries, and Cancer. You three may also have a blunted sensibility and hear agreement where there is none, or see possibility in a closed door.

October

Time for another Mercury retrograde, October 4–24. Those of you who are in school may find that you're mishearing your instructors, and if you don't have a logical system for keeping your email files straight, an event this month may make it imperative that you figure that puppy out! However, the useful part of Mercury retrograde is how it encourages us all to be creative and to come up with an unexpected solution.

Wednesday, October 8, Full Moon in Aries. Shine on, Harvest Moon—you'll bring good luck for Aquarius, Pisces, Aries, Taurus, Gemini, Leo, Sagittarius, Scorpio, and Virgo, although the eclipse this month says "wait before taking action." Aries Moons bring a desire for a fresh start or a new opportunity. However, this Moon also brings out the "get rich quick" desire in even the most stable personalities. Physical fitness should be a pursuit for all, especially exercise that clears your head. But some folks will find that it's hard to focus, and Capricorn, Cancer, and Libra may be (unintentionally) a wet blanket if they're around others who strike them as too enthusiastic.

Thursday, October 23, New Moon in Scorpio. This month has an eclipse, and Mercury retrograde continues through Friday. Are you having quirky insights or feeling like you just want to cut and run? Reducing a project to small parts makes sense. If it seems like others aren't willing to commit, don't press them. Scorpio Moons can make some folks retreat, and for Taurus, Leo, and Aquarius, that's a good thing; the lunar phase is clouding your judgment and bringing out an urge to "fix" others, which may not be in your best interest. Virgo, Libra, Scorpio, Sagittarius, Capricorn, Pisces, Cancer, Gemini, and Aries: give in to your sensual side—you'll be glad you did.

November

With Mars in logical Capricorn—making friendly angles to the Sun, Jupiter (good luck), Venus (attractiveness), and Saturn (learning limits)—work matters should move along swiftly and competently. This month's astrological transits help people to be better workers or be more dedicated to their craft. Personal relationships may have moments of unexpected frankness and sincerity, and if there's something you haven't told a loved one, don't be shy. However, be cautious about airing controversial or half-baked notions to a group. Since Mercury (communication) and Jupiter (generosity) are in a problematic relationship with one another during Thanksgiving this year, there may be tensions on the homefront.

Thursday, November 6, Full Moon in Taurus. This Full Moon rules the home and banking. Interested in a new interior design? Can you afford what you want? This Full Moon offers assistance and can help you create the home environment you crave. Pisces, Aries, Taurus, Gemini, Cancer, Virgo, Capricorn, Libra, and Sagittarius: possessiveness or acquisitiveness could be a strong urge. What is it you need? It's out there somewhere! It's a similar story for Scorpio, Leo, and Aquarius: possessiveness or acquisitiveness could be a strong urge. Do you really need an object? Or just a sounding board and fellowship? Be clear with yourself about what is missing in your life.

Saturday, November 22, New Moon in Sagittarius. A weekend in which sensual delights beckon, as do overindulgence and escapism. With Thanksgiving around the corner, the holiday hootenanny begins, but today's New Moon brings out a desire for solitude or introspection. Taurus, Leo, and Aquarius: no matter how much frankness you are hearing, the whole story has yet to be told. Virgo, Libra, Scorpio, Sagittarius, Capricorn, Pisces, Cancer, Gemini, and Aries: you may need to reconsider a family story—for example, what you were told isn't what actually happened. Pursue clarity as needed.

December

For the most part, we'll all feel things settle down thanks to lots of planets moving into Capricorn, including the Sun (identity), Mercury (messages), and Venus (social cohesion). However, with Mars (aggression) entering Aquarius, everyone's taste in fantasy or quirky entertainment goes into another realm. This will be an excellent month for those who work in computer programming or customer relations—electricians and "trend spotters" will also be at their best. Yule and Christmas occur during the crescent Moon phase, so the waxing Moon will (hopefully) keep the stress and tension some folks feel during Christmas to a minimum.

Saturday, December 6, Full Moon in Gemini. This is the Long Night Moon. Themes during this Full Moon include details and drama, sibling or peer heart-to-hearts, and surprising partnerships. December generally finds people in a mood to celebrate, so even if you're feeling accident-prone (Virgo, Sagittarius, and Pisces), allow yourself some merriment. Aries, Taurus, Gemini, Cancer, Leo, Libra, Aquarius, Scorpio, and Capricorn: work on creating new partnerships or deepening the ones you have.

Sunday, December 21, New Moon in Sagittarius. The New Moon brings hope and possibility, so if you've put off your holiday shopping, it will be easier to get into a groove this week. Sagittarius Moons bring out the restless side of us all, but make sure you have all the information before embarking on a series of visits or traveling. From now through the new year, the Moon is waxing incrementally, and you may find that you're finally in the holiday spirit around December 28! Libra, Scorpio, Sagittarius, Capricorn, Aquarius, Cancer, and Taurus: you're feeling generous toward others, but make sure your giving really is without expectation. Gemini, Virgo, and Pisces: this is a creative period for you, but it's also a time when you will feel overburdened or guilty (in a vague way). Give yourself a break and don't feel you need to "fill in the blanks" if there are silent moments in conversation.

About the Author

Sally Cragin is a teacher and the author of Astrology on the Cusp *for people whose birthdays are at the end of one Sun sign or the beginning of the next. Her first book was* The Astrological Elements, *both with Llewellyn Worldwide. She has written the astrological forecast "Moon Signs" for the* Boston Phoenix, *syndicated throughout New England. Reelected to the Fitchburg, MA, School Committee, she is the only professional astrologer holding elected office in New England. She also provides forecasts for clients that are "cool, useful and accurate." More at Moonsigns.net.*

2014
Moon Sign Book
Articles

The Moon as Calendar and Timepiece

by Susan Pesznecker

Note: This article is Northern Hemisphere–centric, and all points of observation and movement are given from this perspective. Also, these points will be most accurate when seen closest to the mid-latitudes, e.g., the 45th parallel.

To us earthlings, the Moon is a strange, inhospitable place. It's airless and gritty with no discernible atmosphere, and what water is on the Moon is either frozen or hidden underground. Since the Moon has no atmosphere, it never has fog or clouds. For that matter, it has no weather. It also has no global magnetic field and very little gravity. Because the Moon lacks an atmosphere, the Moon's "sky"—to someone standing on its surface— would look black, even at midday. If you were able to walk on its surface, you would leave footprints in a surface that—although dry—felt something like dense, wet sand.

Unusual as these physical characteristics seem to us earthly mortals, the Moon is a happily familiar sight when we gaze into the night sky. And thanks to cycles of rotation and celestial motion that are both constant and continuous, we needn't simply admire them from afar; we can also use the Moon to judge time of day and the passing of each month.

The Moon orbits the Earth once every 27.3 days. This is called its sidereal (sye-DEAR-ee-ull, "with respect to the stars") period. However as seen from Earth, it takes the Moon 29.53 days to complete its phases. This is called the Moon's synodic (sih-NOD-ick, "with respect to the Sun") period, and this is the cycle we follow here on Earth.

Rule number one in tracking the Moon's movements is that it always rises in the eastern sky and sets in the west. However, rising positions may vary by as much as 60 degrees along the horizon; this is due to an 18.6-year cycle of repeated movements between the Sun and Moon. This means that while you may notice a Full Moon rise at a specific point on your horizon, the Full Moon you observe the following month may rise at a differ-ent point, north or south of the previous month's position. If you tracked these risings over 18.6 years, the Sun and Moon's con-stant slow-dance pattern would become apparent.

The Moon also sequences through eight phases over each monthly lunar cycle, which are described in terms of "waxing" (growing) or "waning" (shrinking). Of course, the Moon isn't changing at all; what we see as phases has to do with (a) whether the Moon is visible above the horizon and (b) how much of the Moon's visible surface it lit by the Sun. The latter is determined by the geometrical relationship between Earth, Moon, and Sun. A Full Moon occurs when the Moon and Sun are on opposite sides of the Earth, while a New (dark) Moon occurs when the Sun and Moon are on the same side.

Here is the procession of phases:

New Moon: This is the completely dark Moon, with the lunar face unlit.

Waxing crescent: The first appearance of the waxing crescent is a thin sliver, but eventually up to one-fourth of the Moon's surface appears as a lit crescent.

Waxing half (also called the first quarter): the "right half" of the Moon is lit, with the left dark.

Waxing gibbous: The Moon approaches being full; three-fourths of the Moon is lit.

Full Moon: The round, bright Moon is fully lit.

Waning gibbous: The Moon begins to darken; three-fourths of the Moon is still lit.

Waning half (also called the third quarter): the "left half" of the Moon is lit, with the right dark.

Waning crescent: Only a crescent (up to one-fourth of the Moon) remains lit.

New Moon: A return to the completely dark Moon.

Moon as Timepiece

The Moon phases always rise and set at about the same times:

Moon Phase		Rises	Sets
New Moon	●	6:00 am	6:00 pm
Waxing crescent	◑	9:00 am	9:00 pm
Waxing half	◑	12:00 pm (noon)	12:00 am (midnight)
Waxing gibbous	◐	3:00 pm	3:00 am
Full Moon	○	6:00 pm	6:00 am
Waning gibbous	◗	9:00 pm	9:00 am
Waning half	◗	12:00 am (midnight)	12:00 pm (noon)
Waning crescent	◑	3:00 am	3:00 pm

Do you see the pattern, by which each phase rises and sets about three hours later than the one before it? (6:00 pm, 9:00 pm, midnight, etc.) Of course, there are some Moon phases that we will never or only rarely see. At the mid-latitudes, there is typically enough sunlight available early in the morning that we cannot see the New Moon rise, and it sets before dark; even if it stayed above the horizon after sunset, its completely dark face would make it very difficult to locate. In more northern latitudes, with longer periods of darkness and shorter days, the New Moon and phases closer to the New Moon may be briefly spotted.

Do you see—via the table above—that the Moon always rises and sets in twelve-hour cycles (rises at 6:00 am and sets at 6:00 pm, etc.)? To make these visual calculations even more precise, it helps to know that the Moon rises an average of fifty minutes later each night than on the previous night. Thus, if the Full Moon rises at precisely 6:00 pm, the (waning gibbous) Moon the next night will rise at 6:50, the next night at 7:40, and so forth. In each case, the Moon will always reach its highest point above the horizon halfway (six hours) through each phase.

Once you understand how the phases work and can memorize at least one Moon rise/set time, you can work out the others in your head and can use those to approximate local time. Observe which phase of the Moon you are seeing, then approximately where in its twelve-hour journey it is. Reference the following illustration and these examples:

If you observed a waxing half Moon (with the right side "lit") high in the sky, you'd know it was somewhere around 6:00 pm, give or take an hour. This would be the phase's sunrise (12:00 pm) plus six hours.

If you saw a waxing crescent setting in the west during early evening, you'd know it was around 6:00 or 7:00 pm—sunrise of 9:00 am plus nine hours.

If you were out early in the morning and could see a waning

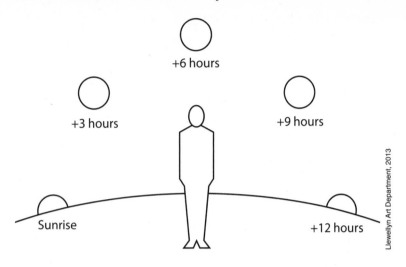

+6 hours

+3 hours

+9 hours

Sunrise

+12 hours

Llewellyn Art Department, 2013

gibbous Moon low in the western sky, you'd guess it was between 6:00 and 7:00 am—rising time of 9:00 pm plus nine hours.

Moon as Calendar

While the lunar phases don't always show anything about the passing of seasons, per se, those of us deeply attuned to the Moon are able to follow the passing of each month by watching the Moon's phases and appearance. Example: the phenomenon known as the Harvest Moon refers to the Full Moon falling closest to the autumnal equinox, which is on or around September 21 or 22. This Moon received its name because the light it sheds was said to help farmers work longer days when bringing in their crops. Many believe the Harvest Moon appears bigger or brighter than other Full Moons, but that's not actually true. The appearance is a visual effect of the "Moon illusion," which means that a Full Moon close to the horizon always appears larger than one higher in the sky.

The Harvest Moon also behaves differently than other Full Moons; because of the shallow angle between the eastern horizon and the solar ecliptic (the path the Sun appears—to our view—to follow through the sky) occurring around the autumnal equinox, the Harvest Moon rises only thirty minutes later than the Moon of the previous night. Because it stays closer to the horizon, it appears bigger than usual (the Moon illusion again), and because it is low in the sky, it is viewed through particulate matter in the lower atmosphere, often causing it to take on a golden-orange color. This early-rising behavior is repeated by the Hunter's Moon, the first Full Moon that follows the autumn equinox. The Hunter's Moon is so-named because the bright moonlight helps hunters stalk migrating waterfowl.

Because the Harvest and Hunter's Moons rise so quickly—right around sunset—the usual long periods of darkness or semidarkness between sunset and moonrise are absent. Compare that to deep winter, when night falls quickly between 4:00 and 4:30 pm, leaving one or two hours of darkness before the Full Moon rises.

Do you want to have more experience with the Moon as a timepiece? Study the Moon table on page 252 until you have it memorized, then practice using Moon phases to tell time. Or, you might do what apprentices used to do long ago: spend weeks, months, or even a year tracking the Moon's rising times, locations, and movements through the night sky, writing down and sketching your observations. There's no better way to deepen your connections to our favorite celestial body.

Resources

Rees, Martin, ed. *Universe: The Definitive Visual Guide*. DK Publishing, 2005.

About the Author

Susan is a mother, writer, nurse, hearth Pagan, and Druid living in northwest Oregon. In her spare time, she is an organic gardener and herbalist who loves to read, take long walks with her wonder poodle, camp, play with rocks, and look up at the stars. Susan teaches astronomy and celestial magicks in the online Grey School and is the author of three books. www.susanpesznecker.com

Ancient World Lunar Myths

by Sally Cragin

Imagine it's thousands of years ago. You're sitting on a beach watching the night sky emerge. There are no electric lights—just a tapestry of stars that covers the sky as it if were a bowl. And then—drama! A gigantic white orb emerges from the east and begins to cross the ebony blanket, obscuring various twinkling lights as it moves along. You look more closely—is that a face? Can you make out eyes and a mouth? But this orb, the Moon, keeps moving until it is overhead. And then it begins its slow descent to the west.

In the far distant past, back when humans lived in small nomadic bands, people may well have crouched in fear at the appearance of the Moon. But some five thousand years ago, when family bands had turned into larger community groups, we began looking at the night sky with curiosity and wonder. The ancient

Egyptians thought the Moon was ruled by the god Osiris, who died and returned every month. They also decided the Moon was ruled by the scarab beetle, the emblem of the soul. The Greeks also came up with the idea of an animal, but they determined that the crab was a better representation. So they came up with the astrological sign of Cancer, whose ruling planet is the Moon.

Since I've been writing a column called "Moon Signs," for the *Boston Phoenix* (and other) newspapers for many years, I've thought a lot about the phases of the Moon, as well as about the rhythms of the lunar transits as they unfold over months and years. One of my aims in the column has been to get readers familiar and comfortable with a 29.5-day pattern. Understanding that it's inevitable that one's energy may be at a low ebb at times is sensible. Taking advantage of opportunities or pushing action forward during the time of the waxing and Full Moons means being in tune with our nearest satellite. Even if we don't live near a body of water, we can "feel" the phases of the Moon as it grows large and then small.

When I speak to groups about astrology, I always begin by saying that every culture on the planet has developed an interesting and dynamic mythology that explains the night sky—the moving planets, the Moon, and fixed stars. What I found when I began researching this essay was marked similarities among some distant cultures' stories, while other tales are completely unique.

Greek and Roman

We must start with the Greeks—key to much of our modern understanding of the world. We have them to thank for many tools, as well as the craft of astrology itself. Without the Greeks, we might not have modern geometry, which is necessary for understanding the mathematics of an astrological chart. The Greeks also provided us with the rich imagery of a system of gods with specific purposes, as well as a fair amount of latitude when it came to capriciousness!

I loved Greek mythology growing up and marveled at how each god or goddess displayed their various traits. My favorite god was Hephaestus (Vulcan to the Romans), the crippled god of the forge. As a child who loved making crafts and working with clay, stained glass, and metalwork, his dedication to his work really spoke to me. (As did his wife, Athena, but man, did she need a sense of humor!)

But I also revered Artemis (Diana for the Romans), the huntress and sister of the Sun god Apollo. Those of us who are nocturnal can always identify with rulers of the Moon, and Artemis was remarkably dedicated to what she did (archery). She was also happily on her own. She was a virgin, she was quick to anger, and she struck me as having more substance than flighty Aphrodite, who was so easily besotted by beauty versus depth of character.

But it wasn't until I took an excellent class in Classical Drama taught by renowned classicist professor Greg Nagy that I learned that Artemis is the goddess you want on your side during childbirth. Here's what Phaedra says in Euripedes's ancient play *Hippolytus*: "In women's difficult tuning [harmonia], a bad, wretched sort of helplessness often makes its abode arising both from birth pains and irrationality. This breeze once shot through my womb, but I called upon the heavenly helper in labor, the guardian of the arrows, Artemis, and she, much envied, always comes to me with the help of the gods." Isn't that a great image? The idea of a goddess shooting an arrow to relieve the titanic cramps and discomfort of childbirth really resonated during the births of my two children.

However, the Moon is such an important player in the night sky that there are actually a host of Greek and Roman gods and beings associated with her. You've probably heard of Selene, the traditional Greek Moon goddess. Selene was a Titan, later replaced by Artemis, an Olympian, as the lore evolved. My research showed that Selene is usually represented as being literally Moon-like, with a round face and figure; she represents the Moon at its most full phase. Artemis usually had a crescent Moon as part of her costume or associated symbols. Selene's siblings are Helios (the Sun) and Eos (the dawn). In Homeric hymns (900 BCE or so), Selene is usually referenced as being "bright" or "richly tressed," which also suggests the idea of the Full Moon.

The Greeks also recognized Pasiphae, the daughter of Sun god Helios, who possessed the magical powers of witchcraft. Pasiphae may not be well known to you, but you probably know about her story. She was the wife of King Minos of Crete, and the gods cursed her to fall in love with a bull. Their offspring, the Minotaur, was then encased in the center of a magnificent maze constructed by Daedalus, the master builder. Daedalus's son was, of course, Icarus, of the waxen wings.

Another goddess associated with witchcraft and the Moon is Hekate (also Hecate), who ruled magic as well as the night Moon. She is best known for assisting Demeter after daughter Persephone was kidnapped by Hades and taken to the underworld. Hekate is often pictured as illuminating the night with a flaming torch. After the rescue, when Persephone needed to return to the underworld to fulfill her part of the bargain (remember, she ate those pomegranate seeds), Hekate went with her as a companion.

Greeks and other communities with agricultural practices had stories about the waning and waxing of the Moon and a connection to crops, planting, and weeding. But the Moon also plays an important role in another regular activity in the ancient world: warfare. Thucydides, the great writer of the fifth century BCE, chronicled a variety of battles and skirmishes in his *History of the Peloponnesian War*. He was scrupulous about documenting the Moon's influence. Here's an extract (translated by Richard Crawley) about an episode that was difficult for the Athenians (the heroes in the narrative): "Although there was a bright Moon they saw each other only as men do by Moonlight, that is to say, they could distinguish the form of the body, but could not tell for certain whether it was a friend or an enemy."

Even today, our armed forces rely on the movements of the Moon for influencing various military sorties, and the small band of Navy SEALS who captured Osama Bin Laden in Pakistan in 2011 were dispatched during the darkest part of the month.

But back to the Greeks. When I talk to groups about astrology, I always preface comments by saying that no matter what your views on the influence of planets and Moon, you have to admit that no other group of people pegged all the quirks, vicissitudes, and characteristics of the human experience as succinctly as the Greeks did in their pantheon of gods and dramatic characters. The Greeks got there first, but let us not forget the Romans, who energetically retold and amplified some of the legends to suit their own purposes.

Every so often, the popular culture gets infatuated with vampires and werewolves, and various creatures of the night. But did you know that the legend of werewolves goes all the way back to the Roman poet Ovid? Every philosopher/poet gave their version of the "ages of man" (beginning with gold, ending with base metal), and Ovid had a lot of fun with the origin of the werewolf—half human, half wolf. In his version, the god Jupiter comes to earth to see what's going on with humans, who have entered an age of decadence (a regular theme in most Classical literature). He travels through wild parts of the country, including remote forests filled with wild beasts. Of course he's in disguise, but the residents slowly recognize a god in their midst and begin to worship Jupiter.

However, some of the villagers resist piety and want to continue their wicked ways. The worst of them is an evil king, Lycaon. He is outraged at the idea of someone "pretending" they are a god, and so he invites Jupiter to dinner. What's on the menu? A murdered hostage. Lycaon does the butchering himself and then boils some joints and roasts others.

When he serves this cannibal's feast to Jupiter—defying the laws of the age and the custom of hospitality—the god can take no more. As soon as the food is on the table, Jupiter summons his weapons of flame and thunderbolts to destroy the palace. Lycaon runs "in terror," and Ovid describes how he foams at the mouth. Jupiter's final avenging act on Lycaon is to transform the blood-thirsty monarch into a partial wolf: he has hair, teeth, and the face of a beast but retains "human shape."

Other Cultures

It's easy to get slightly dizzy when researching various cultural beliefs, especially when you start investigating cultures with multiple gods, such as the Aztecs, Incas, and Hindus. I decided to venture closer to home—for me, that is. I am half Armenian and was curious to see what beliefs governed my motherland. Armenia is an ancient land that was once far larger than it is today. You can find references to Armenia in Classical Greek writings. For example, Xenophon (fifth-century BCE historian/philosopher) observed that the ancient Armenians sacrificed horses to the Sun—a practice that probably was the result of the belief that a chariot drew the Sun across the sky.

The ancient Armenians are thought to have practiced a form of nature worship (praise and sacrifices to Sun and stars) before worshiping idols. But once they began a period of conquest, around 100 BCE, they got into the habit of bringing statues of gods from Greek cities and towns back to the Armenian kingdom. These statues were handed down to a succession of rulers and placed in eight sanctuaries around the country. If you know your history, you'll remember that Armenia was also the first Christianized nation. When St. Gregory the Illuminator began evangelizing the word of Jesus around the fourth century CE, he also marked out locations for the founding of churches—most being conveniently placed where the ancient idols were!

However, Moon worship was still an influence, even in post-Christian communities in various locales in the ancient world. You can find ample references to phases of the Moon here and there in the Scriptures. The holy feast of Zadik was decided by the waxing of the Moon and was set for the fourteenth day of the month, when the Moon is full.

Paying attention to the Moon's phase and color was important for recognizing and decoding omens. It wasn't surprising to find that eclipses have similar symbology and are interpreted as having similar meaning across many a world culture: eclipses bring pandemonium and a shift of power. The Bible reads: "Jesus said, 'there will be signs in the sun, the moon, and the stars, and on the earth distress among nations confused by the roaring of the sea and the waves. People will faint from fear and foreboding of what is coming upon the world, for the powers of the heavens will be shaken. Then they will see "the Son of Man coming in a cloud" with power and great glory. Now when these things begin to take place, stand up and raise your heads, because redemption is drawing near,'" (Luke 21:25–31).

What I find interesting is when ancient beliefs find voice in modern language or experiences. The myth about a lunar eclipse as the result of a dragon or other beast swallowing the Moon prevails in China and the Far East. And I was amused to find the following passage in Maxine Hong Kingston's *The Woman Warrior* (1976). Set in America, there is a scene where the narrator's Chinese mother tells the narrator that she needed to make a big noise by striking pot lids against one another "to scare the frog from swallowing the Moon." When Kingston's narrator tells her mother she doesn't need to do this, because nothing is happening in the world, her mother smugly notes: "The villagers must be banging and clanging very loudly back home in China."

The Chinese lunar-based calendar has all sorts of fascinating practices involving feasting. The goddess Heng O is said to live

2013 © Kia Cheng Boon Image from BigStockPhoto.com

forever on the Moon, and so the Chinese eat mooncakes in her honor each year at the mid-autumn Moon festival (the fifteenth day of the eighth lunar month). Traditional mooncakes will have an egg filling and are made of a taro pastry (there are many variants of this recipe on the Internet if you decide to search for it).

Of course, it's important to remember that the Moon doesn't look the same from week to week, and certainly not from day to day. And depending on where you are situated on Mother Earth, the Moon is going to be higher in the sky (northern latitudes) or lower (southern latitudes). This positioning also changes depending on the time of the year. For nearly half of the lunar cycle, we are all looking at a crescent shape that faces east or west, depending on the phase.

Some Native American tribes believed it was not a good time for hunting if the "horns" of the Moon were upward. I translate this to mean that the Moon would be waning; I've read in a variety of sources that hunting, fishing, and other methods of catching live game are not as propitious during the waning phase as during the waxing Moon.

Nineteenth-century poet Christina Rossetti framed the distinctions between the waning and waxing cycles most elegantly in a short poem frequently anthologized in children's poetry books: "O Lady Moon, your horns point toward the east: Shine, be increased/O Lady Moon, your horns point toward the west: Wane, be at rest." Rossetti came back to the Moon again and again—here's a riddle, where we already know the answer: "I've seen a hundred pretty things, And seen a hundred gay; but only think: I peep by night and do not peep by day!" And this poetic couplet, which again frames the Moon as a feminine entity: "Before the coming of the night/The Moon shows papery white; before the dawning of the day/She fades away."

Since the time that the Greek-speaking peoples ruled the "civilized world," no culture was more in tune to the writing of the Classicists than the English Victorians and their counterparts on the continent. Their poetry and essays presuppose a familiarity with philosophy and mythic legends that most twenty-first-century North Americans and Europeans would find daunting. And so, we update these myths, borrowing a little from Homer and a little from Ovid, and we reframe the characters for a modern age. My son, who is eight, has been enraptured with Percy Jackson's splendid retelling of the Greek myths; the author's knowledge of the Greek gods is delightful, entertaining, and thoroughly accurate.

Speaking of children's stories, Jack and Jill and their unfortunate journey to fetch water on the hill may have derived from a Viking story about "Hjuki and Bil," who were taken all the way to the Moon to fetch water from her well. The Vikings looked at the dark shapes (mariae) on the Moon and thought they saw pools of water waiting to be gathered.

Some cultures I explored (far Eastern, Greenlandic, and African) show no evidence of incursion by anyone with a Classical

Greek or Roman education at any point. Yet many cultures tend to ascribe "maleness" to the Sun (which can be a wheel) and "femaleness" to the Moon. The root word *mens* gives us words such as *menstrual*, *month*, and *Moon*. And though we might think of the Moon as "full" when we think of the image, it's important to remember that the waxing and waning phases also have their own significance—as they did for ancient people.

About the Author
Sally Cragin writes "Moon Signs" for the Phoenix newspapers as Symboline Dai. A regular contributor to Llewellyn almanacs, she is the author of The Astrological Elements *and* Astrology on the Cusp: Birthdays on the Edge of Two Signs. *She can be reached at Moonsigns.net.*

The Moon and Earthquakes

by Bruce Scofield

Most of us know that earthquakes are shock waves traveling through the Earth that are generated by shifts in the Earth's crust. Some are so small that people can't feel them; others kill thousands. The Earth is really quite a dynamic planet with a lot of movement going on all of the time—but mostly at geological speed, which is so slow we humans can't see it. But when there is a sudden, abrupt displacement of rock that has been under pressure for some time, these movements become rapid, producing an earthquake. The places where these sudden shifts occur are called faults—basically big cracks underground where one kind of rock is moving against another.

Earthquakes are the result of the very slow motion of the continents. Alfred Wegener, a German meteorologist in the early twentieth century, first called attention to the strange fact that some of the continents—especially South America and Africa—seem to fit into each other like pieces of a puzzle. Further, he noted that fossils found on different continents often perfectly matched those found on continents thousands of miles away. His Continental Drift theory proposed that the continents had split apart millions of years ago and had moved over time. Today the theory of Plate Tectonics is used to explain the movement of continents over geological history as well as many other geological phenomena, including earthquakes. Over vast periods of time, continents break apart and collide with each other. In some cases (including the west coast of the Americas) one continent in a collision will bury itself (subduct) under the other one. This subduction will stir up the deep underground, producing earthquakes and volcanoes (hence the "ring of fire" around the Pacific Ocean). What is not so well known is *when* the pressures will be suddenly released and the shifting of rock will cause an earthquake. Many think the interplay of the Sun and Moon are a trigger.

Earthquakes have been of interest to astrologers for perhaps three thousand years. Ancient astrologers were more concerned with the cycles and changes of the natural world than they were with the fates of individuals (except for those of the king or other leaders). Weather was a major topic in astrology, and earthquakes were considered an environmental effect, like weather, that needed to be predicted. Ancient Mesopotamian astrologers meticulously recorded such natural phenomena and sought correlations with the positions of the Sun, Moon, and planets. Anaximander, one of the earliest Greek philosopher-scientists (sixth century BCE), is said to have predicted an earthquake and saved the population of a city. It is quite possible that he used the positions of the Sun, Moon, and planets to do so, since he was a serious student of nature. It seemed logical to many historical astrologers that since the tides moved the seas, they may also move the land. By the Renaissance (fourteenth to seventeenth centuries CE), astrometeorology was an important part of astrology. Those who practiced it in lands where earthquakes were common sought correlations of these destructive events with the planets.

The problem with combining astrology with earthquakes is that the latter don't happen everywhere at once. An eclipse or a strong configuration of planets may correlate with an earthquake in China on one day, but a similarly strong configuration at a later date might not. However, it may correlate with an earthquake somewhere else on the other side of the world. Before the modern era of science, there would be no way of knowing that. The science behind earthquake prediction using the Moon, Sun, and planets has a very long history, but in a way, it is still in its infancy. The matter is exceedingly complex and requires a deep knowledge of not only astrology but geology, which itself is a very complex field of scientific inquiry. That being said, let's take a look at some of the ways astrologers have approached this subject.

Seeing that the interplay of Sun and Moon modulates the tides, it seems logical that these bodies could also cause earthquakes. This idea has ancient origins—the Greek philosopher Aristotle (fourth century BCE) even noted that sometimes earthquakes occur around the time of eclipses. The New and Full Moons, which twice a year may also be eclipses, have long been one of the main astrological indicators of a possible earthquake. Modern astrologers also consider perigee—when the Moon is closest to the Earth—to be another factor to consider. The Moon's orbit is elliptical; over the course of a month, its distance from the Earth varies. When it is closest to the Earth, at perigee, its gravitational influence is greater. If the Moon is also lined up with the Sun, as at the New or Full Moon, the strongest gravitational forces are generated. In many cases this combination has coincided with major earthquakes. Today, a maverick geologist named Jim Berkland has taken these ideas further.

Berkland, who lives in California, observed that earthquakes would cluster around the dates of the New and Full Moon, and especially when the Moon was at perigee. He calls this condition a "seismic window." When this condition occurred in 1989, he predicted a major earthquake. Four days later a big one occurred that stopped the World Series in San Francisco. While this prediction earned him fame, it also tarnished his reputation among geologists. The scientific community of geologists are far more focused on understanding the mechanics of the earthquakes, and they tend to look down on anyone making a prediction—which is indeed a risky activity. Berkland's methodology also came to include counting the number of lost pet ads in the newspapers. When these would increase, so would the likelihood of a quake. It has been observed for centuries that animals seem to be able to sense an earthquake and they often exhibit unusual behaviors—which can mean running away and becoming lost.

Earth tides do exist. While the Moon's gravitational effects on the oceans are obvious and can be measured easily by anyone sitting on the edge of a pier, the rising and falling of the land is not. A tidal land bulge moves across the Earth twice daily from east to west. This bulge can raise the surface as much as a foot, and it extends underground as well. In California, at the famous San Andreas fault, this tidal bulge can cause shifts in the rocks that are highly lubricated by groundwater—and this causes an earthquake at the surface. When a section of the fault is just about ready to break off, it doesn't take much to trigger it, and the tidal pull of the Moon and Sun may be all that's needed. This illustrates an important point about earthquakes and tides: The tidal forces are always there, sometimes stronger and sometimes weaker, depending on how close the Moon is to the Earth. But only when a fault is at a tipping point can the tidal pull possibly deliver the final push and give rise to an earthquake. That's why we can't always count on Full Moons or eclipses to coincide with an earthquake—the deep underground rocks must be ripe and ready to move.

Another way that the Moon can trigger an earthquake is through the depth of water over a sensitive area of the coastline. Water is heavy. When the tide is high, there is more water over the shoreline and therefore more weight—sometimes enough to trigger a quake waiting to happen. This is more common along subduction zones, places where the ocean floor is being pushed under the continental plate. The western coastlines of both North and South Americn fall into this category, and many small quakes are triggered by especially high tides like those when the Moon is at perigee and in alignment with the Sun. It has also been shown that earthquakes are triggered when the Moon has a high northerly declination; that is, when it is in the signs Gemini and Cancer. This might be a factor because most of the Earth's land mass is in the Northern Hemisphere—below the Moon when it is at a high northerly declination.

One of the largest, if not the largest, series of earthquakes in the United States did not occur along the West Coast, as most do; it occurred right in the middle of the country with the epicenter near the town of New Madrid, Missouri. These quakes, including three really big ones, struck during the winter of 1811–12 and were so powerful that church bells were set ringing in Boston. There were few people living in Missouri at the time, but residents reported that the Mississippi River's course was altered and that the ground swelled in giant waves. A climatologist named Iben Browning predicted that similar earthquakes might again occur there in 1990. He based his prediction on both the cycles of Jupiter and Saturn and also when the Sun and Moon were closest to the Earth. A big quake did not occur and his reputation was tarnished, in spite of the fact that there were an extremely large number of earthquakes that year—nearly as many as had occurred during the entire past decade.

Astrologers have long worked with solar system bodies other than the Moon and Sun. Ancient astrologers thought that Mars, Jupiter, and Saturn in conjunction was a sign of a quake. John Goad noted in the mid-seventeenth century that earthquake frequency increased when Jupiter was in Taurus, and A. J. Pearce drew attention to Saturn's passage through that sign as a signal of earthquakes. Scorpio has also been considered a significator of earthquakes, often appearing on the Ascendant at the time of the quake. Likewise the sign Aries has also been thought to be important. But, to my knowledge, no one has ever done a thorough study of these claims or has found a fool-proof formula that can be used to predict an earthquake. As mentioned already, the real problem is that quakes only occur when they are ready to; that is, when the subterranean rock is at a tipping point. Then the astrological configurations would, theoretically, activate the quake. But, alas, it is not so simple.

A look at the astrology of some recent earthquakes will illustrate how complex the problem of prediction is. On March 11, 2011, a massive quake hit the coast of Japan, generating a tsunami and killing thousands of people. The Moon was at a high northern declination and in the sign Gemini, and at the first quarter. Jupiter and Saturn were in opposition, but not exactly at that time. Most interesting was the fact that Uranus was almost exactly on the cusp of Pisces and Aries, the vernal equinox, which occurred the next day.

The devastating quake in Haiti occurred on January 12, 2010. Although the Sun was closely conjunct Venus in Capricorn that day, and it was just three days before an eclipse, the other planetary alignments were not so tight, and not much about that day suggested a quake would happen. The huge quake in China on May 12, 2008, happened when the Sun was in Taurus and was square to the Moon (at the first quarter) and Neptune. None of these earthquakes hit when the Moon was at perigee, or at full or new, though two occurred at the first quarter. However, other major earthquakes do have good correlations with New and Full Moons. The December 26, 2004, tsunami in the Indian Ocean occurred at the Full Moon, and the July 28, 1976, Tangshan earthquake in China hit just before the New Moon. Both of these events caused a quarter of a million deaths.

While charts for each of these events would no doubt reveal a few other configurations that might suggest a quake, I think they show that earthquake prediction with astrology alone is not very accurate. It may be that, on average, there are more earthquakes at the Full and New Moons, but to my knowledge, no one has studied this in any great detail. For those interested, much earthquake data is posted online at the National Oceanic and Atmospheric Administration's webpage (http://www.noaawatch.gov/themes/quake.php) and the US Geological Survey webpage (http://earthquake.usgs.gov/earthquakes/map/), where viewers can follow current earthquakes and look up data on past ones.

References

Orey, Cal. *The Man Who Predicts Earthquakes: Jim Berkland, Maverick Geologist—How His Quake Warnings Can Save Lives.* Sentient Publications, 2006.

Scofield, Bruce. "Earthquake Astrology." *The Mountain Astrologer.* April 2012.

Vaughan, Valeri. *Earth Cycles: The Scientific Evidence for Astrology. Vol. 1, The Physical Sciences.* One Reed Publications, 2002. P. 113.

About the Author

Bruce Scofield is a practicing astrologer who's maintained a private practice as an consultant and conference speaker for over forty years. He is the author of seven books and hundreds of articles. He has served on the education committee of the National Council for Geocosmic Research since 1979 and was that organization's national education director from 1998 to 2003. He holds a master's degree in history and a PhD in geosciences and currently teaches at Kepler College and the University of Massachusetts. Scofield and Barry Orr maintain a website, www.onereed.com, which contains articles and an online calculation program on Maya and Aztec astrology.

Natal Moon Sign and the Path to Trust

by Amy Herring

The word *trust* can mean different things to different people. Some people measure trust in reference to how reliable (trustworthy) they think someone is—that they can rely on someone not to lie to them or to keep their promises, for example. Some people consider themselves trusting of others because they have a conviction that people are generally good. People often extend the word beyond relationships with other people and say, "I trust the process" or "I trust the universe," referring to an overall belief that everything will turn out okay. But when it comes trusting another person with our heart, there are three main ideas:

Trust is faith. When we have trust in someone, we believe that they will not hurt us, at least not on purpose. We risk our heart in the belief and hope that another person will not let us down.

Trust depends on vulnerability. When we trust someone, we open up to them and willingly leave ourselves vulnerable to them. That means they could hurt us, but we are hoping (and betting) that they won't. Trust can only be created in vulnerability. If we are closed, then we don't allow another person in. That means they can't hurt us, but we also can't receive their love; emotion simply bounces off a closed heart.

Trust is a process. Trust inherently deepens (or lessens) over time and with interaction. While some people approach the world in a more socially guarded way and others are more likely to extend the benefit of the doubt, trust itself is not simply whether you tend to have faith in people's goodness in general. That's not a state of trust as much as it is an absence of distrust. We develop deeper trust with someone the more times we reveal ourselves to them without being rejected or hurt after doing so.

The Moon and Trust

So why do we look to the Moon in astrology when we want to know about trust in our relationships? How and why does our natal Moon sign affect our ability to trust others and be trusted?

The Inner Child

Astrology has several symbols that speak to relationships, and all of them could arguably have a hand in building trust. Venus is liking someone, and we may use our Venusian wiles to draw someone in. Mars is wanting someone, and we may use our Martial desires to pursue a relationship with someone. But the Moon waits, hidden and protected, until it feels safe to reveal itself and lower the gates. The Moon is our heart, our inner child, and so is inherently vulnerable. It doesn't defend like Mars or deflect like Venus. When it's exposed, we are raw. We open the heart gates to someone when they have proved themselves trustworthy in a way we can recognize. Our Moon sign, house, and planetary aspects provide us with a profile of what leads us to trust another.

An Open Heart

We can infer a lot about trust and the signals of trust from the idea that the Moon contributes to our instinctual makeup (a role shared with Mars). When we trust someone, we are less likely to censor ourselves or hide ourselves, whether it's evident in our behavior, our opinions, our feelings, or even our physical appearance. We are more likely to "let it all hang out" with less fear that we will be rejected for something we say or do. This means we will be following our instincts rather than assessing and editing every move we make; we can truly be ourselves. People with a high level of self-confidence may seem to do this no matter who they are with, but this may be self-esteem or bravado, not trust, since trust requires vulnerability. When we open up to someone in trust, we trust ourselves in their presence.

Trust Is a Feeling

One definition of trust is predictability: can you rely on, and therefore predict, someone's behavior? You can scientifically measure reliability. For instance, you can calculate the number of times someone has shown up at the time they promised and see how many times they've broken that commitment. But true trust cannot be measured scientifically. While someone's regular and predictable behavior can encourage us to feel secure in them, trust is a feeling, which puts trust solidly in the Moon's realm. We feel that we can trust someone, or we don't (even if we want to). Not only does this govern how deeply we trust someone, but whether we even initiate the path to trust or avoid a person altogether. This emotional instinct can also help us gauge whether we should trust someone again when they've broken our trust.

When Trust Is Broken

As we continue to keep ourselves open and have repeated experiences with someone reliably coming through for us, we come to trust them more deeply. But part of being human, of course, is that we are not perfect, nor are we constant all of the time. When trust is broken, logical analysis would tell us that if someone let us down once, we have reason to believe they might let us down again; therefore we shouldn't trust them from now on. But humans give other humans another chance all the time; we forgive and begin again. To forgive and reinitiate trust takes us back to step one: faith. It is the heart, not the mind, that provides the motivation and the courage to "forgive and forget."

Signs of Trust

Read your natal Moon sign for specifics about the kinds of things that make it easier for you to trust, and what things make you feel mistrustful or wary. Read the Moon signs of your friends and loved ones to learn how to build a deeper trust with them. You can do an Internet search for "astrology birth chart" to find sites that will give you your natal Moon sign (as well as a lot of other information) based on your time of birth. The signs here are divided by element.

Fire Moons

The fire Moon signs (Aries, Leo, and Sagittarius) will make judgments about whether they can trust someone or not based on their gut response, and while trust is a process, the fire Moons can move through the process quite rapidly. When their trust is broken, they prefer to deal with it directly rather than sulking or retreating.

If your Moon is in Aries, you trust others when it becomes clear that you don't have to censor your opinions or dampen the full intensity of your personality to please them. You don't tend to trust people who are not forthright, because you don't know where you stand with them. You need freedom to be who you are without judgment. If you want an Aries Moon to trust you, be direct with them consistently. When their trust is broken, they are likely to respond with anger. Weather that storm of conflict with them and hear them out to begin rebuilding trust with them.

If you have a Leo Moon, you open up in trust when you sense someone accepts and has a deep, genuine interest in you. While you can be very expressive, you are not the bold, outgoing, party animal that Leo is often painted to be. This is because no matter what sign it's in, the Moon is inherently our vulnerable spot that we protect until it's safe to reveal. You long to be seen but have to be sure that you won't be ridiculed or discounted when you show yourself. If you want a Leo Moon to trust you, be generous with your feelings and don't hold back. Make them feel like a priority in your life. Don't ignore them or act aloof even if they do so— and they might act that way if they are feeling insecure or their trust has been broken. Sometimes they use pride to mask their lionhearted tenderness, but that is often when they need the most acceptance.

If your Moon is in Sagittarius, you trust people that have an easy-going nature, who are friendly and optimistic. You tend to feel like your heart is an open book, and you trust people who are straightforward and transparent with you. When your trust is broken, you tend to recover quickly, but you may pull back and keep your heart out of reach with a façade of playfulness and a devil-may-care attitude to hide the seriousness of the hurt (even sometimes from yourself). If you want a Sagittarius Moon to trust you, don't bombard or overwhelm them with a lot of expectations. Be open and honest with them, but most of all, be flexible, and they will stay open and open-hearted with you.

Earth Moons

The earth Moon signs (Taurus, Virgo, and Capricorn) are the signs most likely to measure someone's trustworthiness by their dependability. An earth Moon sign feels secure when things in their environment are under control and running as expected,

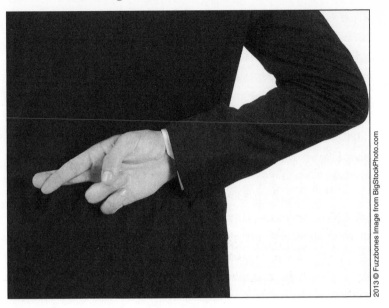

so even well-intentioned surprises can throw them off. Actions always speak louder than words with the earth Moons, because they need to see results, not intentions, no matter how sincere. When their trust is broken, they may show it by holding back warmth, retreating into a more formal "business as usual" attitude, and behaving more independently.

If your Moon is in Taurus, you trust sincerity, warmth, and groundedness. People who seem flaky or are too hard to predict make it difficult for you to open up and relax. You need a sense that someone is steadfast in order to trust that if you open up today, you won't be disappointed tomorrow. When your trust is broken, it takes a while to forgive because you need time to see the "proof in the pudding" that it won't happen again. If you want a Taurus Moon to trust you, don't try to push deeper into their confidence too fast. Just be there with or for them, and ease in. They need to open up in their own time.

If you have a Virgo Moon, you are very analytical, so you trust someone who makes it clear that they are strong enough to handle feedback about sensitive subjects and can give you genuine, thoughtful feedback respectfully as well without being overemotional and shutting down. If you want a Virgo Moon to trust you, pay attention to the little things about them—not just the things they like, but the way they like things done. A Virgo Moon feels loved most when you do practical things for them that make their life easier, but they will trust you if they know you care enough to pay close attention to what makes them feel secure.

If you have a Capricorn Moon, you have a stalwart heart and tend to be the one who takes care of a lot of people and tasks. But even you get sick or tapped out, and you need someone who has your back when that happens. Therefore, you tend to trust people who somehow are able to show you can depend on them like others depend on you. Trust means letting down your guard, letting someone see you are human, and that can be hard to do when you don't want to feel incapable. When you don't trust someone or your trust is broken, you will do all you can to not need (or reveal to them) how much their love and support means to you. If you want a Capricorn Moon to trust you, be true to your word with them. They are realistic and don't expect you to promise them the stars, but they do expect you to deliver on whatever it is you do promise. Appreciate what they do but be capable also.

Air Moons

The way to an air-sign Moon's heart is through their intellect. The air Moon signs (Gemini, Libra, and Aquarius) have feelings just as everyone does, but they often understand and process their emotions by sorting through information and communication—expressing how they feel through words, ideas, and concepts. The air signs build trust with another person through the process of coming to and refining an understanding of what they can expect from another person and what the other should expect from them, like an unspoken social contract. When their trust is broken, they tend to work through the feelings by disengaging and trying to revise their expectations in their own mind.

If you have a Gemini Moon, you tend to be pretty open in whom you trust, as long as they don't have an obviously shady personality. You go further into the process of trust when you feel like you can depend on someone to tell you the truth. You have the mental flexibility to see things from multiple points of view, so you aren't likely to be offended by or argue over semantics, but if someone tells you a bold-faced, intentional lie, it will break your trust since communication depends on honesty. If you want a Gemini Moon to trust you, communicate openly with them. Allow them the room to be spontaneous and to change their mind without trying to pin them down like a butterfly on a board.

If your Moon is in Libra, you are sensitive to another's needs, desires, and emotional states, and often want to be accommodating to them; in order to trust someone, you need evidence that they are not going to take advantage of that. Going deeper into the process of trust with someone means trusting them to respect your point of view when you disagree with them. If you don't trust someone, you tend to avoid conflict and hide your true feelings and opinions. If you want a Libra Moon to trust you, make it clear that you want to know what they want and you want to support them, not just be supported by them. Allow the space for them to bring up issues that may be sensitive and listen respectfully, but don't push them into conflict by attacking them.

If your Moon is in Aquarius, you build trust with someone who is not threatened by your need for freedom and individuality. This means not loading you down with a heap of expectations that encroach on your right to live authentically according to what makes sense to you. When your trust is broken, you tend to distance yourself from another. You can be stubborn but don't tend to hold on to grudges, so a rational conversation about the conflict can be enough for you to decide to extend trust again, as long as you want to. If you want an Aquarius Moon to trust you, communicate with them openly and objectively. Don't "handle" them or maneuver around them in order to get them to do what you want them to do.

Water Moons

The water Moon signs (Cancer, Scorpio, and Pisces) need to feel that someone is being emotionally sincere and honest to trust them. They are going to respond to nonverbal cues such as eye contact, appropriate touching, and warmth. Like the fire signs, they are likely to make judgments about initiating trust based on subjective gut responses to someone, but they will hang back and observe for a bit longer before they open their doors. When their trust is broken, they are likely to retreat into themselves.

If your Moon is in Cancer, thoughtfulness and patience are the winning combination for you to trust someone. Trust unfolds layer after layer for you slowly, through a process of sharing and supporting each other. If this process only goes one way (you "mothering" them or vice versa), trust becomes stalled. You don't recover easily when your trust is broken, but a sincere emotional appeal, an apology, and some extra consideration goes a long way. If you want a Cancer Moon to trust you, provide them with some emotional security that you are planning on sticking around with consistency in being there for them, but don't overwhelm them by pushing too fast. They will shower you with love and care in return.

If your Moon is in Scorpio, honesty is of utmost importance. You need to feel that not only is someone telling you the truth, but they are not holding back or hiding something, even if they are doing so for compassionate reasons. You also need to feel that those you trust are loyal to you, that you can trust them with your secrets, and that they will stand up for you with others, if needed. If your trust is betrayed, you can be ruthless in burning the bridge with someone. Rebuilding trust is an act of will for you. If you want a Scorpio Moon to trust you, don't be needlessly insulting in your honesty with them, but don't pull your punches, and make it clear to them that they don't have to pull theirs. They trust people who are strong enough to acknowledge the deep and taboo stuff. However, as much as a Scorpio Moon values forthright honesty, they also guard their privacy and will not easily forgive if it is violated.

If your Moon is in Pisces, you are very soft-hearted, so gentleness is the key for you to open up in trust. You tend to have faith in people overall, but to really trust someone, you need compassion and encouragement without harsh judgment. You are not one to hold a grudge, forgiving and forgetting easily and multiple times if your trust is broken due to human frailty, since you are compassionate when people are trying their best. However, while you may forgive, you won't forget betrayals out of intentional cruelty or mean-spiritedness. If you want a Pisces Moon to trust you, believe in them and encourage them. Be gentle with your feedback on their ideas and feelings, rather than pummeling them with a "dose of reality for their own good."

About the Author

A graduate of Steven Forrest's Evolutionary Astrology program, Amy Herring has been a professional astrologer for fifteen years. Her book Astrology of the Moon *covers the natal and progressed moon relationship in detail and is available from Llewellyn. Visit http://heavenlytruth.com for personal readings and astrology study resources.*

Extreme Weather and the Outer Planets

by Carole Schwalm

Nature is flexible. If you want paradise, she will oblige. If you want destruction and despair, she will oblige. —Richard W. Langer

Extreme weather involves everything in nature's arsenal. One may endure blazing-hot temperatures and drought. Or gale-forced winds, blinding rains, hail, tornadoes, and lightning. When outer planets transited a combination of cardinal and water signs in the recent past, as they do in 2014, we experienced increased instances of extreme weather. Why? Perhaps because cardinal signs increase activity, and of course, water signs rule water. This article focuses on cardinal signs Aries, Cancer, Libra, and Capricorn, as well as the three water signs of Cancer, Scorpio, and Pisces. The "outer" planets include Jupiter, Saturn, Uranus,

Neptune, and Pluto. Let's look at some examples of the outer planets in cardinal signs and their effect on extreme weather in the United States.

The year 1989 was "weird for weather," according to the National Oceanic and Atmostpheric Administration, commonly known as NOAA (NO-ah). Among other events, Category 4 Hurricane Hugo struck the Caribbean and southeast United States. The northern plains in the United States also endured a summer of drought. Both events resulted in large agricultural losses. Jupiter occupied Cancer in 1989, as it does in 2014. Saturn, Uranus, and Neptune were in cardinal Capricorn, just as Pluto is now. Uranus is in fellow cardinal sign Aries, and Neptune (while not in a cardinal sign), is strong in the sign it rules: watery Pisces. Saturn also moves from cardinal to watery Scorpio.

Another year with emphasis on the outer planet cardinal/water mix was 1994. Tropical Storm Alberto brought torrential rains with extensive crop damage to the entire southeastern United States. The year 1996 (the cardinal/water exception was Pluto here) saw heavy rains, flooding, and Category 3 Hurricane Fran, all causing over $2.54 billion in agricultural damage in the United States.

From 2001 to 2002, Jupiter again transited Cancer. The year was wetter than normal, with increased instances of severe thunderstorms, high winds, tornadoes, and hail. While some areas were deluged with water, others experienced extreme heat and drought conditions.

Extreme Weather Forms

If the "norm" is a general increase in weather activity, it is possible that the 2014 ordinary intense weather will be all the more extreme. We need to be prepared in so many ways. For this article, we are looking at how devastating weather can be on agriculture.

Deluge

Those of us living in drought-stricken areas would like a few strong downpours, but there is such a thing as too much rain. Think back to the pictures of Katrina and Isaac showing water almost as high as street signs and rooftops.

How does excessive rainfall affect crops? Heavy spring downpours damage not only seeds (or delay planting) but also injure plants that are just beginning to grow. Blossoms can't survive standing water, and with enough rainfall, plants literally drown in the fields.

Weeds and fungi also increase during warmer, wetter weather. There is also an increase in parasites and diseases. Moisture-reliant pathogens relevant to bacteria and virus-causing diseases thrive. When farmers are forced to harvest in wet weather, mycotoxins that cause sickness rise.

Drought

Drought and high temperatures go together. Most plants can tolerate up to 90 degrees F, but the hotter it gets, the more they suffer. The longer the heat wave lasts, the greater injury to plants. When hot soil that hampers growth persists, plants are forced to compete for soil nutrition and production decreases. During the 2012 summer growing season, drought resulted in price increases. Typical grocery store corn prices rose from a normal five ears for $1.00 to two ears for $1.00, for example.

The New Normal

Heat waves, warming waters, floods, droughts, wildfires and insect and pest infestations are the new reality of an ever-warming world.

—National Wildlife Federation, August 30, 2012

The UK *Guardian* called the weather patterns "the new normal" in 2011, when drought increased in England and Wales with weather the hottest in a hundred years. Winters were the coldest experienced in three hundred years. And Scotland experienced the wettest weather ever. An August 2012 article in the US *Science Daily* noted that "previously rare high summer temperatures happen more frequently." In Maine, from the *Greenfield Reporter*: "A new study shows that extreme rainstorms and snowstorms happen 74 percent more often (records since 1948)… Biggest storms are getting bigger."

Effects on the Home Garden

If you have things growing in your home garden, whether decorative or for consumption, extreme weather affects you. You need to prepare so your plants do not suffer in 2014. Look around, especially if you are in a drought or rain-soaked area, and be prepared for the effects.

First, your growing season may be shortened by drought or deluge, so you may want to buy seeds requiring a shorter span of time from planting to harvest. Purchase tomato and other transplants with larger, stronger growth. Be ready to protect them against surprise frosts, hailstorms, and downpours. Get used to a regular watering schedule in case of drought and extreme heat.

If you are in the midst of a drought, think about drought-tolerant plants able to withstand the heat. Non-native plants are particularly subject to stress, so opt for plants and varietals that are suited to your growing zone.

Plant roots will rot with heavy rains. A trench around your plants can ease water flow and let it seep in around the plant gradually. Growing tomatoes in containers rather than in a weather-exposed garden, for example, will give you more control over conditions. With hot and dry conditions, bear in mind that container plants are shallow-rooted. Mulch to prevent hot air and dry wind from touching your soil surfaces, which results in moisture loss. Shading also helps, and good soil permits deep water penetration.

Perennial plants condition themselves to endure. Those that survive a first drought season know to grow faster during the second drought season. But sudden weather changes, like damaging rains in a previously arid area, upset that plant's ability to survive. You have to monitor growing conditions. It is important to think ahead rather than wait until you are right in the middle of extreme conditions. If the forecast shows heavy rains on parched soils, consider shielding plants for part of the rainfall, or use rain barrels to save the water and distribute it over a longer period of time, so it can soak into the soil rather than flood and run off. If your area has been seeing excess rainfall and no rain is in the forecast, be ready to let plants dry out for a bit, but then water more than you might normally, since those plants growing are used to lots of water.

Look around you while your memory is sharp about the previous growing season. Watch when it rains and observe how the water flows and keep records. Alter the flow as needed with new landscaping or water-capturing systems, or at least make notes so that you won't forget. It isn't just rain you should consider—don't forget about spring snow melt from winter, whether large or small, and excess water just when plants are beginning to send out new roots.

Sources

Langer, Richard W. *Grow It!* New York: Noonday Press, 1994.

About the Author

Carole Schwalm lives in Santa Fe, New Mexico. She has contributed self-help articles and horoscopes for many people through America Online and other websites. She provides a variety of astrological works for astrocenter.com.

Natal Ceres Sign and Your Relationship to Food

by Michelle Perrin, Astrology Detective

Our relationship to the celestial body Ceres is as complicated and volatile as our relationship to that which it rules: food and nourishment. Ceres was discovered by the Italian astronomer Giueseppe Piazzi on New Year's Day, 1801. Piazzi named it after one of the Roman goddesses most deeply connected to the scientist's native Sicily. Ceres ruled plants, the harvest, fertility, and motherly love.

Pluto is not the first orb to lose its planetary status. For approximately fifty years after its discovery, Ceres was also considered a planet before being downgraded to an asteroid. In 2006, however, it was once again reclassified by the International Astronomical Union, along with Pluto, as a dwarf planet. Interestingly (and somewhat confusingly), it is still simultaneously deemed an asteroid by NASA.

The intertwined fates of Ceres and Pluto as heavenly bodies mirror the myths that gave rise to their names. Ceres, the Roman equivalent of the Greek Demeter, was happily living with her daughter Proserpina, and Earth enjoyed a year-round bountiful harvest. One day, Proserpina was kidnapped and taken to the underworld by Pluto, who desired to marry her and make her his queen; this caused her mother, Ceres, infinite grief and sorrow. In the pain that resulted from being separated from her daughter, Ceres stopped the growth of all crops and fruit trees, while Proserpina entered into a fast, refusing all food and drink. Without food, the entire human race was at risk, so Jupiter commanded Pluto to release Proserpina, and Pluto acquiesced. Before leaving to return to her mother, Pluto offered Proserpina a few pomegranate seeds to quench her thirst, which the girl gladly accepted without realizing that that those who ate from the underworld were bound to it forever.

As a compromise, Proserpina spent part of the year with her mother on Earth, during which time plants bloomed and food grew, and the other part of the year in the underworld, when the land would grow desolate and barren. Today, words such as *cereal* are derived from this goddess of the harvest.

In astrology, Ceres represents how we approach nourishment—physically, emotionally, and psychologically. It also represents nurturing, the mother principle, and the way we receive and give emotional support. The word *nurturing* comes from the Latin *nutrire*, "to feed," and one of the most innate acts of nurturing humans experience is when the mother instinctually holds her newborn to her chest to feed. Proper parental love should be secure and unconditional. If it is not, low levels of self-esteem, anxiety, fear, dependency, perfectionism, or control issues may manifest. All of the above are also root causes of eating disorders such as anorexia or bulimia, and it is no surprise that Ceres rules not only nourishment, but also eating disorders and our relationship to food in general.

Negative manifestations of the Ceres energy may result in the manipulative use of food as a control mechanism, such as withholding food or using food as a reward device. In such cases, the naive will stop listening to their own hunger instincts and instead seek to nourish themselves guided by external programming, in an almost Pavlovian way. By becoming aware of this cultural or domestic conditioning, people can free themselves from unhealthy eating habits and move to a better state of overall wellness.

In its best, most harmonious manifestation, Ceres represents food that is used as a conduit of love, such as a home-cooked meal, as well as the use of good nutrition as an integral part of a healthy lifestyle. Here we examine how Ceres manifests itself through the signs. Search the Internet for sites that will give you a free natal chart based on your time and date of birth in order to find out your natal Ceres sign and that of your loved ones. You may need to choose an option to display secondary asteriods or lesser bodies in order for Ceres to be drawn into your chart. Try AlwaysAstrology.com's free birth chart, for example.

Aries

People with Ceres in Aries use food not so much for nurturing others but for gaining a competitive advantage, as well as acceptance and increased popularity, with their family or social group. Due to their generous and encouraging natures, they may also use food as a form of motivation, such as by giving a piece of candy to a child for finishing their homework. Ceres in Aries people are highly active and may feel trapped at the dinner table, probably preferring to eat on the go. Mealtime is not really a focal point of their lives, but a process they must undergo to keep the machine humming smoothly. Therefore, they are happy eating fast food just to get full so they can quickly move on to more exciting things. Individuals with this placement may also be extremely spoiled and impatient—they want their din din and they want it now! They can have a childlike innocence toward proper nutrition and may want to eat their dessert before finishing their peas; if they don't get their way, they may throw a temper tantrum. Imbalances can occur if their independence was restricted by a family member who overnurtured them with food, which may have caused them to rebel. For this reason, these people might refuse food from others, as they don't want to have to eat by other people's rules or deal with the strings that are involved by accepting generosity. By supplying the flow of nourishment to others, they maintain self-reliance for themselves.

Taurus

Meatloaf, a baked potato, maybe even a piece of apple pie for desert—those born with Ceres in Taurus are all about comfort food. For them, food is a grounding experience, and eating is their way of plugging into the security of life's routine cycles. Anything too outré or nouvelle is not their thing. That is not to say they do not indulge from time to time in luxury products, but when they do, it is not for the food's inherent status, but because they realize that laziness cannot produce first-grade comestibles. While they might be put off by the price tag at first, they ultimately admire the effort involved in creating high-quality foodstuffs and the hard work needed to prepare something so complex and top-notch that they will gladly pay the fair market price for such goods. This is one placement where a person may have a tendency to put on weight and not really care—possessing a few extra pounds merely signifies they are fully taking advantage of Earth's abundance. A slightly rounded figure may also conjure up idyllic images of nurturing, home, and mother. In any case, they are put off by superficial appearances and care more about every-day living and achieving results; they don't have time to be sitting around counting calories. They care for others in a pragmatic way by providing necessary nourishment, but they don't place too much importance on chic presentation, new dietary trends, or exotic spices. They prefer food that is healthy, hearty, and filling.

Gemini

Ceres in Gemini has an intellectual approach to food. They may prefer to indulge in complex, slightly fussy foods such as French cuisine, where their mind, even more than their taste buds, can fully appreciate the interesting, complicated flavor combinations and culinary methods. They enjoy cooking most when tackling a highly involved recipe where each step must be mastered in order to create the final, spectacular result. They may develop an anxiety to food preparation if asked to create a meal off the cuff, and they'd rather learn the craft through cooking classes and careful study. When dieting, they prefer to research the underlying hows and whys of each meal plan in order to fully understand the logic behind the hype. Gemini Ceres folks tend not to be taken in by junk food, because they cannot rationalize eating something that does not give any nutritional content in return. They also have a slightly sophisticated or even snobby attitude toward food, and they would not want to be seen with a lowly takeout hamburger. A high metabolism and tendency toward agility and movement also helps these individuals burn calories; foods that are overly heavy or high in fats and carbs tend to drag down their naturally vibrant energy and so are intuitively avoided. Food is often best when used as an accompaniment to great conversation. Dining can be synonymous with socializing and intellectual engagement with one's companions, and eating alone may be a more isolating experience for this placement than for other individuals.

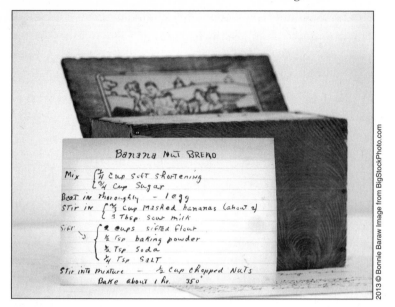

Cancer

For the Ceres in Cancer individual, food is highly connected to nurturing. They are the family member most likely to be given grandma's recipe box in order to keep long-standing traditions alive and make sure these treasures are passed down to the next generation. While their siblings may have spent their childhoods outside playing, Ceres in Cancer individuals were most likely to be found in the kitchen next to their parent while they prepared the evening dinner. As an adult, food is synonymous with family, and they insist that mealtimes are an almost-sacred occasion when the entire clan can spend time together engaging over home-cooked goodness; they will not put up with children wanting to eat on their own schedule in order to attend sports or after-school activities. Food has a highly emotional quality for them, so they should beware of using it as a kind of reward mechanism. Perhaps when they were growing up, they were awarded dessert if they ate their vegetables or did well in class and have kept this link between nourishment and self-confidence into adulthood. This can lead to an unhealthy relationship to food if they are not aware of it; once they become conscious of this connection, however, it will be easy to control it. They should also try not to use food as a guilt mechanism with their children, as it could lead to the development of complexes for their offspring as well. Instead they need to nourish their youngsters with their culinary output and love—but without strings.

Leo

Ceres in Leo individuals have a joyful, hedonistic approach to food that would rival Epicurus himself. They see food as the fundamental nourishment—for the body as well as the soul—that is the spring of life itself. They love highly luxurious foods, not for the snob factor, but for the sheer enjoyment of delighting in the apex of human culinary creativity. These individuals are highly inventive and able to whip up delicious concoctions from the most basic ingredients. When cooking, they are probably better at the preparation of savory foods that can be put together intuitively rather than baked goods that require precise measurements or heating instructions. Individuals with this placement are also very generous with food and enjoy hosting lingering, festive dinner parties that are lively and decadent—and accompanied by plenty of wine. While normally drawn to foods that are prepared with fresh, nutritious, and quality ingredients, they won't say no to indulging every now and then in a bit of low-brow junk food—after all, life is too short not delight in all its pleasures. People with Ceres in Leo have an overriding inner confidence in their relationship to food and will not use it to influence their self-esteem. They may put on a few extra pounds here and there but prefer to enjoy life rather than count calories. The best diet for this placement is one in which herbs and spices are used as flavor enhancers instead of salt and fat, so that low-cal food can still have a zesty tastiness to it. A home herb garden would be perfect for Ceres Leos.

Virgo

People with Ceres in Virgo can be finicky eaters who have a very complex, almost controlling relationship with food. They are fussy eaters whose quirks may veer into OCD territory—that person who won't allow the various foods on their plate to touch may very well be a Ceres in Virgo. They can be extremely regimented in their eating plan, preferring to eat three meals every day at the same time, and perhaps with a set, stringent diet. They are not ones to go off the beaten path into the exotic or decadent but prefer the security and safety of the well-known and routine. They have an austere approach to food and most likely do not enjoy anything too spicy or fatty. They may do very well with a macrobiotic regimen, as they prefer to eat nutriments in their natural state so as to enjoy their natural flavors without any added herbs or finery. Their restraining attitude towards nourishment, however, may lead to anorexia or other eating disorders based on withholding and control. By following a natural, wholefood eating regimen, they will be able to get all the nutrition they need without the discomfort of eating overly calorific food. They also have a tendency to possess an active metabolism caused by excessive anxiety and should be careful of nervous snacking. Their one downfall may be baked goods. They can find comfort and clarity in the precision of baking but then may also indulge in eating the results.

Libra

Those born with Ceres in Libra will be the first ones to open the caviar and pop the champagne but the last ones to don the apron. They enjoy the hedonism and decadence of luxurious food but are a bit too lazy to cook anything too fussy. Luckily, they don't mind spending lavishly on restaurants or hiring a private chef or caterer for a special occasion. When they do prepare their own meals, however, they are capable of making exquisite concoctions out of relatively few—but high-quality—ingredients that require as little preparation as possible. These folks also understand the inherent diplomacy of food. After a misunderstanding, they will be the ones that show up on your doorstep with a tin of cookies or a bottle of wine. When trying to close that must-do business deal, they realize it will be easier over a lingering lunch rather than in an austere boardroom. Libra is a highly aesthetic sign that enjoys the good life. These individuals are, therefore, blessed in knowing how to balance an indulgent culinary lifestyle with their weight on the scales, and a few extra pounds will not be the end of the world. In a way, they are saved from excessive weight gain by their own extravagance—by spending a lot of money on high-end food, they cut down on their ability to overeat. Also, the high-quality nature of the food they enjoy tends to be inherently tasty, and thereby satiates with less quantity.

Scorpio

Ceres in Scorpio individuals will not readily buy into food snobbism. That is not to say they do not enjoy good food, but that they are not going to be fooled into paying a bloated price at the specialty store for what they can get at the farmers' market much cheaper; sure, gas may be quite costly these days, and they may need to drive over an hour to get there and will probably only eat a small fraction of that bushel of green beans—but at least no one took advantage of them! Ceres in Scorpios love hunting for a bargain and may be happiest when buying foods at discount outlets with names like The Dented Can. In fact, it will fill them with a feeling of warmth to save these little culinary rejects by giving them a loving home in their pantry. Scorpio is a highly intense sign, and these individuals may link food to mood—especially bad moods. If upset, they need to be careful not to overeat in order to wallow in their misery. These folks can also harbor secret eating habits, especially binge eating, that would surprise those who know them because they always seem to have everything under control. Ceres in Scorpio may enjoy eating alone or only with their family. These individuals will be found inside the dark interior of an eatery instead of on the sunny garden terrace, because they don't like people watching them eat; likewise, they may prefer takeout to actually eating in restaurants.

Sagittarius

People who have Ceres in Sagittarius use food to expand their consciousness. They love to travel, explore new horizons, and encounter new cultures through a firsthand experience with exotic foreign foods. They will be the first to step up to taste anything strange, eccentric, and hard-to-find, from Indonesian Fruit Bat Soup to Thai Deep-Fried Grasshopper or Bolivian Broiled Alpaca. They prefer to eat foods that are rooted in cultural authenticity as opposed to dreamed up by a celebrity chef and are happier at the street-level noodle bar in China Town rather than at a Michelin-star restaurant. They may find long seated dinners a bit of a bore, and prefer to partake in tapas while standing at a vibrant bar filled with interesting people, live Spanish guitar, and maybe even some flamenco dancing. People with this placement may rebel against lovers or family members who try to nurture them with food; for them eating is an act of freedom and adventure. It is best for those who live with these Ceres signs to not insist on a strict eating schedule or serve bland, tasteless food—and not take it to heart if their place at the dinner table is often empty. If you are in love with a Ceres in Sagittarius, instead of vainly trying to domesticate this wild beast, join them in their culinary globe-trotting adventures—if you dare to break the boundaries of polite food etiquette, you will win their heart faster than baking them a five-course luxury meal from scratch.

Capricorn

For Ceres in Capricorn individuals, food should always bring with it a certain status and respect for tradition; there exists the proper food for the proper occasion. When entertaining people of a certain hierarchy, the correct food must be offered to suit their standing. If they need to impress their boss, they will take them to the best and most stuffy French restaurant in town—the one where the waiters refer to everyone as Monsieur or Madame—and order the full tasting menu, complete with a different wine for each course. When hosting friends of a lower income bracket, however, a more relaxed, low-budget spread is possible. This does not mean that they look down upon certain individuals; it's just that they respect the social order and know what they need to do to most efficiently maximize their position in the system. People with this placement are sticklers for tradition. The latest trendy restaurant with stark minimalist design and ethno-fusion cuisine is the last place you will find them. There will also be no tofu turkey at Thanksgiving; instead, everything will be served properly, and with that certain grace and dignity that comes from following historical conventions. These individuals do not believe the culinary status quo should be challenged; certain foods and eating habits developed over centuries for a reason, and they are not arrogant enough to call into question these habits. As much as they find comfort in the rituals of eating, they do not indulge in comfort food, as it may seem too lowly and calorific.

Aquarius

Individuals born with Ceres in Aquarius are fascinated by innovative food products and the use of technology to transform the way in which food is used in society. Instead of keeping issues regarding health and diet to the individual, home, and family, they prefer an impersonal, universal approach to the culinary realm that embraces the entire global community. They envision the entire world's population sitting at one universal banquet table—and therefore wish to increase the bounty of the earth so that everyone can be fed equally. They may particularly enjoy engaging in humanitarian aid, such as community gardening or working for a nonprofit in Africa. They are not afraid of "Frankenfood" and believe technology and genetically modified food products—if used in an ethical, charitable way—can greatly help in the fight against world hunger. These folks are not massive "foodies" and bristle against the exclusivity and costliness of the celebrity chef culture—but they are deeply fascinated by food science. For them, the most delightful food comes from a high-tech lab filled with a scientist instead of a mere kitchen. They greatly appreciate cutting-edge concoctions, such as those that could be found at Spain's famous elBulli restaurant, where technology transformed food and flavors into a completely new experience. Food technology that is used for evil, corporate, or strictly monetary purposes, or that crushes small farmers or messes up the natural ecosystem, is an anathema to these individuals. They may find a great

2013 © Fedor Kondratenko Image from BigStockPhoto.com

sense of purpose as activists against the agro-chemical industrial complex.

Pisces

People who have Ceres in Pisces often have a deeply emotional attachment to food, and they may view mealtime as a sort of spiritual communion with the highest vibration of Earth's bounty. Food can have an almost messianic quality for them, and people with this placement often approach food with a eucharistic sanctity. The poetry and beauty of the food chain, with its cycles of birth, harvest, and regrowth, are not lost on these individuals. They realize that nourishment starts far before the food arrives on our plate. Sometimes, there may be psychological issues relating to food that arise if the individual is harboring any repressed feelings regarding a lack of proper nurturing from their parents. Food addictions may create a sort of mask used to hide emotional pain, and they may replace love with food. These folks truly understand the meaning of the phrase "The way to a man's heart is through his stomach." They may use food to create the illusion of nurturing, when in fact they are using it as a means of manipulation in order to achieve their own emotional aims. In the kitchen, Ceres in Pisces is a highly inventive and fantastical chef who can take commonplace ingredients and transform them into one-of-a-kind, never-before-seen creations. They also value the aesthetic side of food preparation and will decorate and garnish their dishes in a way that is as inspired and unique as the recipe itself.

About the Author

Michelle Perrin, aka Astrology Detective, is one of the world's most popular astrologers. She writes the "Love—Money—Health" column for Dell Horoscope Magazine, *the biggest astrology magazine in the United States. She is also a featured blogger for astrology .com, with her blog, The Astrological Edge. Visit her website at astrologydetective.com.*

2013 © Georgijus Pavlovas Image from BigStockPhoto.com

Growing Roses

by Misty Kuceris

Roses are special flowers that evoke emotions and memories. On Valentine's Day or special occasions emphasizing love, you'll see red roses given as a pledge of affection. During time periods when you want to show your loyalty and trust of another individual, you may decide to send a dozen yellow roses. At other times, you may want to celebrate the simplicity of life and send white roses, which symbolize purity and virtue. That the symbol of the rose is so ingrained in our culture is not surprising. Walk in a planting of old garden roses and close your eyes. Smell the fragrance of cinnamon or citrus that is so common. Look at new world roses with their flowers and see the perfection of nature in its very design, as most keep blooming throughout the season.

Roses have a noble history, whether in fact, mythological stories, or religious events. Rose fossils have been found that are over 35 million years old. While not all fossils are that old, roses have been found in Europe, North American, North Africa, and Asia. In the times of the ancient Greeks and Romans, roses were used during days of festivals with their petals strewn on the streets. They've been used for pharmaceutical purposes, as well as incorporated into perfume and food products. Rose hips are known for their vitamin C. Their essential oils, according to Homer's *Iliad*, were said to have covered Hector's body upon his death. For people experiencing the historical miracles of St. Thérèse of Lisieux, roses or their fragrances were often said to appear.

Roses have a reputation for being a difficult plant to grow. Even though they can be grown from zone 3 to zone 10, they are very particular about their environment. They need at least six hours of sunlight a day. The type of sun they need actually depends on where you live. In some locations, roses need six hours of continuous exposure. In other locations, roses like some of the six hours of sun in the morning, a little respite during the hottest time period of the day, and the rest of their six hours of sun in the afternoon. The best way to find out the sun requirement for roses in your area is to contact your local rose society. Many of the local rose societies are listed on the website of the American Rose Society, www.ars.org, or one of its links.

Roses really don't like to be in a drafty location, especially in climates that have cooler summers. At the same time, they need enough air circulation, especially in humid climates, to avoid fungal diseases. While they need a lot of watering, they don't like what gardeners call "wet feet." This means roses don't like to have their roots sitting in water. While roses can actually tolerate most soils, many roses prefer a soil that is high in organic matter. But even if you don't have quite the right soil conditions, you can overcome this by building raised beds or growing roses in containers.

Before you start planting roses, think about what type of roses you'd like in your garden, your patio, or your home. The first questions to ask are totally subjective:

Do you want fragrant roses?

Do you want one-time, remontant (one vigorous bloom followed by sparse blooms), or repeat bloomers?

Do you want depth of color in the flowers?

Old garden roses, also called heritage roses, are cultivated from wild roses. They are known best for their fragrance but often were limited to basic color choices: white, red, pink, and yellow. They were popular during the eighteenth and nineteenth centuries but soon gave way to the modern rose when hybrid tea roses were developed by French hybridizer Jean Guillot in 1867. The hybrid teas roses were known for greater vibrancy of flower color, more bloom cycles during the growing season, and longer stems, which made them popular for floral arrangements. The good news is that, thanks to individuals whom many call rose rustlers, old garden roses are making a comeback. Rose rustlers go to cemeteries, old properties, and other locations to rescue and cultivate the old garden roses.

The other questions to ask yourself focus on the type of property you own:

Do you want large shrubs or a hedge?

Do you want standard roses (a rose tree)?

Do you want climbing roses for a trestle or an arbor?

Do you want ground cover?

Do you want container roses for a patio?

Do you want miniature roses for a patio or your home?

When you review various publications to determine the best roses for your area, you may not find roses categorized by shrub, standard, ground cover, or container plants. But these, with the exception of hedge rose, will be the classifications you often find at nurseries.

The waning cycle of the Moon (decreasing in light) is always one of the best times for planning. If you started planning in the waxing cycle (increasing in light), you may have come up with some very grand schemes. However, the time to re-evaluate your plans is during a waning cycle.

When you have a large yard with the right lighting conditions, you have a wide choice of roses. You may decide that you want an entire rose garden. You could start with a climbing rose that anchors the wall of your house, moving out farther to include some shrubs roses, until you finally border the garden with carpet roses. Or, you could get a standard (tree) rose and place it in the center of your garden with small carpet roses forming a blanket at its feet.

The good news is that you don't have to despair if you live in a townhouse or other small space where your best garden location is a patio or indoors. You can grow the roses in a container! Standard roses can look nice as pillars near the patio door, and climbing roses might be grown on trestles near the edge of a patio. Even miniature roses can look great in pots around the various parts of the patio. In your home, with the right lighting, miniature roses make a beautiful statement. They thrive in pots and can bring hours of joy.

When you do get ready to plant roses in your garden, you have one of two choices: bare-rooted roses or container roses. If you decide to plant bare-rooted roses, soak them in water overnight before planting them. They are also better if planted early in the season so that the plants don't start growing while still in the box. For indoor pots or container gardening, consider miniature or miniflora roses. Whatever type of roses you decide to plant, the best time to plant is after the New Moon and before the Full Moon, during the waxing phase.

For bare-rooted plants, create a little mound in the hole you've dug. The reason for this is that the roots will drape over the sides of the mound rather than lie flat on the bottom of the ground. If you live in zones 6 through 10, make sure that the bud union (that bulbous part between the main stem and roots of the rose) is either a little above or even with the ground. In zones 3 through 5, this bud union needs to be 2 to 4 inches below the surface.

If you've purchased a container plant, you don't need to worry about the mound in the hole. Just dig up the soil about twice the width of the pot and place the plant in the hole.

Remember that roses prefer loamy, well-drained soil. They also like a pH of about 6.5. If possible, take a sample of your soil before you plant your roses so you can analyze the pH level, macronutrients, and micronutrients content. By doing this first, you'll know exactly the type of organic matter to put into the soil to amend it properly.

To keep your repeat bloomers vibrant during their growing season, it's important to remove the old blooms, called deadheading. Always cut the spent flowers just above the five-leaflet leaf on that stem. The time to stop deadheading is about one month before the first frost; you want your rose to start going dormant at that time. Don't deadhead single-bloom roses, because the spent blossoms will produce very ornamental rose hips.

If you live in zone 5 or colder, you may need to winterize your rose. In some cases, this means covering the rose for the winter with a cone developed especially for this purpose. In other cases, it means placing 6 inches or more of soil or mulch around the base of your rose. If you have container or pot roses, it means bringing them into your house.

As your rose comes out of dormancy and spring starts announcing itself, you'll need to prune the rose. The right time to prune your rose depends on your zone. Warmer zones can prune as early as Valentine's Day. But since frost dates vary, it's best to check with your local rose society. Try to prune during a waning Moon phase.

The environmental requirements for miniature, potted roses are not all that different. When you decide that you want an indoor garden of roses, you can find some Old World varieties as well as modern roses. They like a sunny location, so your house either needs good natural lighting or grow lights. During the evening, the house temperature needs to be between 60°F (15°C) and 70°F (20°C). During the day, the temperature needs to be a little warmer. The potted roses also like a lot of water. Besides directly watering them, it's a good idea to place them on a moisture tray and occasionally mist them. Some people will even circulate the air with a fan. If you decide to do that, keep the fan off the plant directly, since roses (like most indoor plants) don't like to be in a drafty area. Be sure to fertilize them about every two weeks during their growing season.

I have a feeling roses will continue to evoke emotions and memories for centuries to come. Their beauty continues to astonish people. Whether you choose to give roses as a gift or to plant them in your own environment, you'll never regret adding more stories to the history of roses.

About the Author

Misty Kuceris is a Certified Horticulturalist and ISAR Certified Astrology Professional working with individuals in understanding the cycles found in nature and life. She has worked as a plant specialist during the past several years for various nurseries in the Greater DC metropolitan area. As a plant consultant, she meets with homeowners to assess their property and gardens in order to develop a sustainable environment. She also lectures at garden clubs and senior citizen centers, giving guidance and advice on how to create healthy home gardens and lawns. You can contact Misty for her gardening expertise at plantinvestigations@gmail.com and for her astrological expertise at misty@EnhanceOneself.com.

The Rich Flavor of Tea Gardens

by Charlie Rainbow Wolf

It's morning and you're ready for the first cup of tea to start the day. Imagine going into your own garden and picking the herbs fresh, with the dew barely gone. Sound too good to be true? Well it isn't! Even the smallest space can accommodate a few herbs so that you can really connect with your favorite herbal infusion.

There are numerous benefits to growing your own herbs. For me, the most powerful is the connection I find when nourishing a garden that is in turn going to nourish me. I get a real sense of a sympathetic relationship knowing that the plants I tend are going to reward me with a lovely cup of tea.

It is also very nice to know from where your tea comes. When tea is bought in a supermarket, sometimes it is hard to discern whether the parent plant was of good quality or how long it has been between picking and packaging. You may also be concerned as to whether it was grown compassionately and harvested with fairness to the workers. These concerns are not an issue when you grow the herbs yourself.

Tea gardens can be breathtakingly beautiful, too. Many of the herbs make great companion plants when grown together. The striking colors and exquisite flowers are as refreshing as the teas that can be made from them. In addition, some of the herbs are very aromatic, and it is possible to derive pleasure from their sweet scent while also indulging in their appearance and taste. The smell permeates the garden, and it is delightful to sit among the plants and bathe in their fragrance.

Herbs for tea can be grown according to their purpose, as well as their appearance. Check on how amiable the herbs are with each other, and combine those that are good garden companions and that serve the same healing purpose in a well-designed cluster. Patterns could include a living patchwork quilt, spaces between a labyrinth that could be walked, or any other design that is pleasing to your eye. Garden designs have come a long way since the rigid rows of the past!

The herbal tea experience can start the moment you set the seedlings into the soil. Know your plants' characteristics before you start, though; tall plants need to go at the back so they do not overshadow smaller ones. Also pay attention to the location; different herbs have different requirements for light and moisture. You want to get things off to a good start.

It is sometimes difficult to find herbs that grow well in shady areas. I have comfrey growing under my crabapple trees, and it seems to do really well there, as does the anise hyssop. I think this is more because the plants are indestructible rather than shade-loving, though! Mint may be another hearty shade grower, though it can get out of control if not tended well. Foliage herbs are the best selection for areas that do not get much sunlight, but be sure you have chosen them well. Woodruff is an excellent ground cover for a shady area. Remember your climate zone while select-ing herbs for shade. What grows in full sun in the north may need shade from the hot summer sun in the south.

Annual herbs versus perennial ones is another consideration. Some plants that are perennial in the warmer climates will grow as annuals in the north. A heavy mulch in the autumn as the frosts approach may help the plants to winter over, but this can often be trial and error. What survives a mild winter—or even a mild sum-mer when taking heat and sunlight into consideration—may not make it through more extreme weather conditions. If in doubt, treat the plant as an annual; if it returns, consider it a blessing.

As if all these concerns weren't enough, the soil conditions also have to be contemplated. Some plants—such as echinacea or chicory—are going to prefer dry soils to moist. Others, such as violets or mints, need more moist conditions.

A mint garden can make a very simple garden plan for those who are just starting to experiment. Mint has a wide variety of uses, can be easily obtained, and is fairly easy to grow. A bit of care is needed, though, for mint can be invasive in the right conditions. The stronger plants will overpower the more delicate ones if you're not careful. I recommend planting mint in tubs. These don't have to be fancy or expensive, but they do need to be fairly deep, and they do need a drainage hole in the bottom. Old toilet tanks are ideal for this! Fill the container with soil, bury it about two-thirds into the ground, and then plant your mint. Another option is a deep-running garden edge to prevent the plant from crossing over it.

For the most part, mint is a perennial, though some of the more tender mints are best treated like annuals. Square stems bear scal-loped or serrated leaves, and it is the young leaves that are used for mint tea. In late summer the plants will produce fairly insignificant flowers varying from purple to lilac to nearly white. Mints vary in height, some as tall as four feet, so be sure to plant accordingly.

Once mint has taken root, it is hard to move, as the hairy roots will keep coming back with new growth. This is another reason to plant in buried containers: so you can remove the plant fully if you find it doesn't suit the spot or your tea preferences.

There are many types of mint, and it's fun to experiment. Banana mint has a rather creamy minty flavor with a mild smell of bananas, while a good chocolate mint will taste like an after-dinner candy. These mints tend not to be as strong as their peppermint or spearmint counterparts. All mints have the traditional cool taste, some with more bite than others. I have the stronger mints—peppermint, spearmint, and melissa—planted around my fruit trees as a deterrent for wildlife, who don't seem to like the pungent odor. The more fragile mints—chocolate mint, banana mint, ginger mint, apple mint, and orange mint—reside in more sheltered areas. Some are in raised urns, to add visual appeal. Mint actually makes a very good container plant for those with limited space. Several pots grouped together, varying in height and each growing a different kind of mint, can be very rewarding.

Catnip and catmint can also be added to a mint garden, as well as the anise hyssop. Trial and error will tell you what is pleasing and what isn't. Mint makes a very good base for a lot of teas. Sage can be added to it and consumed hot or cold. Mint and sage tea over ice with a slice of lemon makes a lovely refreshing drink on a hot summer's evening. If a themed design is being planted, all mints make a great addition to a garden whose theme is to aid digestion or to help relieve headaches.

Like mint, sage comes in different types, too, and makes a tasteful and colorful addition to the tea garden. Things that are often thought to be culinary herbs—sage, basil, rosemary, thyme—will all make nice additions to herbal teas. Rosemary and ginger with a bit of honey is one of my favorite teas for the colder weather.

Plants often valued simply for their fruits or their flowers can make wonderful teas. The berry and the leaf of the raspberry plant can be used. The flowers of the beautiful hibiscus steep into a rich fruity flavor. Both the flowers and the hips of the beautiful *Rosa rugosa* have lovely—but very different—flavors. Try a rugosa with mint growing in front of it and woodruff or violet as a ground cover. Sprinkle anise hyssop among the hibiscus, with some violets peeking out from between them. Put parsley among the raspberries. Create a blue-themed garden, or one that is low growing, or one that will provide herbs for relaxing teas. Study your climate and soil, then set your imagination free and paint a living picture of beauty for all five senses to appreciate.

The best teas are made from younger leaves harvested early in the morning, when the plant's essences are at their highest. You may choose to harvest excess leaves and dry them (as you would any other herb) for the winter season. After you've found a combination you like, this is a nice way to create gifts: combine your favorite herbs in a jar along with a tea ball for steeping. Keep in mind that while some herbs lose a bit of their punch when dried, they also lose a lot of their volume, so you'll need less dried herb per cup than fresh.

The flavor of the tea garden, like the flavor of the teas it provides, is always an individual taste. There is no right or wrong way; if you listen to the plant, it will let you know where it wants to grow. Tuning in to that connection can be a reward unto itself.

About the Author

Charlie Rainbow Wolf is happiest when she is creating something. Knowledgeable in many aspects of healing, she is most keen on using meditation as medicine. Charlie is the Dean of Faculty at the Grey School, where she teaches subjects in most of the sixteen departments. She is drawn most to the Tarot, a subject that has captivated her for more than two decades. Charlie has a flair for recycling, and is keenly interested in organic gardening and cooking. She feeds her creative muse with writing, pottery, knitting, and soap-making. She lives in the Midwest with her husband and special-needs Great Danes.

GET MORE AT LLEWELLYN.COM

Visit us online to browse hundreds of our books and decks, plus sign up to receive our e-newsletters and exclusive online offers.

- **Free tarot readings • Spell-a-Day • Moon phases**
- **Recipes, spells, and tips • Blogs • Encyclopedia**
- **Author interviews, articles, and upcoming events**

GET SOCIAL WITH LLEWELLYN

 Find us on **Facebook**

Follow us on

www.Facebook.com/LlewellynBooks

www.Twitter.com/Llewellynbooks

GET BOOKS AT LLEWELLYN

LLEWELLYN ORDERING INFORMATION

Order online: Visit our website at www.llewellyn.com to select your books and place an order on our secure server.

Order by phone:
- Call toll free within the U.S. at 1-877-NEW-WRLD (1-877-639-9753)
- Call toll free within Canada at 1-866-NEW-WRLD (1-866-639-9753)
- We accept VISA, MasterCard, and American Express

Order by mail:
Send the full price of your order (MN residents add 6.875% sales tax) in U.S. funds, plus postage and handling to: Llewellyn Worldwide, 2143 Wooddale Drive Woodbury, MN 55125-2989

POSTAGE AND HANDLING

STANDARD (U.S. & Canada):
(Please allow 12 business days)
$25.00 and under, add $4.00.
$25.01 and over, FREE SHIPPING.

INTERNATIONAL ORDERS (airmail only):
$16.00 for one book, plus $3.00 for each additional book.

Visit us online for more shipping options. Prices subject to change.

FREE CATALOG!

To order, call
1-877-
NEW-WRLD
ext. 8236
or visit our
website

newworlds

Discover True
Soul Mate Relationships

PLUS